# Love&Stardust

## A MEMOIR: TWO HEARTS,
## ONE SOUL AND A PROMISE OF FOREVER.

Paul Marshall

Paul Marshall
paul@paulmarshallwrites.com

Website: www.paulmarshallwrites.com
Facebook: www.facebook.com/paulmarshall writes/
Instagram: www.instagram.com/paulmarshall_writes/

Printed in the United States of America.
First Printing, 2020

ISBN Paper Back: 978-1-7353822-0-3
ISBN Hardcover: 978-1-7353822-1-0
ISBN E-book: 978-1-7353822-2-7

Cover design: © Tim Simic, Green Light Creative, Hammond, IN.
Cover photograph of Dolly Marshall © Paul Marshall.
Formatting by Polgarus Studio

The book Love & Stardust is not in any way intended as a self-help guide. If you are in need of help or guidance, please seek it from a trained, professional source.

First Edition

*For Dolly,*

*AMOUR NOSTRA AETERNA*


"DOUBT THOU THE STARS ARE FIRE,
DOUBT THAT THE SUN DOTH MOVE,
DOUBT TRUTH TO BE A LIAR,
BUT NEVER DOUBT I LOVE.

Wm. Shakespeare

# ACKNOWLEDGMENTS

Writing a book is essentially a solo journey. However, others do generously contribute and deserve thanks and recognition:

First, my Mother and Father, Leona, and Henry Marshall, for without their love there would have been no Paul. Without Paul to love Dolly, there would have been no marriage, no children, no grandchildren, and no love story to tell. Love & Stardust, the story of our lives, was a seed planted in good soil long ago by my mom and dad.

To Ann and Louis Czahor. They were the channel that brought an angel into this world and for this miracle I am forever grateful.

My love goes out to daughter, Gabrielle, and son Tyler for being patient with a father who for six years talked ad nauseam of the book he was writing and rewriting, and little else. Each day I feel blessed and rejoice that you are my long-suffering family. I'd be lost without you and love you both.

I'm grateful to my siblings, Ann, John, Leona, their spouses, and their children, all important in my life and there when I needed family most. Also, to our grandchildren, Veronica and Marshall. You've made me proud. Being related to me requires infinite patience as does being my friend. For years I've bored everyone with two topics, the book, and my late wife Dolly. Thanks for suffering along with me in our common loss, and in my literary obsession; it can't have been easy.

A special tribute to sister Leona, my sounding board for all I've written, and an ever-faithful cheerleader whenever I had doubts, which was often. You have my gratitude and love.

To our many nieces, nephews, Aunts, Uncles, relations, and friends; I wish I could name all of you, but space is limited, and you are so many. Please know you have been a much loved and appreciated part of the lives of Dolly and Paul.

Thanks to sailing friends Doug and Senn Gee. Senn was Dolly's dearest friend and a loved and treasured part of our family for 50 years and counting. Thank you both for the fun we've had together, for your generosity and caring and most of all, for loving Dolly as I know you did.

Sincere thanks to Bryan Dunigan, faithful friend for many years. My gratitude to you Bryan, for reading the eulogy I wrote for Dolly but was incapable of delivering at her funeral mass. You have been an important presence in our lives and a treasured gift to our family.

Hugs to friends Rebecca and Greg Kozlik. It was Greg, who told Dolly that it was a scientific fact she was largely made of stardust. Thank you Kozmos, for supplying half the title of my book. For the remainder of her beautiful life, Dolly rejoiced in the knowledge that she was in fact, stardust from heaven.

Thanks to our Sarasota friends on Modena Place, and especially to our Florida family, Rick, Debbie, Kate, and Ryan Butor. Also, a heads up to Lisa, Andrew, Bit, Sunny and Mia Risner and the Jazz Juvenocracy family for all you added to our time in FLA.

First readers helped me refine the book, and each was appreciated for their feedback. In no special order they are, Gabrielle Marshall, Leona Marshall, fellow writer Richard Stepan Kiebdaj, Marge Winfield, Marsha Harrington, Colleen Miltenberger, Veronica DeBone, author David Hoppe, and my very first reader, Johanne Dunigan. Thanks to all of you for improving my work.

My gratitude to Sara Noë, author of the *Chronicles of Avilesor* series, who generously shared her advice and experience of self-publishing with me. Freshmen writers like me need friends like Sara who have been down the road before. I'd have been lost without her guidance.

It's impossible to give excessive praise to editor Susan Krawitz. She went far beyond her assignment of structurally editing my manuscript and gave me many valuable writing lessons, including the wisdom of removing the unnecessary and remaining focused on the arc of the story. Susan, I've learned much from your mentoring and am deeply in your debt. It was a good day for me when your friend recommended you. Huzzah!

Additional thanks also to editor Stephanie Parent for her final line edit, proofing, and many positive and encouraging comments about my work. As I was pushing toward the finish line her polish took LOVE&STARDUST that last step. I desperately needed both these talented editors and am grateful for their patience, endurance, and counsel in pushing this beginner to a finished manuscript.

Thanks also to Marina Anderson at Polgarus Studio, Australia, for guidance and to Jason Anderson for formatting my brutal treatment of WORD into something that I can now call a book.

To Tim Simic of Green Light Creative, friend, former client, and graphic design artist, a huge thank you for the beautiful book cover. I had a dream vision for the cover and your genius made it reality. Through *far too many requested changes* on my part, you remained ever patient. I'm certain Dolly would have approved of her cover. Refusing payment Tim said, "It's for Dolly and was an honor. From my heart Tim, thank you and the staff you worked with.

Finally, to the best part of me, my beloved Dolly. She was my wife, lover, best friend, guardian angel, mother of our beautiful children and the most extraordinary woman I've ever known. She added joy, love, and happiness to my days and to the lives of all who knew her . Dolly was goodness itself; beautiful in mind and body, always faithful, steadfast, and as near perfection as a woman can be. Kind, charming, spirited, and magnetic, everyone wanted to be her friend, and I, more than anyone, understands why…her loving way of living life inspired all of us, even to the writing of this book. In life she completed me, helping me grow and become a man; even now in death, she continues to encourage me to do and be more.

The words *thank you* are too feeble when measured against the priceless gift she shared with me during our 55 years together. She not only gave me herself and her precious love, but she also showed me what true love can be in its perfection.

This book is for Dolly.

# FORWARD

Our culture doesn't do happily-ever-after very well. According to current statistics, nearly half the marriages in this country end in divorce. Long-term marital love is apparently becoming a rare thing. And yet, when scientist's scanned the brains of seventeen long-married women and men who claimed to still be deeply in love with their spouses, the regions associated with intense, early stage romantic love were just as active as those of newlyweds. But I didn't need science to convince me of this. My marriage was living proof. "How do you two do it?" friends would ask my wife Dolly. "After all these years Paul still looks at you like he's just fallen in love yesterday."

We'd met young and married early, not the ideal scenario for a successful lifelong marriage. And yet, for us, the music of love never stopped playing, not when separated by service during the Vietnam War, nor through struggles with finances, career, a stillborn child, and a debilitating bout with acute anxiety disorder. Like all great love stories, through it all we remained deeply in love and committed to each other. Even as we aged Dolly remained for me the same beautiful girl I'd met in 1959.

As we approached our fiftieth wedding anniversary, suddenly, with little warning, death took Dolly, ending our fifty-five-year love affair and with it, my desire to go on living. To survive and continue without her was the greatest challenge I would ever face.

PM

*"Once Upon a Time, a young girl with the face of an angel, took the hand of a shy, brown-eyed boy and promised to love him forever. That was a lifetime ago...*
*I am the brown-eyed boy,*
*and this is our story."*

Paul Marshall (with Leona Marshall)

# 1.

"Her eyes kissed mine,
I saw the love in them shine…"

The Joy of Love/Traditional

The moment I saw her I knew there would never be any other girl for me. Is that crazy? Of course it is, and yet when it happened, I knew. With the absolute certainty of youth, I knew.

June 8,1959 was one of those perfect spring mornings when every aspect of it made me happy to be alive. I'd arrived early to Thomas Kelly High School on California Avenue in Chicago for the start of the summer session. Still sixteen for a couple of more months, I was between my junior and senior years of high school and there to make up a class in chemistry. My plan was to locate the chem lab, then have a leisurely lunch before class began. While killing time hanging out with other kids on the main entrance steps, I saw a friend from my neighborhood named Patsy walking toward me so stood to greet her. It was at that moment, my life changed forever.

There was a girl with her and when she came into view, I suddenly felt I couldn't breathe. I will admit now, at the outset of our story, that one of the great truths in life is that beauty is in the eyes of the beholder. Sometimes we see what our heart wants us to see. So, forgive me if I seem over the top in describing this moment, but I was in fact convinced I was seeing an angel,

1

one so dazzling that to look at her was like trying to stare at the sun. Someone else might have described her as just another pretty teenager... but not to me. Unbelievable it may be, but when our eyes met, I felt like I'd been kissed, and my soul was awakened for the first time by a beauty I now believe I was meant to find. So, how did I respond to this revelation? I fell in love of course, with a girl whose name I didn't even know.

It was obvious to me this young goddess was way out of my league, so the question was, should I quietly surrender now, accepting the inevitable, or try and convince her I might be worthy of her consideration? These thoughts raced through my dazed, befuddled brain in the few seconds it took to catch my breath again.

Some experts say love at first sight is a cliché and never happens. And yet, isn't the beginning of young love beyond reason, beyond explanation? If we accept what the ancient Greeks and Romans called fatum or fate, then perhaps we feel a sense of recognition when first we encounter that one ideal soul we were meant for. No one really knows, and yet four hundred years ago, playwright and poet Christopher Marlowe wrote, 'Who ever loved, that loved not at first sight.'

I was a shy, callow boy and she an angel of such perfection, I knew I was seeing true beauty for the first time.


Warm sunlight caressed her face like golden paint flowing from an artist's brush, glazing her skin with a luminous glow. She was blonde, petite, perfectly proportioned, had sparkling, laughing eyes, and was without doubt the loveliest, most feminine girl I had ever seen.

Inexperienced with females, and genuinely bashful, two questions begged answers: Did she have a boyfriend, and could I convince her to grant me an audience? Patsy made introductions: "Paul, I'd like you to meet a really special girl." The special girl surprised me offering her hand to shake, an unusually confident gesture for a teenage girl in 1959. Smiling sweetly, she looked unflinchingly into my eyes, and in a warm voice said four words that changed my world:

*"My name is Dolly."*

Only four words, none more than five letters, and yet they stamped *the end* to all that had come before, opening my heart to a new world filled with infinite possibility. I took the offered hand, touching her for the first time. My reply was far from inspired as I mumbled, "Hi Dolly, I'm Paul." As I spoke her name I thought, *Well, of course, she's a beautiful tiny porcelain doll, so her name had to be Dolly.* Introductions complete, our matchmaker friend Patsy said, "Sorry kids, must run. I'm in a rush to meet my boyfriend! But knowing both of you as I do, I've got a strong feeling you two are really going to like each other." With that she blended into the crowd of kids on the street. I stood gazing at Dolly, struck dumb by how pretty she was.

Her hand was soft and warm in mine. I knew I should release it but having never held the hand of an angel before I was reluctant to let go. She glanced with amused curiosity at our joined hands, then at me, and drawing out a short word into a long one asked, "*Welllllllll...?*" Finally finding my voice, and not stopping to pause or breathe I blurted, "Dolly if you're not doing anything right now I was on my way to the diner on the corner and I realize we've only just been introduced but may I buy you lunch and before you say no I promise I'm actually nice well trained already housebroken and I seldom bite... so please, please say yes." She started laughing at the silly way I'd asked her to lunch with me so in desperation I punctuated my speech with a Mr. Nice Guy grin, waiting for the answer I knew would disappoint, instinctively understanding that angels do not lunch with mortals.

Brushing away a few tiny laugh tears the angel surprised me saying, "Well Paul, you've made me laugh *and* aroused my curiosity with that funny invitation of yours. In my experience, teenage boys are seldom that witty, so your cleverness has won me over and my answer is yes... I would love to have lunch with you." "Really?" I said, astonished.

"Well, why not? You seem pleasant enough; you're clean and nice looking, so I'm reasonably confident I'm safe joining you for lunch. You will be nice to me, won't you? Oh, and by the way, as I'm certain I'll be finding a use for it soon, do you suppose... in your own time of course... you might consider giving me my hand back?"

And that's how it all began.

As we started to walk the short distance to the diner, Dolly said, "You're one fast worker, Paul. We've only just been introduced, and you've already convinced me to have lunch with you. That's not like me at all, so I can't believe I said yes. After all, I don't know a thing about you. Maybe, you're one of those hoodlum gang members I've been hearing about."

Now…I'm not terribly quick but did recognize this confident and clever little beauty was baiting me. I'm sure she sensed I was a somewhat shy boy, so she was going to have some friendly fun teasing me. We were approaching a park bench, so I suggested, "Can we stop here for a bit and I'll tell you a little about myself?" As we sat down and turned toward each other, I struggled mightily to keep my voice even and my hands from shaking.

"First of all, I'm not one of those bad guys you mentioned; I'm actually quite civilized. And second, I don't know how I managed to find the guts to ask you to lunch, and I'm still wondering why a girl like you would consider having lunch with a guy like me?"

"What sort of girl *is* a girl like me," she asked, "and what's so wrong with a guy like you?"

"Well, obviously there's not a single thing wrong with you; you're flawless and make me feel like a flat tire. Also, I'm no Casanova with fancy come-on lines to use, and I'm painfully shy with girls. But today I refused to let shyness hold me back and I had a special reason why."

"And what might that special reason be, I wonder?"

"It's you. You're the reason, Dolly. The minute we met I could see you were perfect and out of my reach, yet I was determined to try and capture your attention anyway. If I'd let you walk away, I might never have found you again, and when I say it's hard for me to talk to a girl like you, I'm telling the truth. Normally I'd be hopelessly tongue-tied right now, yet today, somehow I've managed to find a little courage." I shook my head, embarrassed, and surprised at my own words.

"I can't believe I'm telling you all this stuff because just looking at you, it's clear Patsy didn't exaggerate when she described you as a 'special girl. I agree with her description."

Apparently embarrassed by my flattery, for a moment Dolly looked at her hands resting in her lap, and shaking her head as if to say no, she whispered softly,

"I'm not special… or perfect."

In that moment, I must have lost all presence of mind because I did the unthinkable; I reached out, and touching her face lifted her chin gently until she was looking at me again.

"Dolly… to me you are special, and absolutely perfect. It's not even debatable."

I've no idea what possessed me to think I had any right to touch her or even speak to her that way. It just wasn't me. I guess for once I hadn't thought; I'd just reacted. Gazing at her while considering my faux pas, I feared at any moment she was going to stand and walk away because of the liberty I'd taken. But instead she jumped up pulling me with her, and looping her arm through mine as if we'd known each other for years she said,

"Come on Mister Shy Boy, take me to lunch."

While walking arm in arm Dolly asked what my surname was. Now why, I said to myself, would she suddenly want to know my last name at this time? Girls are such a mystery to me.

"Marshall…my last name is Marshall," I said. I watched her considered this for a moment, her lips moving quietly, saying words to herself I couldn't hear, until finally she said, "That's a nice name; I like it. If you saw mine spelled out, you wouldn't even be able to pronounce it. It's Polish, spelled C-Z-A-H-O-R. The C-Z-A is pronounced *Cha* like the dance, *cha-cha*. The HOR is pronounced like the slang name for a prostitute which," she added blushing, "is not so nice. It's not a pretty name like yours, but it is what it is. So, tell me Mr. Paul Marshall, why are you attending summer school?" I hated to tell the truth because she'd think I was stupid, but I did the honest thing…

"To make up a class I failed due to laziness and lack of interest. At my school I'm required to pass chemistry to graduate. What about you?" I asked, trying to shift the conversation back to her.

"Oh, I like art," she said, "so I'm taking a class for fun. Paul, it's obvious to me you don't go to Kelly High because I would certainly have noticed you, so where do you go?"

"Why would you have noticed me," I asked, genuinely curious.

"Well… you're definitely cute and girls notice a cute boy." I thought to myself: *one thing is certain…there's nothing shy about this girl.* I continued on, saying nothing about the cute boy remark.

"To answer your question, I go to Tilden Technical, and now it's my turn to ask you one. Why would you attend a class during summer vacation if you didn't have to? You must really like school."

"I do, and since I'm a social kind of girl, I didn't feel like sitting around doing nothing all summer. I'd rather be with other kids." I didn't believe for a moment that a girl like Dolly would ever want for companionship. There had to be an army of guys vying for her attention, and even though I didn't know their names, each one of them was competition and therefore my dreaded enemy.

"May I ask how old you are, Dolly, and what year you're in?

"I'm going into my senior year and still sixteen but will turn seventeen in August." .

"Me too," I replied.

It occurred to me how unlikely it was that we had met at all. Our neighborhoods were miles apart and with millions of people living in Chicago, the chance of our crossing paths had been unlikely. This meeting was pure serendipity, a fortunate piece of luck for me. Looking back, I've often thought that *if* I hadn't failed chemistry, and *if* my mother didn't insist I make it up in summer school, and *if* Kelly High hadn't been the only school offering chemistry that summer, and *if* Dolly hadn't decided to take an art class…well, maybe there was more to our meeting than simple chance. My Italian friend Vincenzo's mom was always shouting some word in Italian about her life…what was it? Then I remembered: "'Destino!'" Is what's happening to me now meant to be? Was this my destiny. Now that was an interesting question.

The grill (called The Huddle… what else?), was one of those classic late 50s teen hangouts with a black, white, and chrome interior. They served the usual burgers, fries, shakes and Cokes, largely to students from the high school. As we entered, Elvis was soulfully crooning "I Can't Stop Loving You" from the jukebox. Was it an omen?

"Gee, this place is packed," Dolly said. "I don't see an empty table or booth anywhere, do you?" As we stood there looking around, two girls got up to leave. "Quick," I said, "let's grab that tiny table in front of the window."

I held Dolly's chair for her, and a look of surprise crossed her face, as if no guy had ever done that before. "This is really a small table," she said as our knees rubbed together underneath. Physical contact with her was causing additional erotic shock to my already overstimulated senses. I didn't recall the touch of other girls causing a similar effect, but with this girl, the game had totally changed. Very strange.

From my current adult perspective, I know scientifically what was happening. A potent neurochemistry of attraction was being produced inside me, likely containing some mix of dopamine, oxytocin, adrenalin, serotonin, and lots of testosterone. This cocktail raced through my brain and body, creating chaos in my system. The ancient Greeks called this sensation "love madness," the feeling that you're drowning in ecstasy. It's an accurate name.

So, high on nature's chemicals, I now found myself sitting across from a stunning, nearly seventeen-year-old beauty in a teen hangout on California Avenue in Chicago, all the while being possessed by Eros, the god of love.

A soft, indirect, Vermeer-like light from the big window was caressing Dolly's face as softly as a lover's whisper. I felt as if I were seeing her through one of those soft-focus filters used in old black and white movies to make the starlets look flawless and dreamy. Did Dolly need help from a filter to look beautiful? Oh no… she was beyond perfect.

"Dolly," I said, "I didn't mention it before when you asked about schools, but in my freshmen year I attended an all-boys Catholic boarding school before transferring to Tilden. And for some reason, I just remembered something we'd discussed in religion class; it was a quote from St. Augustine."

"What was it the saint said that made it stick in your mind?" she asked.

"*We can't help loving that which is beautiful,*" I quoted.

"What in the world made you think of that at this particular time?" she asked.

"I don't know. I guess I was just wondering what causes romantic attraction to occur."

"Are you flirting with me, Paul Marshall?"

"Who, me? Nooo!"

"You know, for a shy boy you're not that shy, and I'm fairly sure you're flirting with me."

"Come on, Dolly. I'm just making friendly conversation," I mumbled before continuing to dig myself in even deeper. "For example, how about love at first sight? Now that's an interesting question, don't you think? Do you suppose it can really happen? And I'm sure you've heard of Cupid, the Roman god of attraction with his love arrows. Or, what about Eros, the Greek god of love? Do you think we should believe in the influence of any of those ancient gods?" Her answer came in the form of a question...

"You seem to know all about the gods of love, Paul. Why?"

"Oh, probably because I'm a romantic kind of guy. I like poetry, love sonnets, romantic books and movies, and those ancient people and the gods they invented intrigue me. The early Greeks and Romans were interesting people, especially the Greek philosophers. I'm terrible at math, but I do like history and English and literature are my best subjects; I'm a voracious reader."

"We have that in common then," Dolly said. "I love books too." I was glad we were finding common interests. Our conversation hit pause when a waitress came to our table and said,

"So, whatta youse kids wanna eat taday?" Her way of speaking was what I called "Chicago Speak, sort of a midwestern form of cockney, not uncommon in certain Chicagoans.

"I'm not really that hungry," Dolly said, "so I'll just have a cherry Coke and a large order of French fries we can share? Is that all right?" I nodded, adding a chocolate shake for myself and we began to talk, my eyes never leaving her angelic face. To use an old-fashioned word, I was smitten.

In conversation, as I learned more about her, it became clear that Dolly had an unusual aura about her. As young as we were, I could see how confident and comfortable she was with herself, and not self-conscious in the slightest. She laughed easily and often, displaying a warm, happy disposition, yet there was also a serene quality about her. As for me, I was an ocean of nervous anxiety, the opposite of her sea of tranquility. Obviously, she was intelligent, but not the kind that can become boring or overly intellectual. She was also completely female, and if I were to add the words, highly desirable, they would be a gross understatement. I was aching to touch the contours of her face, smell her, feel her skin and hair, and taste her lips, all the wild urges of an over-revved teenage boy. I was punch-drunk and staggering, just basking in her light. I must have been experiencing love madness, because at that moment, the description fit me perfectly.

I'd had lunch in this diner before and knew that the owner, like me, was a jazz music fan because the jukebox was well stocked with jazz offerings. When a lull in a series of rock and roll tunes came, I went to the jukebox and inserted coins, selecting a few songs, the first a favorite of mine titled, "You Go to My Head." It contained a highly descriptive message in the lyrics, my subtle way of telling Dolly the intoxicating effect she was having on me. I didn't believe she'd pick up on my little game, but noted she was clearly listening carefully to the song's words. Soon she smiled, raising her eyebrows in a questioning sort of way. I got the feeling I was being read like a romance novel.

"That's an extremely romantic song," she said, her voice suddenly soft. "Can I assume you like jazz?"

"No... not like, I love jazz."

"Well Paul, it occurs to me that those are really suggestive and amorous words in your song choice, so I was just wondering... Did you have someone *special* in mind when you chose it?"

"I might have," I said. *I could tell she was playing with me again when she emphasized the word special. I decided to play the game too, so asked...*

"Were you thinking that someone special might, be you?"

"Well, I don't know. But I seem to remember being called a 'special girl,' by a boy named Paul, so naturally, since that's your name I wondered if you were thinking of me, that's all." But the torture she so smoothly doled out didn't end there. "Gee Paul, are my questions upsetting you? You're looking kind of nervous." This slick operator had maneuvered me into a corner and continued to prod.

"So? Were you, or were you not, thinking of me... mister charming, brown-eyed boy? Well...come on. This girl would like to know."

"I think I'll let that question go unanswered for now," I stated. Her expression clearly said she already knew the answer anyway. Why did I feel like I was standing in front of Little Miss Smarty Pants, totally naked?

"I have a feeling that later on you will get around to telling me who you were thinking of," she said, smiling confidently. Yep, I said to myself; definitely too clever by half. We took a short pause and sipped our drinks. Then the sparing continued.

"How many brothers and sisters do you have?" she asked.

"One brother and two sisters. How about you?"

"There are five of us, four girls and one boy, I'm the oldest, and by the way, I'm Catholic too."

We went on like that for a while, playing getting to know you. When we were introduced, I'd noticed her eyes were an unusual color; not blue, brown, or green but something different, so I asked what color they were. Her answer was kind of funny.

"The sort of boys I usually meet don't spend much time looking at a girl's eyes. I'm not sure they even notice we *have* eyes if you get my meaning, nor do they ask about their color, but I've always called mine hazel."

"Really? Well I think they're golden with flecks of amber, but I'm going to go with golden." She just smiled. I got the impression she was always one jump ahead of me, as if she could read my mind, Was I so transparent or just predictable? I found her very mysterious.

"Is Dolly your given name?" I asked.

"It's Anna Louise, but I've been called Dolly since I was little. I'm not crazy about Anna so in school I officially use Louise, but I prefer Dolly. I like it and I'm used to it. Everyone calls me that, even some of my teachers."

"I like it too," I said, "and besides, it suits you perfectly because let's face it, you're definitely a living doll." *Whoops, I thought, that is over the top? But I was sure I was getting the hang of this flirting thing, the clue being that if I didn't sound like me, I must have it right.*

"You sure flatter a lot, Paul; you're making me blush. Although it is sweet of you to say that, so thank you."

"You're welcome," I said. In silence we sipped and nibbled as the jukebox began playing another of my song selections, "When I Fall in Love." I was swinging for the fence with this tune too. The lyrics spoke of falling in love forever, or not at all. I watched Dolly smile at the message. I'd never encountered a girl like her before. I think I'm being subtle and clever, and yet she instantly picks up on everything I do and is smarter about this boy-girl thing than I will ever be.

"I'm a fan of Nat King Cole, too" she said, so I know this song. "The people I sometimes nanny for have lots of his records and I play them when I'm babysitting." She leaned back in her chair and looked at me thoughtfully, finally saying, "It seems you like romantic songs, so you're certainly not like other boys. It's rather refreshing, and nice, too." Gee, I thought... I think I've just won a round.

"When were you born?" she asked.

"August First, Nineteen Forty-Two, right here on the southwest side of Chicago."

"That is an interesting coincidence... me too, but on August Twenty First, also Nineteen Forty-Two. It seems we're both astrological lions, born under the sign of Leo. Did you know Leos often have large egos? It's also a fire sign, so lots of heat." After a pause she added with a sly little smile, "But... when male and female Leos do manage to connect, they nearly always mate for life." *Whoa,* I thought. *This is really getting heavy. Is she serious or just teasing again?* Why did I feel like she was the huntress and I, her game? I was the male and supposed to be chasing her. We ignored our cooling French fries as Dolly continued to explain astrology to me. While she spoke of stars, I fantasized about lips, her lips.

"Paul, you're staring at me with such intensity it's making me feel like a biology specimen."

"Sorry," I said, "I know I am. But if you're a specimen you're the most attractive one I've ever seen." On impulse, I stood up and began to lean over our small table toward her. She instantly got a watchful look on her face as I got close, and perhaps thinking I was going to try and kiss her, she began to turn her face to the side which was perfect because I put my lips to her ear and whispered, "No girl has any right to look the way you do. It's not fair to helplessly vulnerable boys like me. I simply can't help myself…you're just too pretty," and I sat down again.

"Well, I'll say one thing, for a boy professing to be shy, you've really got an effective technique. You sort of sneak up on a girl using your bashful, Mr. Nice Guy image, but I think it's all a trick. I've never been flattered and flirted with so much in my entire life. And even though we barely know each other, for a second there, when you leaned over the table… I was certain you were going to kiss me."

"Kiss you? I mean…you were going to let me?"

"No, Paul Marshall, not just yet." That comment sounded like a promise and was also the third time she'd used my full name. Why? Did she just like saying Marshall, or could she be trying it on for size? That thought pleased me… a lot. I was shy but still knew a little about girls. They make these leaps into *pretend* to test how certain things feel to them, like maybe trying out how a guy's name fit with theirs. I've seen girls do that… write their first name and link it with a boys last name inside their school notebooks, just to see how it looks. Girls like these little games of love. So, if Dolly was testing her name with mine in her head, I didn't mind. Still, we'd just met so wasn't it kind of quick to wonder about stuff like linked names? What kind of girl is this, I wondered? Is it possible she's feeling about me as I do about her? I've known my feeling since the moment I first saw her. Is it possible she's feeling that way to? Then I thought, *dream on big boy. This girl is class.* And yet, I wasn't ready to give up that easy. Stay in the game, I said to myself. You haven't struck out yet. Just keep swinging.

I stuck my bottom lip out in a pout, looking sad like a disappointed little kid who didn't get the kiss he wanted. My antic made Dolly giggle; the sound was irresistible. "Well, spoilsport," I went on, "you said, *'not just yet,'* so does that mean you might give me a kiss sometime soon?" To be honest, I knew I'd never have the guts to kiss her. Dolly would have to kiss me first. I was intimidated by her beauty and understood that guys like me don't get to kiss earth angels like Dolly unless invited. She confirmed this informing me with a sweet smile,

"No kissing yet brown eyes."

"Well then, can you answer one little question honestly?"

"If I can."

"Are you currently dating anyone?" For a moment there was dead silence.

"Not exactly," she finally said. "Is it any concern of yours, and why should you care if I am?" This feisty porcelain doll was testing me again, so I cranked up my courage and answered,

"You know I'd care, Dolly, and I'm going to be honest with you. You're the prettiest girl I've ever seen, and must have a million guys after you, which, by the way, is a deeply depressing thought." She said nothing, just smiled sweetly as I went on. "You're too smart to pretend you don't know I care because you've been reading me like Cliff's Notes all through lunch. I know that to you, I'm already an open book and you have me all figured out. But I think we both feel there's something going on here, so why pretend there isn't?"

*I never understood where these bursts of courage came from when I said things like that; it just wasn't like me.* She stared silently, apparently thinking about what I'd said. Suddenly I remembered we'd been sitting together for at least an hour or more and it was time for my class. A glance at my watch confirmed this. "Dolly," I said, "I'd love to sit here staring at your lovely face forever, but unfortunately I have to get to class."

To my surprise, she didn't seem ready to let me go. "You just don't quit flirting, do you," she said. "First you tell me your bashful and then you come on like a battalion of Marines? Have I missed something here?" She'd asked a fair question, and I had to think it over for a bit before deciding how I'd answer her. After a moment I screwed up my courage and said...

"Dolly, here's the whole truth. Something has happened to me today and you're the reason why. I've become like that cowardly lion who finally finds courage. My flattery is sincere because you deserve it. You are an amazing girl and all the wonderful things I've discovered about you today... how smart you are, and how heartbreakingly pretty…how funny, happy, and fun to be with…all those things are true. Honestly, I've never flirted with a girl like this before, but with you, I've forced myself because I desperately want you to like me. Oh, and by the way, remember earlier… when you asked me who the special girl was that I was thinking of? Well, as you knew all along, it was you Dolly. I've been thinking of nothing but you since the moment I set eyes on you."

"Well, well, Mr. Charmer. "Will the flirting never cease?" she said shyly dipping her head down a little. I once again glanced at my watch. "Unfortunately, today the clock is my hated enemy," I said, "because as much as I don't want to leave you, not ever, I really have to go." At the words, *not ever*, she looked slightly up at me again through those long lashes and a hint of a smile appeared, but she didn't comment. Making eye contact with the waitress I raised my hand making a little scribble sign in the air indicating *check please*. "I can't afford to screw up summer school," I said. "My mother wouldn't think twice, she'd kill me."

"Your mom sounds scary," she said, knowing I was almost certainly exaggerating the truth.

"Yeah, well, she's actually quite nice," I said, handing money to the waitress showing off a bit by adding, "keep the change." Who was I fooling? It was only small change, not big bucks.

"I'm happy to hear that," Dolly said, "because I'll probably be meeting your mom one of these days." Wow. Another big hint of a future for us, which encouraged me to say,

"Listen, Dolly, do you think you might consider meeting me here tomorrow, same time, same place?"

"Absolutely. I'd really like that," she said, "but before I go, I have something to say as well, and uhm…darn it, now I'm feeling shy." She covered her face in her hands for a moment, then composed, she raised her eyes to mine, and said,

"I can't believe I'm going to tell you this after only knowing you for what, an hour or so, but as you've asked me to be honest, here's the truth. Paul Marshall, I find you different from other boys in a really nice way. There's something intriguing about you. You're thoughtful, sensitive, kind, and I've already experienced your good manners. In fact, if anyone around here is special, it just might be you. And since you've been sending me endless hints that you're interested in me, I admit, I'm interested in you too, and I'd like to get to know you better, a lot better. In other words, if you want to, I'd like to spend more time with you to see what develops." It seemed that any uncertainty Dolly had felt moments before had gone now and all her usual confidence had returned in its place. She was in control again.

"Really?" I said in happy disbelief.

"Yes, really. And now, my charming new friend, I too must get going, but I will see you tomorrow, I promise. About eleven, and I'll save *our* table." As she began to rise, I said softly,

"I'll be counting the hours." She dropped back into her chair and looked at me, slowly shaking her pretty head from side to side.

"Paul, Paul, you really are too much. How can I resist all your flattery?"

"Don't you get it, Dolly?" I said. "I don't want you to resist… I want you to like me." She looked at me without saying a word, all the while grinning like the Cheshire Cat, with a look that said she'd just drawn the winning card she wanted in a game I didn't know we were playing, nor did I understand the rules. But I did have an idea we sought the same prize so if she'd won, so had I. Preparing to leave she turned, and locking her eyes on mine, she added in a sexy, theatrical sort of voice,

*"I'll be seeing you soon, Paul Marshall."* Then she winked, followed it with an air kiss, and laughed happily knowing it was game, set, and match, and she'd won, getting exactly what she wanted. Walking toward the door, she glanced back, wiggled her fingers over her shoulder in a cute wave, and swinging her hips a little more than necessary, she walked out of the grill, knowing perfectly well I was watching every mesmerizing movement of her lovely bottom. Girls know where boys are looking. They always know. As she passed by on the sidewalk outside our window, she was shaking her head and although I couldn't hear, I could see well enough and what I saw was that Dolly was laughing out loud!

Looking back, I have a feeling that even then, teenage girls knew how to play the game better than boys. Dolly was already aware that I was hers for the taking. I wasn't experienced at being charming or mysterious with girls, but I think I'd made it clear that I was enchanted with her. Sure, I'd have a little influence in the game of seduction we'd just set in motion, but it was Dolly who would decide each new step along the way. I remember how happy I was with how things had developed. I never in my life thought a girl like Dolly could ever be interested in me, and yet it had just happened. It was now obvious she liked me and wanted to spend time with me. So, what you may ask, was the one thing that occurred to make me so sure? That's easy, because...

*I'd just shared French fries with an angel!*

# 2.

"Oh, thou art fairer than the evening air,
clad in the beauty of a thousand stars."

Christopher Marlowe

My new chemistry teacher was nice and explained to us what we would be covering in his class. Then he started right in on the dreaded Periodic Tables. Well, of course, more memorizing of things I didn't really care about. I spent that first chemistry class *not* memorizing the symbol for carbon. All I could think about were the embarrassing words, "I'm counting the hours." Where did *that* come from? The rest of my lunch behavior played in my head in excruciating, embarrassing detail. What had happened to me? I'd somehow become a ventriloquist's dummy with no control of what was coming out of my mouth. Then I realized…it's that girl. Maybe she's not an angel at all…maybe she's a witch and she's cast a spell and is now in control of me, making me fall in love with her. But wasn't that exactly what I wanted to happen? Angel or witch, I didn't care. She was the girl I wanted; I was now more certain than ever.

I was a weird kid in my teens. Even though I knew I was just an ordinary guy, I had an all-consuming desire to be cool; not the black-leatherjacket, gang-member kind of cool, but the poetry-reading, jazz-loving, intellectual beatnik type. I wore the beat uniform of the era: Clarks Desert Boots, turtlenecks, or black T- shirts, and sunglasses much of the time, all part of the hip image I was trying to project. Unlike most guys I knew, I liked reading books, enjoyed poetry, romantic movies, and love songs. I was a sensitive kid rather than the cocky jock type. Not a wimp, however; I could play rough when necessary. But what sort of teenage boy reads sonnets without having them assigned in class? The answer, I decided, is a romantic guy like me. What could be more beautiful than words like: "Shall I compare thee to a summer's day? Thou art more lovely, and more temperate."

Like most boys I was crazy about cars, specifically hot rods and, in my case, also two-seat English sports cars. I was in fact, an incurable Anglophile obsessed with most things British. Not an overachieving student, I did well in subjects I liked such as literature, English comp, physics, machine shop, and architectural drawing. I was satisfied with just getting by in subjects I didn't like such as math and chemistry, all that boring memorization and god knows I didn't want to be a chemist anyway, and as for math? I had no talent for it. No specific life direction had yet occurred to me. I was still trying to figure myself out. I'd also been a bit slow in realizing that females were mysterious, and delightfully different. I was thirteen years old when I discovered that girls acted kind of goofy around boys; they were like flowers that decided the time to blossom had arrived. And oh boy, bloom they did, getting my attention in the process. Although there had never been a girlfriend in my life, I'd met a pretty heartbreaker who lived one street over from me while skating at the local ice pond. I think she was fourteen and she started inviting me over to her house after school with the express purpose of giving kissing lessons on the couch in her living room before her parents got home. "*Don't make your lips so hard,*" she'd instruct. "*Make them soft and open your mouth a little.*" Wow, this is fun, I'd thought. Yum. Kissing was also stirring sexual thoughts in my young brain while causing certain awkward responses to my body.

She was the first girl I ever kissed, and exactly what I needed, someone to show me the ropes. She smelled good, tasted like peppermint, and liked to wear tight sweaters of some soft fuzzy material to show off the fact that she had developed grown-up breasts. She took pleasure in pressing this abundance against me while we kissed. I didn't mind.

Crushing on her, I began to volunteer to walk the family dog at night after the evening meal. This enabled me to stroll past her house, hoping to get a glimpse of her through the big picture window that was a standard feature of many of the houses in our neighborhood. I thought this girl was hot stuff and my new girlfriend, until, that is, some guys at the ice pond told me she'd tried out quite a few boys on her famous couch. And here I'd thought I was special. With that knowledge my passion for her quickly faded. No more nighttime dog walks and no more kissing lessons. Even after that experience, I remained slow with girls compared to other boys. I'd been brought up to behave like a gentleman, so I was not pushy or aggressive where girls were concerned. Oh, all right; I admit it, I was also a big shy chicken about females. They intimidated me.

My freshmen year of high school was spent at boarding school, a Catholic, all boy's college prep academy in rural Illinois. It was not my choice but my moms, who believed in boarding school. Because I wanted to fit in as one of the guys I learned to smoke there, as many other boys did. In the process I developed an addiction that would take me half a lifetime to kick. I disliked boarding school, too many rules and too much control, so I begged my mom and dad to let me transfer to Tilden Tech, the public school my dad had attended in Chicago. Happily, they allowed me to register there for my sophomore year.

While attending Tilden Tech I turned sixteen, got my license to drive, and with money I'd been saving for a year from part-time jobs, I bought an already souped-up car from an older guy in my neighborhood. Most boys who became my friends in high school were gearheads. We spent lots of time fiddling with our cars, in my case, improving a Ford on which the prior owner had performed a swap to a powerful Oldsmobile V8 engine. Hanging out in each other's garages did not leave much time to worry about girls. But of course, they were an ongoing topic of conversation that went along the lines of, "So, did ja kiss her yet, ya loser? Har, har, har!" We were not the most sophisticated group when it came to girls. I'd already figured out that females were much smarter than we were, and they made up the rules of engagement, not us.

So it was, that on a warm day in June late in my sixteenth year a miracle occurred. An angel named Dolly had appeared and thrown open a new door, immediately taking ownership of my foolish heart. I rushed right in, never considering what the consequences might be. There's a voice in my head sometimes. I suppose it's my conscience or maybe just the voice of common sense, but after this miracle had occurred the voice appeared and reminded me that Dolly was no ordinary girl. *This one's serious, boy,* (The voice always called me *boy*). *So be warned, she won't be toyed with. She plays for keeps. She's also a lot smarter than you are about this romance thing.*

Of course, I ignored the voice. After all, I was nearly seventeen, the age of knowing everything. I'd met a girl so wonderful it made my heart hurt to be near her. It had only taken one arrow plucked from Cupid's quiver and shot from his golden bow to pierce my heart, infecting me with an acute case of love madness.

We did meet again the next day, and the day after, and all the days and nights that followed through the summer of 1959. If there'd been a boyfriend, he was long gone. It was obvious we were drawn to each other like roses to sunlight, and the strong attraction we felt was looking a lot like something much bigger than simply, "I like you." In my world, no other girl existed, only the one I secretly thought of as part angel who'd come from the stars. I wanted to learn everything about her as fast as possible. She told me she was of Polish, Slovak, and Hungarian decent, not uncommon in my part of Chicago. I loved the look of her; fair, blonde, with eyes of gold and skin so fine she seemed to have no pores. My grandfather Marshall had been of British descent, giving me an English surname, but two of my grandmothers were Polish and my mother, a great beauty in youth and old age, was half Polish and half German, so perhaps attraction to northern European girls was in my DNA.

Soon, few thoughts that weren't of Dolly ever entered my head. Days and nights were a time of discovery. We talked excitedly, on the phone and in my car, about books and our love of reading. We both appeared to be well-read, even precocious considering our ages. Dolly was reading the Russian author, Nabokov which amazed me as I found him difficult. Later she became a great admirer of Solzhenitsyn books. There was something about the Russians that appealed to her. At the time I was reading British classics. Authors like Hardy, Waugh, Austen, and American novelists like Herman Wouk and J.D. Salinger. We both liked music and art and were not much interested in ball sports.

A key to our strong connection was that we shared romantic natures. This was made obvious by the books, movies, and music we each liked and the tender way we were already treating each other; gently, with kindness and caring. I'd bring her a few flowers, stolen from someone's garden, or a 45rpm record of a Nat King Cole song she liked. She'd sometimes rub accidentally (?) against me, thrilling me down to my Clarks desert boots, her touch giving an electric shock sensation every time. It was a game we were playing, she was good at it, and I loved it. It seemed we fit together like peach pie and ice cream. I wanted to be with her all the time. My focus was on her happiness, comfort, and pleasure. I found myself behaving like one of those male birds who strut about puffing up his feathers to attract the female. I tried my best to paint myself in a good light. Without question, Dolly was an endless pleasure to look at, yet I found her much more than just a beauty. For the first time in my life, I cared about someone else more than I did myself. This was a major discovery. I was addicted, enamored, in awe of, and even somewhat intimidated by this confident little girl. She was fearless, and so sure of herself it was almost frightening, yet she showed little tendency to outsized ego. Rather she was unpretentious, kind, and endearing.

At the time we met I knew for certain I'd experienced love at first sight. There was no doubt in my mind. But now I was getting serious about the question of true deep love, the enduring kind. Is it possible I'm truly in love with Dolly? I'm only seventeen, I thought, and not even sure I can define real love? Then suddenly I recalled something we'd discussed in religion class at Catholic high school: "To love is to will the good of the other." This quote was from Thomas Aquinas, and I finally understood it at last.

We didn't see each other in school during the summer session, only before or after class. Then in the evenings we began to spend every possible hour together in my black Ford. Sometimes I'd take her to a DOG & SUDS where lots of hot car owners hung out, the area saturated in testosterone. The hot Oldsmobile V8 engine in my Ford made it quite fast so occasionally I was able to earn extra folding by picking up an eighth mile drag race for money on deserted factory roads at night...prize money only if I won of course. I'd arrange a race with some guy, then after I'd dropped Dolly at home, I'd go meet the competition. Surely Dolly would not have approved as this was totally illegal. I was, all things considered, a good kid, but I did have a weakness for drag racing occasionally.

I was proud of my car. The exhaust from that big engine rumbled through glass pack mufflers and out twin chrome-tipped tailpipes, singing the song every motor head loves. Hanging from the rearview mirror were the requisite fuzzy dice, popular at the time, and the car sported blue dot taillights. It was the style among hotrodders to put a name on his car, so I'd paid an artistic kid at school to paint *WILD CHILD* in inch and a half tall white letters with pinstriping around it, under the rear side windows of the Ford. I thought it looked cool but got the feeling Dolly couldn't care less about the name. And beyond its use as a magic carpet that afforded us freedom and privacy, she didn't really care about the car either.

Fortunately, I did matter to her, a fact far more important to me. I quickly abandoned my gearhead buddies, and soon stopped the racing too as nearly every night the two of us weren't at our part-time jobs, we'd drive to Marquette Park, a nearby urban paradise, to be alone together. If a friend needed me, he knew where to find me; just cruise through the 323-acre park until you spot the black Ford parked in some dark secluded spot. What good the dark spot did for me was not much; I still hadn't found the courage to kiss Dolly. But I knew that once I did, I'd want to go on kissing her forever. There was no question about that fact.

Landscaped with large grassy areas, a golf course, trees, flower gardens, and recreational facilities, the park was an oasis of nature surrounded by housing. An unofficial lovers' lane, it was used by young people who'd park along the curbs after dark and do what kids have done in lovers' lanes since cars were invented. The police cruised through but if nothing publicly unacceptable was going on they left the lovers alone.

As it was summer, Dolly would often wear the white tap shorts she favored, the kind you see on girl dancers in movies from the '30s and '40s. They fit her sexy little body amazingly well; snug on her bottom, then flaring a little at the leg openings. I was as susceptible to sexiness as the next guy, so when she wore them, I'd grow weak at the sight of her. Dolly had a beautifully shaped bottom, so when walking her little "Dolly Walk" away from me in those shorts, I'd feel my pulse rate go up. It was a little frightening; this power girls have over the male. Song writer Cole Porter gave us a hint of what it was when he wrote the words, "You've Got That Thing!" The question is, what exactly is *that thing?* I couldn't describe it, but I knew that Dolly had it… an abundance of it.

She'd curl up on the passenger side of the car, sometimes with her knees drawn up, hugging her legs, and we'd talk for hours while DJ Sid McCoy played jazz on the radio show he called *The Real McCoy.* He would open the program with his theme music, a Frank Sinatra vocal version of the Cole Porter song, "At Long Last Love." After the lyric line "…or is what I feel the real McCoy?" the music would fade, and in a dark, warm, honey-coated voice he'd purr,

"Hey, Hey old bean, and you too, baby… It's the Real McCoy." I loved his program. He had great taste in jazz, and that mesmerizing voice and the wonderful music he played became background to our endless sessions of shyly (on my part) dancing around each other playing a subtle game of "I know you want to kiss me so what's the holdup?" I will forever associate jazz on a car radio with warm summer nights spent happily with my living doll. I felt so incredibly grateful that she'd chosen me to be with.

I've often wondered what we could possibly have had to talk about all those hours, but talk we did, and I got to look endlessly at those wonderful legs. Once I got bold and said, "Doll, have I mentioned I think your legs are beautiful?" She smiled with a pleased look, so I decided to risk even more… "Even your feet are pretty. They're so small with perfect little toes. And your ankles are delicate and fine too."

"There you go, making me blush again. Guys don't usually tell girls such things, Paul. It's kind of personal. We know they may think it, but they seldom say it out loud."

"Well, I'm different, so thought I'd tell you. Sorry if I've embarrassed you."

"Oh, I'm not embarrassed. I like that you like things about me…a lot. I really do." She reached over and squeezed my hand; as usual, my heart missed several beats. Why did her touch cause such a reaction in me? Time spent together was slowly encouraging these small intimacies. Step by step we were growing closer but, not being an aggressive guy, I didn't rush it. I didn't have the courage. The truth is, there was no part of her I didn't want to kiss and touch. Being with her was like a religious experience, and I was a convert, ready to worship at her altar. I longed to call her my "steady" girlfriend although we had no official understanding…yet. Young Paul's emotional state at the time could be summed up in one word: enraptured.

Dolly had to know she already owned me, heart, and soul. Aching to kiss her, I was too shy. The few girls I'd kissed in the past had been practice, but I instinctively knew that kissing Dolly held major significance and would be a life-altering experience. I couldn't botch it up. Bumped noses or teeth would spoil everything. Still, what was I waiting for? I knew she wanted me to. I was cowardly, but not stupid.

In my defense, I understood certain realities. Dolly was no ordinary girl. She was a teen goddess, whereas I was just a shy mortal. Shy mortals don't just grab goddesses and kiss them. She had to know I was hers and like a ripe apple on a low-hanging bough, I kept hoping she'd pick me, and soon. Girls understand these things instinctively. They're all Eves at heart, playing love games with their lustful Adams in Gardens of Eden like Marquette Park, and it seemed to me the young female always holds all the power cards. They're smarter than we are and in control of the game of love.

As weeks passed into midsummer our romance was approaching a new level. I was holding Dolly's hand at every opportunity. I know, I know… modern young people laugh, as according to today's standards, handholding is from the dark ages. Back then we'd never heard the term "hooking up," which is considered common practice today. But this was 1959, and some well brought-up boys were not as aggressive then, at least I wasn't. Manners and morals had been drummed into me at home and Catholic school, so holding hands was a breakthrough. After all, this was not one of my sisters. Oh no. This was a real girl, and I was so obsessed with her that simply holding her hand was exciting to me. I had also begun putting my arm around Dolly when she sat tight against me as we drove in the car, another breakthrough instigated by her of course as she tried to move me off first base. The truth was, for me, a boy whose hormones were in overload, the simple act of touching Dolly, any part of her, was a confusing mix of pain and ecstasy. We weren't intimate yet but were moving in that direction a little more each day. I knew it was only a matter of time.

Dolly radiated sexiness without studied intent. Her doll-like size, beautiful figure, and soft prettiness made me want to squeeze, cuddle, and love her. It also made lots of other boys want to do the same. She attracted guys without effort, a phenomenon I wished would go away. I'd come to despise all males, no matter their age. When we went to The Huddle or were just walking back to school for my class, lots of guys who knew her would wave or shout greetings like, "Hey Dolly, looking good." In my frustration I broached the subject one day. Pleading with her I said,

"Doll, how about not wearing makeup to school? Or maybe you could wear less pretty, girly clothes, or try to not look so incredibly cute?"

"Why?" she asked, not understanding such a crazy request.

"Because you attract guys like ants to sugar and it's driving me crazy, that's why."

She laughed and said, "You have nothing to worry about, Paul. It's you I'm with, and not any of those guys you worry about so much. I don't care about any of them the way I care about you, so you can relax and trust me." I liked that she'd said she cared about me, so I determined I'd have to learn to trust and pay the price of having a beauty for a girlfriend. Males, I decided, were all barbarians who would stare at or even approach my beautiful girl, usually with that dumb, mouth-breather Neanderthal look on their stupid faces. I hated them.

One warm evening in late July, I sensed a change in the air. I'd picked Dolly up for an evening in the park. She was wearing a full loose skirt of a soft lightweight material, taupe in color, that had a way of shaping itself around curvy parts of her anatomy as she moved. She also wore a black camisole top held up by a thin strap around the neck. It plunged quite low behind, revealing a flawless back. It was made of a soft material, perhaps chiffon I think, and it teased because it was almost but not quite see-through (darn it). It hung softly, draping over her breasts which shivered like Jell-O when she moved, and that plus the lack of a bra strap across her back made it obvious she wasn't wearing one. On her feet were strappy sandals with little heels. Quite honestly, I'm surprised her mother had let her out in this get-up. The sexy fashion show was too much for Mr. Shy Guy. Did I say, "Oh my god, you look gorgeous?" Not a bit. I said nothing, just mentally drooled over this sweet young girl who had suddenly metamorphosed into a femme fatale, an enchanting creature of the night, and I... well, there was no excuse for me. When it came to this oh so desirable creature, I was a plodder, and she was obviously growing impatient with my plodding. Her tempting dress was shouting, *Look at me! I know I'm the girl you want, so do something about it!*

We entered Marquette Park as a beautiful evening began to unfold, the sky slashed with bold brushstrokes of red, gold, magenta, and Dolly's favorite, lavender. It was right after the sun had dipped below the trees, so soon the first evening stars would be points of burning light glittering in the blue-black dome that covered our secret garden of Eden. The Old's engine was growling away nicely as we idled along. We were like a black night bird in search of that perfect perch on which to land near the flower gardens. Locating a secluded spot, I parked, shut the car down, and the hot engine began making popping and pinging sounds as the metal cooled. Settling in, music on the radio, we began taking those special mental steps only two kids in the first stages of young love know. Where would the steps lead us tonight—that was the burning question. It was obvious, even to me, that tonight. . . a new game was on and we'd be taking things up a notch.

Dolly had kicked off her sandals, placing her bare feet on the black dashboard. Her toenails were painted a pearl color. Normally one does not think of feet as particularly sexy, but to me, Dolly's were so small and perfect, I wanted to kiss them. In fact, I wanted to kiss any part of her she'd allow. I craved every bit of her and needed only a good dose of confidence to let her know. Surely, she recognized I was a young buck in rut, and she was the doe I'd singled out from the herd.

Most young guys don't understand the power of soft music, tenderness, moonlight, and pretty words. That's because most young guys are barbarians. Being a romantic guy, I understood all those things. What I lacked was the courage to put them to work. Dolly had adjusted her skirt so that much of the fabric was gathered between her legs, revealing nearly all her smooth, flawless thighs. It was a lot of skin she was exposing to my hungry eyes. Actually, it was no more than if she had shorts on, but when a girl is in a skirt and it's gathered up that high…well, that's a game changer and a major tease. She had one tiny scar on her left knee, received, she'd told me, in her tom boy days when she fell off her bike in the cinder alley behind her house. One tiny flaw to contrast and magnify the perfection of the rest.

Part of the chemistry of attraction is olfactory. The perfume Dolly wore at the time was the popular *Hypnotique,* by Max Factor. It was a warm floral with a hint of balsam, and I loved it. Knowing it was her favorite, I'd gifted her a bottle of this balm, which she used to cast a spell over me.

I didn't know how far she was planning to take this game, but the wondering made me dizzy. Looking back now, she was hammering me on the head with *green light go* signs, and I was slow off the mark. Truth is, her overtures tested my insecure nature, so we continued to dance around each other, the tension in the car palpable. My beautiful girl was like a spider in a web waiting for her prey to land in her trap. Every so often she'd casually run her hands over those legs as if she were applying lotion. I'm certain she did this intentionally, drawing my eyes where she wanted. It was an effective ploy.

I watched, mesmerized, imagining how it might be to run *my* hands over those glorious thighs the way hers were doing. This was all part of a mating dance between two young animals in heat, but what to do, what to do.

I confess the closeness of all that skin made me harbor what my parish priest would call impure thoughts. Why, I wondered, is every food that tastes good bad for our health and everything we really desire, mortal sin, at least for a Catholic? A priest in the confessional would have told me that sweet, loveable little Dolly was in fact a dangerous and seductive temptress, the very occasion of dreaded mortal sin, so I should avoid her, or end up in hell. My reply, assuming I ever saw the inside of a confessional—I didn't believe in that practice—would have been something like, "Are you kidding, Father? According to church teaching, God made her just as she is. I believe it's God's intention that I find her adorable, completely irresistible, and yes, even tempting, so if she's mortal sin, so be it. Give me my sin."

Dolly turned and, stretching her legs across the seat (*my god, I thought, that's a lot of skin*), she began gently kneading my thigh with her toes. When readjusting her skirt material, I'd been given a brief glimpse of very pretty white, lace-trimmed panties. Was it intentional? With girls, even nice girls like Dolly, you just never knew how far they'd go in teasing a boy they wanted. They were unknowable creatures….unsolvable enigma's. Suddenly, it felt extremely hot inside the car with the result that I became quieter still. She continued this seductive new game, purring in a soft, sensual voice, "Well-l-l, Paul-l-l, tell me, what are you thinking about so hard?"

"Oh," I said innocently, "I'm just sort of…daydreaming."

"Oka-a-a-y…so tell me what you're daydreaming about?"

"I think I'd rather not say."

"Oh, re-e-a-ally?" she teased. "I'll help you out then and tell you what I think. Since I saw your eyes wandering all over sweet little me, I'll just bet you were thinking hard about my bare legs, that's what I think, and didn't you just take a peek at my panties when I accidentally provided the opportunity? I didn't notice you turn your eyes away, did I? Wouldn't a nice boy have turned away instead of staring greedily? And maybe you were even daydreaming naughty thoughts about other parts of me as well. Hmmm? Am

I right? Tell the truth, now." She'd revealed my deepest desires, and the kneading of her toes against my leg continued. Young Paul just sat there in a state of confusion. Maybe she really was "mortal sin," but I didn't care. I was so hungry for her I was prepared to burn in hell to have her for my own. Her boldness made it apparent that she was getting tired of waiting for me to do something…anything.

"Do you read minds," I asked, "or are you guessing? Maybe you're teasing me intentionally with that gossamer top, your beautiful legs and that unfair trick you played by letting me see your fancy pants, and if you are…well, I admit, I don't mind one bit. Tease on."

Dolly placed a foot against my side, and giving a playful push said, "Well, well, this is getting interesting. I already know you like my legs; you've told me so, but what else are you wishing you could see or touch ? Oh, and by the way. . . I also saw you staring at the front of my camisole with what I'd call hungry eyes. My top can't be that interesting unless you have X-ray vision, so maybe you're trying to form a picture of what the fabric is covering up, you bad boy." I couldn't believe what I was hearing. I had a sudden desire to quietly fly out of the window. She was exposing me because she knew what I really was… a sex-crazed but cowardly teenaged boy. The torture went on.

"So, tell me Mr. Greedy Eyes, what other parts of me do you find interesting?" she asked. "I'm beginning to think you're not the sweet guy you pretend to be after all. Have you been fooling me all this time, trying to make me believe you're such a nice boy? Well? I'm waiting. What have you got to say for yourself?"

It was plain this sweet but tricky girl had planned this production. Trying to gain some control of the situation, I gently moved her legs aside, which of course required touching them, making me tremble with desire. Sliding close, I gazed intently into that angelic (?), innocent (?) face and forced myself to make a true and honest confession. How I found the courage I'll never know.

"Dolly" I said, "you have beautiful *everything*. "At least everything I can see. And at night I do dream of you, trying to picture the rest of the delicious places you keep hidden from my eyes." I knew this was the perfect moment and I was preparing to kiss her. Alas, I was sabotaged by a sound that began deep in her chest and stopped me cold. She'd begun laughing softly… It was instantly apparent I was being toyed with… suckered into a game of her invention called *tease Paul mercilessly but don't give anything away, at least not yet.* She'd been manipulating me all along, getting me to admit I found her body beautiful and that I fantasized about things I hungered to see but could only imagine. There was clearly a devil in my angel; one who knew exactly what it was doing. She knew she had complete power over me. Before things went any further, and to salvage my pride I said, "Okay, you bad girl. You've had your fun getting me all excited and worked up with your hot clothes and your tease Paul game. But now, my clever, sexy young beauty, it's such a beautiful night, why don't we take a walk in the gardens?"

"That sounds perfect," she said. I went around the car and as I opened her door, she asked, "Pretty please, Paul, would you buckle the straps on my sandals?" *Oh lord I thought, you're killing me girl. You know I'm going to have to touch you and what that does to me.* With shaking hands, I was struggling to complete the task when she asked.

"Paul, is that how you picture me? Am I really your sexy young beauty?" She was casting her hook in the pond and once again, I dove on the bait.

"Oh yes," I said softly, "You most definitely are… sexy, incredibly beautiful, too smart for your own good, and you're my girl. That is… I'm hoping you want to be my girl."

"I already am, foolish boy. Haven't you figured that out yet? You're so slow… I can't believe how slow." Her declaration that she was my girl made my heart leap, but I could also hear real frustration in her voice. She was right, of course; I was slow, but I couldn't help it. I lacked confidence in this game of love. However, I promised myself firmly I'd be bolder in future. As it turned out, in a few moments, courage and the future arrived, flying in at Mach 1.

I'd placed an arm around her shoulders, and she'd put hers around my waist, leaning against me as we strolled the winding pathway deeper into the park gardens. I lowered my face to her silky hair, inhaling its clean fragrance, like warm, flower-scented sunshine. There was nowhere else on this earth I wanted to be than right here holding this captivating, enchanting girl. At that most inopportune moment, my friend the faceless voice popped up and said, *Boy, this is the moment you've been waiting for . . . don't blow it.* This time the voice was correct, brief, and to the point.

It was a magical evening, what the Irish call a *soft night*, one just made for romance. The sky was dotted with billions of stars beaming down and softly touching us as if we were the only two people in the world. At last I found courage and turning I took Dolly in my arms, slowly drawing her to me until our two bodies merged into one. We were a perfect fit, like two halves of the yin-yang symbol joined at last. She did not resist, just looked at me, liquid eyes filled with anticipation. I knew what they were telling me; *Now, my brown-eyed boy; don't think, just do it."*

"I want to kiss you," I whispered.

"I know you do, and I want you to. You've made me wait much too long."

Our faces moved together at a glacial pace, my eyes still open, absorbing the beauty of her angel face, my lips anticipating that first touch with hers. It was as if we didn't want to hurry what we'd both craved for so long. When lips did melt into lips, merging at last, the joining was fire devouring fire, our mouths like crucibles enduring the heat and the awakening of a desire so intense it would prove impossible to extinguish…ever. Kissing Dolly was, for me, an experience so incendiary I felt she was consuming my soul in the heat of her flame, a feeling I never wanted to end. When we paused, our panting mouths remained close, hot breath mingling as she whispered, "It took you long enough, Paul Marshall." So, of course I kissed her again, this time our tongues shyly touching. The dam inside me had finally crumbled and bursting free were an ocean of desires and emotions, long pent up but free now and completely out of control. Intensely aroused, my hands moved over her bare back, fingertips tracing lightly the smooth perfection of her flawless skin. I continued to inhale the heat and fragrance glowing from her excited body. Her lips were as soft and sweet as the flesh of an overripe peach left in the sun. I was intoxicated and prayed silently to Venus and all the various goddesses and gods of love man has ever conceived of... *please, don't ever let this feeling end.*

It never did... not in all the years that were waiting for us in our future.

# 3.

"Sin from thy lips? Oh, trespass sweetly urged!"
Give me my sin again!"

Shakespeare/*Romeo and Juliet*

We kissed our way through the last days of July and into August, never getting enough of joining our faces at the lips, tongues still shy, yet daring hungrily to touch, searching for the very soul of the other. Once the flame of desire had been lit, it refused to be extinguished. It was a fire edging dangerously out of control.

"Doll, I can't get enough of you," I told her one night. "No matter how much we kiss it doesn't ever seem enough. I have a cannibal-like urge to devour you. I don't think I'll be satisfied until I've eaten you up."

"I know, I know," she whispered, "and I want to let you." Then our lips would start the dance again, in anxious anticipation of that yet-to-be-experienced connection our bodies longed for, but self-control and a little fear and uncertainty would not allow. Biology intends us to feel this desire; it's programmed into us, encouraging procreation, and at the same time giving two lovers a way to bond in a most intimate and beautiful way. The lamp of love had been lit and it had sparked a powerful mating urge. Resisting desire and denying our body's longings was one of the most difficult challenges we faced at that time. We did our best at self-control…for a while.

Our first real date, and by date, I mean a dress-up-in-our-finest, night-out kind of evening, happened August 9, 1959. Dolly wore a pretty summer frock, perfect for evening. "You look exceptionally beautiful tonight. You take my breath away" I said. "In fact, if you stand there much longer, and I continue to stare, I may not be able to breath at all."

"Thank you, kind sir. You look extremely handsome too, so let's go have some fun." She was being generous. I couldn't hold a candle to this earth angel.

We had dinner at the famous Diamonds Steak House on South Wabash where grilling steaks was a production performed over an open hickory charcoal fire. Dining at Diamonds was just the beginning of the evening. After our meal we drove to Chicago Stadium where I felt so sophisticated escorting this lovely girl to the first (and only) jazz festival sponsored by *Playboy Magazine* in Chicago. I was now seventeen years and nine days old and Dolly would remain sixteen for twelve more days. The crowd in attendance was older and seriously hip. I'm certain they were thinking, *Aren't those kids just too cute.* But I was thinking, *Man, I am one cool cat with the prettiest girl in the place on my arm.* We felt glamorous that night, two swinging jazz lovers out on the town, or as Frank Sinatra would say, "Ring a ding-ding!" Though we felt very uptown, the reality was that we were still two teens role playing what we'd learned watching movies.

The music that night was a once in a lifetime experience. We heard Ella Fitzgerald, Stan Kenton, Coleman Hawkins, and other jazz giants making our first formal date one we'd recall for years.

There was a popular song at the time called *"Too Young to Go Steady,"* performed by Nat King Cole. Going steady was the hot ticket among teens in 1959. I'd asked… Dolly had said yes, and we were "going steady." Being "steadies" meant a girl was presented with her guy's ring, a senior class ring if he had one, which she'd either wear on a chain around her neck or wrapped with tape or angora on the back so it would fit her smaller finger. It was a sign telling everyone that she was one guy's girl and not available. Dolly wore my

senior ring on a gold chain, and I was king of the world. She was all mine…
well, sort of. A problem was brewing.

One day my Mother asked, "Paul, where's your senior ring? You're not
wearing it." "Mom, I whined, as if the answer were obvious, "Dolly and I are
going steady!" "Lord, give me strength," she said. "That ring cost $35.00."


We were now into September. I'd passed chemistry, summer school was over,
and our senior year of high school had begun. I was back in my own school
and Dolly in hers, but I'd developed a problem I found impossible to control,
possessiveness. I didn't want other guys near my girl. This became an issue
that threatened to drive a wedge between us. Dolly went to a co-ed school
where she was popular, and well liked. It seemed she knew just about everyone
and was, unfortunately, a magnet for the attention of boys. My youthful
inexperience and unreasonable lack of trust in her caused more than one
argument, though we rarely argued about anything else. When I picked her
up from school, I found she was often talking to some boy…frequently more
than one. I voiced my frustration that guys were always around her, and this
began a barrage of angry words, even shouting as she said,

"You don't trust me! You don't believe me when I tell you I'm only with
you. Why can't you understand that I have friends who are boys, but they're
just friends and I'm still faithful to you?" She was frustrated and blazing mad.

"My school friends are respectful," she continued. "Practically the entire
senior class knows I'm going steady with a guy from Tilden Tech. Some boys
are envious of you but do respect we're going steady. It's like an honor thing
with them. And most of the girls think you're lovely, So where's the
problem?" This comforted me for a time, but it seemed I could not control
my jealousy. By late September things had gotten so bad I don't know why
she stayed with me. I assumed every guy was after her and lived in constant
fear she'd be tempted away. I'd heard plenty of stories about that happening.
I would have locked her up in a little jewel box if I could. The unbearable
thought of losing her turned me into a jealous monster. I had read once that
jealousy has no place in true love, but it didn't seem logical to my young brain.

If you love someone and want to hold them close as your own, you just naturally protect and guard them from others.

We were in the car in Marquette Park when she brought up the topic of the dance. Before we met, she'd promised to go to the first fall dance at her school with some boy who was a classmate and neighborhood friend.

"His name's Danny and he's genuinely nice, so you don't have a thing to worry about. It would be wrong of me to break my promise now, at the last minute. Think about it, Paul, it's nothing, just a dance. A few hours and it's over. No big deal." Darn that kind heart of hers.

"Dolly, you're killing me," I said. "Your promise to him doesn't matter to me. The thought that he'll be touching you, holding you, makes me crazy. I'm not stupid. This kid is interested in you and I want to murder him." Looking back, it's obvious that at that time I had a boatload of growing up to do. The discussion grew even more heated, a fusillade of words flying from both sides. Eventually however, arguing and anger lost momentum as usually happened when my affection for her calmed me, so finally, with a few humiliating tears trying to form I abjectly begged forgiveness for my lack of trust. It was at that moment that Dolly did something which elevated us to a new plane; something I'd never have anticipated. After kissing and making up, she stopped for a moment, looked intently at me, and whispered,

"Give me your hand, Paul." I did as she asked and slowly, her eyes burning into mine in a way more intimate than I'd ever seen before, she placed my hand under her sweater covering one of her breasts. She wore no bra, and the shock of this reality took my breath away. Keeping her hand on mine, she began to tremble a little, taking short, fast breaths as her excitement increased. For the first time, I was beginning to experience what true physical passion with a lover is like. I couldn't imagine how the ultimate joining of my body with hers would be; just the thought made my head spin.

"No one has ever touched me like this...not ever. I'm giving you something I would never have allowed anyone but you. Her eyes were sparkling as she squeezed my hand making it even tighter on her breast. It's because I want you to understand how much you mean to me and I'm trying to make you believe me when I tell you, Paul, I am for you alone. I'm yours and don't want to be anyone else's. You can trust me completely." Her words were important to me, but this level of intimacy and closeness was new territory, and I could barely think about what she was saying. She removed her hand and let me continue to gently caress her breasts as our kisses took on a hungry urgency that bordered on sweet insanity. I wanted to become a part of her, to be absorbed into her through her lips and mouth. This intimacy was beyond anything I'd ever known. Blood was pounding so hard in my veins I thought they might burst. The hunger I was feeling, a desire to possess her completely, was nature telling me something profound. Once again, the voice:

*Now you know why you're alive, boy; she is your reason for living. What you have just begun is going to take you places more beautiful than you've ever imagined.*

This first experience of passionate intimacy with the girl I loved will stay in my memory forever. It was one of those times in life a young man never forgets. I should add I'm glad I'd never known this feeling before and would only know it with the girl I loved. Why waste such a tender, beautiful thing on a casual encounter? At least that's how I felt about it then, and still do.

In the end I accepted that the school dance must happen. You will survive this, I told myself over and over. It's no big deal and nothing bad is going to occur. Dolly is faithfully yours alone.

She was right, of course; she always was, and yes, I did survive. But I couldn't do it with grace. Years later I overheard my beloved telling our daughter Gabrielle the story of that dreaded dance, including the embarrassing ending. They couldn't see me standing just outside the open door of the room they were in, listening.

"Your dad was overcome with jealousy over this kid he didn't even know, a nice boy who was nothing more to me than a casual friend. Daddy was right about one thing though: Danny did like me and at the dance he even tried to kiss me, but I said no so he knew it was hopeless.

Finally, your dad agreed I would go to the dance. However, when the evening ended, there he was in his car outside the school gym, sitting in the dark with just the parking lights on. He was waiting there for me, like my own personal taxicab. That big engine was growling away, and I remember thinking that black car sounded alive, like some wild animal. I walked up to the open window with my date, intending to introduce them, but your dad said, 'I've come to drive you home. Just you.'

"Oh my god, Mom. Really? What did you do?" Gabrielle asked.

"Well, it was rude of your dad, I suppose, but also kind of cute, like a scene out of the James Dean movie, *Rebel Without a Cause*. Your dad took off those sunglasses he wore, sometimes even at night, and just stared at the boy, fire in his eyes! I didn't dare refuse to get into the car, so I told Danny, 'Thank you for the dance, it was fun, but this is my steady boyfriend Paul, and I've got to go with him now.' He nodded without saying a word. I think he sensed his best option was to quietly walk away. So, your father's Ford, with us in it, eased from the curb and slowly rumbled its way down the dark street. Your dad was such a little boy about these things, and jealous in the extreme. But he was my jealous little boy, and so cute!" Fortunately for me, they couldn't see my ears burning red. They laughed themselves silly for a time over my pathetic performance that night during our senior year of high school. I admit, young love was never a simple thing for me.

# 4.

"I would not wish any companion
in the world but you."

Wm. Shakespeare

In describing Dolly, it may seem I paint a picture of a girl too near perfect to be real. I don't. All I say about her is the truth. Beyond her physical beauty there was a goodness in her that made her immensely attractive. Petite at only five feet tall, when she entered a room, her presence was palpable. It had little to do with size; there was something about her that refused to be ignored. Often laughing happily, she made me wonder if the infant Dolly had entered this world laughing or perhaps life was just one long playful farce to her, something to enjoy and laugh about. She genuinely liked people, was friendly, and truly kind, but also in possession of a formidable personality. Metaphorically, I liked to imagine her to be a fine steel blade cast in fire, but she was a sword with a positive purpose, a tiny warrior goddess for good. And all these qualities were present in a young woman whose background was far from stellar.

Dolly was the oldest of five children. Her sibling's names were Jerry, Diane, Joy and Lillian. These kids didn't have a smooth path growing up. Louis, Dolly's immigrant father, was a crude man with little more than a third-grade education. A mason by trade, he loved his family in the best way he knew how. His problem was an issue with alcohol. In his defense, he did avoid drinking when employed and working every day. However, he was often laid off due to the seasonality of his work so would collect unemployment compensation and drink lots of it up at the corner tavern shooting pool with his drinking buddies. He was tender and loving toward his children at times, but when under the influence, he'd become demanding, unreasonable, and ignorant.

On the flip side of the parental coin was Dolly's mom Ann, a patient sweetheart, even considering that her husband made her life a constant challenge. An even-tempered woman, she liked reading poetry, and possessed the kind of wisdom people acquire after they've seen a lot of life. That wisdom was passed on to Dolly, helping her become who she was; clear eyed, determined, and sensible. Dolly's mother was also a lady. When she went out or to church, she wore white gloves in the old way. I had great respect for her mom, who was a candle in the dark of that marriage.

Soon after we met, I'd paid my first visit to the interior of her family's old three-story frame house. It told me volumes. On a heavily trafficked city street, her house was part of a row of similar houses, probably built in the late nineteenth or early twentieth century. Over the years it had been poorly maintained, and although spotlessly neat inside, it was apparent there wasn't a lot of money available to care for it. The oriental-style carpets in the living room, like the furniture, were clean but well worn. I'd been taught not to judge others by their circumstances, so I tried not to. It didn't matter where Dolly came from, as I saw nothing beyond the amazing girl she was. My family wasn't wealthy either, just middle-class working people. We did, however, live in a new brick house on a pleasant residential street in a neighborhood of brick houses. My parents, Henry, and Leona, both worked, and owned two cars, paid for with cash. They'd built for us, a shell of a summer cottage near the shores of Lake Michigan, which my father was finishing, working on it weekends and summer vacations. There was no summer place in Dolly's family, and no cars; they traveled by bus or occasionally, cab. Dolly told me her father didn't drive any longer because he didn't trust himself due to his drinking. Very sensible.

Considering their circumstances, Dolly and her siblings were surprisingly happy kids. She always spoke lovingly of her home life, describing it in positive ways. She'd talk of the stately old tree in front of the house, the drone of traffic at night that lulled her to sleep in her attic bedroom, and all the fun she, her siblings and other neighborhood kids had when young and playing in the alley and nearby Illinois prairies, a few of which still existed then at the far edges of the city.

She was by nature, a happy girl, so if there was good to be found, she'd find it. To me, her family was borderline poor. My comments are not a judgment of them or a prejudice on my part, simply what I observed. Life in that house was flawed but had its good sides also.

Tolstoy wrote, "All happy families are alike; each unhappy family is unhappy in its own way." Dolly's life at home was unpredictable. You never knew what you were going to walk into. Family life seemed a seesaw of feast and famine, flaring tempers and sometimes laughter, yet Dolly and her siblings remained happy, which was a bit of a mystery to me as I felt they had cause to be unhappy. Dolly loved her family, including her father. She found tender sensitivity inside his rough hide. She was very forgiving and tolerant.

There were, at times, overt displays of love in that house. She often shared happy stories of her mother and aunts singing and harmonizing old songs from their girlhood while cooking ethnic foods such as Kielbasa, and Pierogi. Her dad, a baker in the Navy during WW2, would sometimes make homemade pancakes and bake bread on a Saturday morning in a sun warmed kitchen, surrounded by his kids, the smell of coffee filling the air. They were able to be themselves on those days when the focus of the parents was not on the hard realities of life but rather on the joy of being a part of a family. Dolly had a natural way of clinging to all that was good and ignoring the rest. I tried to understand how she accomplished this, sensing there was some lesson for me in her background that I needed to understand and adopt. I think now, part of the answer was to be found in the love that somehow managed to exist there, like a determined flower that grows happily through a crack in the sidewalk. Even when times are hard, people do love each other with determination and to the best of whatever ability they have. We all need and therefore seek love. It is the most important thing in life and without it humanity would be doomed.

Dolly was often caregiver to her siblings. In an unpredictable house the oldest often takes over what should have been parental responsibility. She saw that they were clean with hair combed, and on school days had lunches and got off on time. In my opinion, accepting responsibility at an early age helped make her the reliable, organized woman she became as an adult. Because of the challenges in Dolly's home life, I envisioned her as a glorious phoenix who had risen from ashes to soar above most of us, yet she never seemed aware of how truly special she was.

I had a rather typical, average middle-class childhood, growing up in a stable home environment. My sister Ann was the oldest and the best behaved, always doing what our parents expected of her. She was a good student. I was next in the lineup and a good kid overall, rarely getting into any real trouble. My brother John and I roomed together. I have vague memory of being a terrible tease at times, so perhaps not the older brother I should have been. Later in our teens and as adults, we always got on fine and still do. He must have forgiven or forgotten my poor behavior when we were boys. Leona was the youngest and the most rebellious. As a young teen it seemed she was always doing something she shouldn't. She and mom never agreed on much of anything. Today, we are a close family, all successful people who never argue among ourselves and get along well. My biggest problem as a kid was with grades…math especially. I always felt I'd dropped the ball and been a disappointment, especially to my mom who felt I was not giving proper effort to school. Those feeling of not being a good son weighed on me and I carried that sense of being a disappointment into adulthood. Being perceptive and sensitive, Dolly saw through the invisible wall I'd built to hide my negative feelings of being less than I wanted to be . She understood and believed in me, always trying to gently boost my confidence.

"You're a much better person than you think you are, you just don't realize it," she'd tell me. Your kind, intelligent, and sensitive to the feeling of others, so have nothing to be ashamed of. Still, the latent issues I tried to hide were a portent of things to come and would eventually cause me serious setback for a time.

Perhaps it's obvious to make this observation, but parents have much to do with forming us. My mother adopted certain attitudes and methods, learned I think, from her father. She felt that strict academic discipline could force a child to achieve in any subject. I don't agree. I think we each have individual *gifts*, things we will excel in and other things that will challenge us. Force and discipline have little to do with it. We don't fully comprehend how a Mozart can look at a piano, understand it and begin to play. Or how a chess prodigy, once he learns how the pieces move can instantly play the game at an advanced level. It's a gift; we all have them in varying degrees.

My father was, in my opinion, a great guy, although, like most of us, he had his moods. Handsome and a charmer with women, my personal memory of him concerns his devotion to family. He spent weekends and vacations working on finishing the summer cottage for family use. If he found me in the garage struggling with something on my car, he'd join in to help me, even when exhausted after work. I loved that about him. I also admired that I never heard him use vulgar words around the family. I've inherited that discipline from him and have rejected the use of offensive language throughout my life. The inability to express a thought or emotion without being reduced to the use of obscenities was beyond me. I've always strived to be a refined gentleman. I don't say this with arrogance; it just seemed to me the right way to be. Today it seems the opposite is in vogue. Crudeness is the new normal. Our culture seems to have abandoned elegance and grace for sloppy dress and common or even bad behavior. We have largely discarded the beauty of our language. In my opinion, *'Have a nice day,'* does not qualify as having good manners. And someone should tell waitresses that, "How are WE doing," and "How's everything tasting?" are truly brutal uses of the English language. Didn't they pay any attention in school? But then I remind myself they may not have had the advantages I did so I've no right to judge. It may not be their fault, and our current culture doesn't help.

A hunter and gun enthusiast, dad was an accomplished competitor in shooting events with target pistols and shotguns. He wanted me to hunt with him as he saw this as a manly pastime for father and son. I have vivid memories of Dad coming home from hunting trips with whatever he'd shot that day, leaving a trail of blood drops down the snow-covered sidewalk leading to our garage. The sight made me sad because it meant some small animals were dead. He taught me how to skin and clean rabbits, a terrible job, as their insides smelled awful. I couldn't understand why anyone would want to kill critters to eat when perfectly good food is available at the store. Perhaps it's an instinct present in some men, one left over from when humans lived in caves. I lack that hunter killer instinct. I wasn't a wimp, but shooting living things held no appeal.

When I reached the proper age, eleven or so, dad bought me a used single shot 16-gauge shotgun. I refinished the stock with his guidance. I enjoyed that time spent with him in his shop in the basement. As we worked, sanding, staining, and varnishing, he would smoke a pipe of *Whitehall* brand tobacco, a smell I really enjoyed and found more pleasant than his cigarettes. He'd also turn on the radio and we'd listen to shows like *The Shadow* and *Green Hornet*. I was so proud to have my own shotgun. Wanting to please my dad, I agreed to go hunting with him. It turned out to be only once.

We were joined by a couple of hunters he worked with. I felt manly in my lace-up high-top leather boots with the little knife pocket on the side. In my flannel shirt and wool-checked jacket and cap, I looked and felt the part, but that would not last through the day. On a farm, walking a fence line through some trees, a bird was flushed up. In truth, the gun that brought the bird down could have been any one of us as we all took a shot, including me, my first. When we got to the bird, it was not a pheasant as expected but a beautiful owl, and it was fatally wounded, but alive. My dad said we would have to put it down, and he twisted its neck. I tried not to show un-manly emotion, but this was heartbreaking for me. A thing of beauty was dead, and it might have been my fault.

That night I told my dad I didn't like hunting, did not like killing things, and did not want to hunt anymore. He looked at me for a moment and said: "OK, Paul, if you don't like it, that's fine. It's up to you, of course." I never went hunting again. I was surprised when my father took that position, one I now consider filled with wisdom. He was a good man with enough sensitivity to understand the kind of nature I had. I took no pleasure in killing. I was not the kind of male who had to prove his masculinity by killing animals. And yes, I know that some hunt not only for sport but for food. I also understand that thinning the herd has a positive effect in nature.

Later I would engage in different but equally manly pursuits such as offshore sailboat racing and sports car racing. As for the rabbits and birds, I left them in peace. But I kept the shotgun and passed it on to my son. It still doesn't get any use, as he's not a hunter either.

Dad had the owl stuffed by a taxidermist and I was always proud to show it off to my friends as if killing a bird were heroic, though I knew it wasn't. Still, I used my boy hunter story to bolster my status with my pals, taking credit (without evidence) for the kill. It was often about image with me. Perhaps even then, this was a sign of compensating for self-doubt, some insecurity I didn't understand; the desire to project a persona that wasn't necessarily my own, but one I thought others would respect and be impressed by. It was like putting on a mask.

Our parents provided for my siblings and me, taught us ethics, morals, manners, and frugality, yet were generous where it counted. An example of their generosity was the summer cottage where, as kids, we spent all our summers watched over by our grandmother, an unforgettable experience for us. Mom and Dad worked hard in the city so we could have idyllic summers in the country and at the beach. Back then, for us kids, it was just how our life was; now we know it was a gift to us and sacrifice on their part, and we're grateful for their goodness. They were also savers ready to spend on our educations. In short, my siblings and I were loved and cared for by good, reliable parents.

None of these background gifts made me excel in math, however. I was constantly being told by my mother that I had capabilities I wasn't tapping. "You have an above average IQ, so have no excuse for not excelling in school." I understand now that this was my mother's way of "bringing me up in the right way." She wanted me to be an achiever like my older sister Ann, an obedient child who did well in school. I had a quietly rebellious, unconventional spirit, which I now think is part of the creative temperament. Some of us are not destined for a conventional life. How many artists and authors seem predictable and normal in the usual way? It's fair to say most are not. They dance to a different beat and it's not much of a stretch to think I did too, but it went unrecognized. I'm now convinced that hearing different music is a gift to be nurtured, not discouraged.

I came away from my youth, not as a disaster, just not the star I was expected to be. Not to suggest any cruel behavior in my mother. Far from it. She always meant well, only desiring that her kids live up to their potentials. My mom was an intelligent, loving, and charitable woman, but looking back, I think some of her methods were misguided when it came to nurturing confidence. A kid craves and needs parental approval. He does not want to feel their disappointment.

Although math made my brain hurt, I always loved to read. I was one of those kids who read under the bedcovers with a flashlight at night. I learned to read early and could never get enough of books. As a boy, if I had Conan Doyle, Dickens, or Robert Louis Stevenson, I was happy. Later, as a teen, I developed a taste for Scott Fitzgerald's short stories and dipped my toe into the works of authors like John Updike and Hemingway. I remember realizing I needed to live a bit longer to grasp Updike. He was out of my league.

Dolly was also an avid reader. I recall her telling me she'd read *Gone with the Wind* several times as a young girl. She told me her father had grown tired of seeing her with her face always buried in the pages. "Not that damned book again!" he'd complain.

All through high school I performed well in English, literature, and writing. I also did well in architectural drawing and shop classes, but never math. Still, I managed to muddle through algebra and geometry. I would in the end, discover and pursue a creative path.

During my grade school years and before my mom became a teacher, she worked for Sunbeam on the toaster assembly line. She and Dad both chose to work second shift because it paid a bonus for the poor hours. I was required to put my math homework out for her to check when she got home after midnight. If she found mistakes, she would wake me up and work with me on corrections at twelve thirty to one o'clock in the morning. I call this child abuse. She called it helping me. I hated this practice of hers, absolutely hated it. It was cruel but she didn't see it that way.

I suppose it's possible I was emotionally frustrated by parental good intentions. There is no doubt Mom loved me, and I loved her. Still, I think I was angry with her. She meant well and was a wonderful mother in every other way, but she pushed so hard on education that I began to dislike the very mention of school. My mother failed to understand she was raising four children who would have above average abilities in their life pursuits. For her at the time, grades on a report card were the primary yardstick by which we were measured. Only Ann fit her mold. The rest of us danced to different tunes. Time would prove that we all succeeded in our own way, making her proud of each of us…eventually. I think she finally understood that different kids have different gifts, and we must pursue our own light.

Dolly could speak her mind if she felt it necessary; she was honest and never lied. However, her approach to me was always kind and loving; she would encourage without judgment. It seemed my great good fortune was to be loved by a girl who possessed a wise yet gentle heart, one truly kind in every way.

# 5.

"It's beauty that captures your attention,
personality which captures your heart."

Oscar Wilde

The 1959/1960 senior school year was marching forward. As the calendar changed, fall colors and the smell of burning leaves at the curbs segued into traffic rolling quietly through snow-covered city streets. Colorful lights were everywhere as Christmas grew near, the city aglow and sparkling like an urban fairy village. I loved this time of year.

Dolly worked part-time as a salesgirl for *York's*, a women's clothing shop on Archer Avenue in Chicago. She liked her job and being a people person and stylish dresser only added to her success. Arriving outside the boutique to pick her up one evening, I waited in the soft muffled silence that falling snow creates in the city. While admiring holiday store decorations Dolly came bouncing out the door with the beautiful, radiant smile that told me how happy she was to see me. Jumping into the car, she said,

"Hello, handsome."

"Hello to you, gorgeous girl." She delivered the longed-for kiss that always stopped my heart for just a tick. Then off to lovers' lane to let falling snow transform our black Ford into an igloo lump of white, idling quietly at curbside. We kept a blanket or two in the car to keep us warm, and periodically, I'd run the engine long enough to heat the interior, then shut it off until it started to get cold inside, when I'd repeat the process. Fortunately, gas only cost 25 cents a gallon back then. I can only guess at the number of hours we spent in my car in the park, but for me, each was paradise, cuddling under blankets with the sweet girl who held my future and my life in her hands, even if she knew it not.

I obsessed over Dolly's needs, possessing a burning desire to take care of her. Her family didn't go to doctors unless it was a pressing issue. Doctors were an expensive fee to be avoided. So, when Dolly developed a toothache, I took her to my family dentist who rejoiced in the name Dr. Weary. A friendly, energetic old guy, he liked to talk, asking questions while he had his dental instruments in your mouth. You would attempt to answer him, and it would come out something like "muga fublle doplat soba," which he mysteriously seemed to understand perfectly. A filling was necessary to cure Dolly's toothache, and he quoted the cost. Quietly, Dolly told me, "I can't afford this right now, Paul."

"I'll take care of it. Don't concern yourself."

"Are you sure?"

"I'm very sure, my beauty. Just get the work done. I can't bear the thought that you're walking around in pain."

Truth was, doing this gave me pleasure because I felt I was being responsible for her. I wanted to demonstrate my desire and ability to take care of her. I felt confident that one day I would discover my talent, become successful, and then I'd be able to watch over her in a way this special girl deserved.

Dolly enjoyed fashion and dressed well in stylish clothes and shoes, all paid for from her own earnings. I often observed that when girls got together, they liked to look at each other's shoes. Most guys couldn't care less but I paid attention. Fashion had become important to me because Dolly was a fashionable girl, and I wanted to fit in with her. I'd begun reading *GQ* to keep up with male styles. I leaned to a classic British look, no surprise there as I now fancied myself a bookish intellectual type and tried to project that persona. For winter, when it was called for, I favored wearing a tweedy three-piece suit with little watch pockets in the vest. Cary Grant was my style hero, so his famous pale tan trench coat found its way into my closet too. I have a picture of us taken by one of those street photographers that used to work Chicago's famous State Street. Now badly faded it does show my Cary Grant trench coat. We were all of 18 years old and in our minds so sophisticated.

I'd found a little card from York's in my car; it must have fallen from Dolly's purse. On it appeared all her sizes, even undergarments. The thought of panties made my temperature rise but that pleasure response I kept to myself. I quietly slipped that card into my wallet so I could buy her things. I can sense you're thinking she dropped the card intentionally... I never thought so, as Dolly was not devious. If she wanted me to have her sizes, she would have given them to me, so I'm reasonably certain it was accidental. Then again, I admit, she is female, and that mysterious sex moves in unfathomable ways, making them even more interesting and a loveable challenge.

I discovered she wore adult women's size 5 shoes. I knew her foot was small after we'd played a little game in the car one night. She let me hold her bare foot and rest it across my hand to see how small it was. In truth, I'd invented this exercise, not to observe how tiny her foot was, but because I wanted to hold her bare foot in my hands. I was sure this would prove a highly sensual experience. It was. Now, I can hear todays boys saying, "dude, it's only a foot." That's true, but that little foot happened to be attached to an angel.

Dolly's bra size as listed on the card was 34B. What I knew of bra sizes was not much, but I did think about that number 34B.... a lot. On occasion she would describe something that had just come in at York's that she really liked. Often, she'd find a package in my car a few days later, containing items like the olive green, lined, and hooded winter coat of some soft velvety material with fur around the cuffs and hood that she had told me she coveted. I popped into York's when she wasn't there and bought it for her. The other sales ladies had gotten to know me and as they all loved Dolly, they made it easy for me to shop for her. After excitedly putting on her new coat, she put her arms around my neck and whispered, "You're much too good to me."

"That, my beauty, is simply not possible," I said, which earned me another of her sweet kisses. I loved her warm lips, but in fairness to me, they should have come with the warning sign, *danger ahead.* It was a constant battle to keep my hunger in check and her desirability didn't help.

She was mad about her new coat, looked very romantic in it, and wore it through a couple of winters. I loved to see her with the hood up, her face surrounded by white fur, looking like the heroine on the cover of a Russian novel.

How did I find money to pay for Dolly's gifts and dental visits, you ask? I worked. Every Saturday I hand-washed cars at a gas station in my neighborhood. That was good for twenty-five to thirty dollars per week, a nice sum for a kid in 1959 money. I had other part-time jobs during the week. At various times I was a dishwasher, pizza maker, and breaktime coffee cart boy in a factory. Fortunately, I was usually free early enough to pick Dolly up for an hour or two alone in the park.

Often, I'd try to analyze my relationship with her, wanting to understand if the intense attraction I felt for her was love or physical sexual desire. Both love and sex were on my mind all the time. I'd be lying if I said I didn't want her physically because I did. At the same time, I never tired of talking with her; she was so wise, bright, and fun that simply being with her was satisfying enough. Most guys my age lived in constant pursuit of sex. If all systems in our young bodies are functioning, that drive is built into us and impossible to ignore. I liked to think in my case, sex wasn't the only attraction. It was a powerful one to be sure, but I loved the girl herself and all that made her who she was. I was confident she was in love with me too, and that fact is an intoxicating motivation to love someone in return. To be loved is the ultimate proof that one is loveable. I would have been content simply to watch her cook or do her laundry, so decided I wasn't after that one thing only. What I felt was far deeper emotionally than just the pursuit of bodily pleasure. Still, I recognized that as certain as the sun rises each morning, I wouldn't say no if she offered herself to me. On that point I was absolutely, positively certain.

Dolly was the first and only girl I ever brought home to meet my family. Everyone was taken with her, including my mom. Still, I could see her thinking, *so this little cutie is the reason Paul never comes home on time anymore.* My mom was tough about house rules, which I was breaking regularly. We had lots of arguments about curfew time and I was at the age where I thought I knew everything and wanted to be free to make my own decisions. During that period, my mom and I were often miles apart on what defined acceptable behavior. .

Once, after an argument with her about curfew, I charged out of the house (petulant boy) and slept in my car, which I parked in a space behind Dolly's house where a garage would have been if they'd had one. Her sister Joy spotted my car out there, told Dolly, and out the two girls came, in their pajamas, robes and fuzzy warm slippers. She knocked and I lowered the window. "Paul, what are you doing out here?" she asked. I winked and said, "I missed you so much I had this sudden need to be near you."

"You're crazy," she said, shaking her head which was covered with those awful hair roller things most girls used then, perhaps some still do. Joy was obviously enjoying this "boyfriend, girlfriend" drama, a huge grin on her cute young face. Then I told Dolly the truth about arguing with my mom. "That's not good," she said. "You'd better go work things out with her," and with a quick kiss, she and Joy went back to bed. She'd smelled fragrant and clean, like bath soap, and warm like a cuddly girl who'd just come from a bath and a cozy soft bed. I had an irrational desire to follow her up the back stairs that led to her attic bedroom. I imagined how easy it would be to slip into bed with her. I didn't follow this mad impulse, but oh how desperately I wanted to. I slept in a cold car all that night, with dreams of a certain teen goddess so close I could almost feel her.

My tantrum helped, because when I went back home the next day and apologized to my Mom for staying away and worrying everyone, she agreed to be more flexible about curfew rules. I argued that I had never been in trouble: no drinking, no speeding tickets, no run-ins with the law, so she must have finally concluded I deserved some space. I pointed out that at night I wasn't doing bad things. I just wanted to be with Dolly. I wasn't a kid who went looking for trouble. Of course, to a mom any pretty young female is trouble, simply because she's pretty and Dolly was all of that in spades. Soon they became close as they got to know each other, and mom relaxed, realizing what a fine girl she was.

Both of my mother's parents lived with us, and Dolly and my grandmother became great friends. Dolly had a gentle, caring way about her and a natural respect for the elderly that allowed her to easily relate to my Gram. They enjoyed spending time together in her kitchen just talking, or sometimes Gram would teach her cooking tricks, a skill Dolly was interested in improving. My grandmother was from a bygone era and looked the part. Plump, with a jolly face, she had long steel-gray hair she kept on top of her head in a kind of wound up birds' nest. Typically, she wore what we used to call a house dress, cotton, usually with a pattern, plus an apron. She was a grandma from a Norman Rockwell calendar, but wise about the way of things.

It was spring and near the end of my senior year, and as graduation drew near, Grandma pulled me aside in the kitchen one evening and said, "Paul, I want to tell you something just between us. In Dolly, you have found a special girl."

"I know that, Grandma," I said.

"So special that you might want to consider marrying her one day." I was floored. My grandma was suggesting that I marry Dolly, and I wasn't quite eighteen yet. In truth people did marry younger in those years, and I knew my gram was an experienced, wise old lady and usually knew what she was talking about, but marriage? Wow!

"Grandma, I'm still in school," I said. "I haven't found what I want to do in life. What's more, I haven't told Dolly yet, but I'm in love with her and have been since I met her. And Gran, it keeps growing stronger every day."

"Oh, I know you're in love, Paul," she said. "It's written all over you. I see love in your eyes every time you look at her. I see it in her eyes too when she looks at you. I wouldn't worry about it too much because believe me, she knows. Just remember what I'm saying. Dolly is special. I know quality when I see it and she has it in abundance. Most girls her age tend to be self-centered and frivolous, but Dolly has her feet firmly on the ground. I know you're young, Paul, but I have a feeling that for you, she is the right one, and you would be happy with her all your life. She will complete you, filling in things you might lack." Grandma smiled at me then, and added, "Oh… and one more thing, Paul—she's Catholic!" Well of course. To my grandmother, who was more religious than my mother (if that's possible,) being Catholic was a must. I was surprised she hadn't added, *and she's Polish too!* It was clear my grandma was enamored of my girlfriend. "Just remember what I've told you," she said, patting my hand.

"I will, Grandma, I promise." Grandmas always know, at least I believed mine did. Still, telling Dolly I loved her would be awfully close to the bigger question of asking her to marry me, and I still harbored a fear of rejection. Then again, if she didn't want me, she wouldn't be in my life, and yet at this moment I could hear her in the next room, happily laughing about something. Gran was right; Dolly was a rare creature, and I knew it in my bones.

So why did I have such a difficult time putting what I so obviously felt into words? I'd only kissed her about a million times, and little about our bodies went unexplored by hungry hands. We were quite intimate and yet I had never used the word LOVE with her. I recognized that I loved her almost from the second I first saw her. At first young love and then deeper enduring love. Perhaps it was because in my family it would have been unusual to say the words, "I love you" to one another; it just wasn't done. Maybe we were embarrassed to express that emotion or just never got into the habit. I have no idea why. We just weren't as touchy-feely as some families. We expressed our love in ways other than verbal ones.

Our culture was different then. Today, "love you" is tossed about so casually it loses its deeper meaning. It's nothing to hear a girl shout out *"love you"* on departing from someone she met a couple of hours ago. What she means is: *It was nice meeting you and I hope to see you again.* In 1960 the words "I love you" spoken to a girl, were one step from *will you marry me*—a sign of commitment. I loved Dolly and according to my grandma, she already knew. Still, it was the males responsibility to tell the female first, why I don't know. Old tradition I suppose. I finally accepted it was time to say what should have been said months before.

June arrived, nearly graduation time. We'd made plans for dinner out on a Friday night.

"Dolly, you look gorgeous as usual, like a *Glamour* magazine cover."

"You look gorgeous yourself, brown-eyed boy." At least my wardrobe had improved, as I was now sporting gray flannels, navy-blue blazer, a pale blue shirt, and a deep red regimental striped tie, all of which she had helped me pick out at Carson Pirie Scott on State Street in downtown Chicago. I felt good about myself; slim at five feet ten, I thought I looked like an ad for Carson's men's department. I was learning.

At a favorite restaurant of ours on the far south side (they had real candles on the tables,) we each ordered filet mignon for dinner by candlelight and later drove to a beach on Lake Michigan near the Museum of Science and Industry on South Lake Shore Drive. Parking the car, we joined hands and took a stroll out near the water's edge. "It's such a beautiful evening," Dolly said with a sigh, resting her head against me, "and we even have a full moon. It's as romantic as a scene in a movie."

"Better," I said, "because it's all real." Dolly nodded in contentment. We continued gazing at moonlight dancing in the water ripples, listening to the small waves lap against the shore. It was the perfect setting for what I'd carefully planned to say. Trying to remain calm, my heart refused to cooperate, threatening to leap from my chest as I turned to her and began.

"Doll, I want to say something to you, words I've been avoiding for a long time because I lacked the confidence… but not anymore." She looked at me with anticipation, her eyes glittering in starlight, her angel face kissed by moonlight. With all the courage, warmth, and tenderness I could muster, and struggling to control the tremor in my voice, I said,

"Dolly… Anna Louise… I love you. I *am* in love with you. I knew the moment I saw you that you were the one. I had an intense feeling that we were meant to be together and the longer we are, the deeper my love for you has grown. We dream the same dreams, want the same things, think the same thoughts. Dolly and Paul, Paul, and Dolly. Our names even sound right together. If you can read my mind you know I want to be with you always and you need look no further for a faithful lover because here I am, standing before you now begging you to love me."

I'm sure she knew what I had been planning to say because with a patient sigh she said softly, "You know perfectly well that I love you Paul and have from the hour we met." She took both my hands in hers. "Remember the day

Patsy introduced us in front of Kelly High School and we shook hands and exchanged names and you took me to lunch?" I nodded saying "Are you kidding, of course I remember. It was the day my life began."

"Well, I quickly discovered kindness, sincerity, and earnestness in you, things that boys I'd met before lacked. You were different and charmed me so completely my love for you began to form at once. I had an unusual feeling about you, one I'd never felt before, a feeling that when I was with you I had come home, and I knew I wanted to be with you always. I was sure, even then, that we were meant to be together." I remained silent as she pressed our joined hands to her breasts and declared, "Paul, my sweet, shy, brown-eyed boy, I believe it's my destiny and my future to love you, and to travel through life with you, so if you want me, I promise… I will love you forever."

There they were, the seven words I longed to hear; *I promise I will love you forever.* I know it's not considered manly, but at that moment I think a few tears welled up in my eyes, I was that happy. We kissed under a star-laced sky, each knowing, with the confidence of young lovers, that Dolly and Paul were going to be in love until those stars ceased to shine. I was the happiest guy in Chicago that night, and as I drove her home I asked, "By the way, have I mentioned that I love you?" "Not nearly enough," she said, cuddling close, "Not nearly enough. Just keep saying it for as long as we live." My god, I thought, she's just confirmed without any reservation that we are going to be together for life. I wanted to shout at the full moon: *She loves me and she's going to love me forever!* I parked in front of Dolly's house and after lots of kisses and countless goodnights followed by multiple firmly stated declarations of *"I mean it this time, I'm really going in,"* I finally cruised home in a dream. Still kids, we were confident in our love for each other. How could we possibly be so sure? I don't know the answer…I only know we were. Love is sometimes beyond reasonable explanation. Would our love always be this intense, and would life always remain as perfect as it seemed in that moment? Only time would tell.

It was spring and high school graduation arrived with pomp and circumstance, at least for Dolly. It turned out I was still one credit short to graduate, another disappointment for my poor mom. The credit shortage was due to religion credits from Catholic school that did not transfer. I received the final needed credit in night school that fall, and my diploma came in the mail without fanfare. I was unable to watch Dolly walk down the aisle in cap and gown. Space was limited to parents.

In that era in middle-class neighborhoods in a city like Chicago, high school was as much education as many kids received. Today the thinking is, everyone should go to university. But in 1960, not all went on to college. Instead, life as an adult began. Guys found jobs, went into training programs, trade apprenticeships or joined the military. Those were the facts of life for a large part of the young middle class in the city; we went to work. Of course, my parents wanted me to go to college, but I told them I wasn't ready, and they finally accepted that.

We had attended Dolly's senior prom in May. She looked like one of those little porcelain figures that rotate in a music box when you open the lid. Her dress was pale lavender, with a little tiara of faux diamonds in her hair, and seeing it made me immediately think of Cinderella. Alas, no glass slippers, just two-inch heels in lavender satin. I wore my first tux, white of course, as high school boys thought white the height of cool. It was the last white dinner jacket I ever wore. My dad let me use his Buick for the night, so I'd cleaned and polished it to ultimate perfection. Prom. Such a big deal when you're seventeen, as it should be. It's an earned rite of passage and a sign of pending adulthood.

On the last day of school, many kids signed Dolly's yearbook. Some had written funny little sayings, but most offered best wishes and good luck. After more than fifty years I still have Dolly's yearbook; it contains the note I wrote to her. In it I said that many of her friends were wishing her the best of everything, but that I wanted to *give* her the best of everything. I also said I wanted to be with her forever and would never want anyone else. Those were brave promises for a boy not quite a man, and yet I'd made them in all sincerity. Fortunately, we couldn't see into the future so had no way of knowing that at times our life would prove an uphill road that would test us. Mostly however, it would be filled with love and genuinely happy. There's an old cliché' that say's, *Love is Blind*. If that's true then in my opinion it's a good thing because many marriages, the ones based on real love, become truly devoted unions that prove successful. Yet they might never have happened if the couple worried about the messy bits. Those that do fail were probably built on sand from the beginning.

Dolly read what I wrote, gave me a hug, and although optimistic, still thoughtfully asked,

"Paul, if we could look into the future and see the difficulties life inevitably hands out, do you think we'd still press on bravely?"

"I'm certain the answer is yes." I answered, "because we believe in and have faith in each other. This is a fork in the road of our life together and we're bravely choosing a path marked commitment, fearless in our conviction. I believe that, and I think you do too?"

"I do, and you've put it so nicely. I just love the way you express things. It gives me confidence."

"Oh sure," I laughed, "I can charm the moon into shining whenever I want." I got a kiss for my boyish eloquence but honestly believed that for us, there was no turning back. This was the girl I wanted for life. Dolly felt the same about me. We were so young, and she was so beautiful, that perhaps I was blinded by that beauty and my youthful optimism. But I continued to believe we were setting the right course for us. I was sure of it.

High school was a thing of the past, so I was expected to pay a minimal room and board as my contribution to the family household, as was Dolly to her family. Adult responsibility was expected. In 1960, parents didn't provide any free rides. This wasn't out of miserliness, but so we learned the facts of life; if you're not going on in school, you must support yourself. So that summer we both began looking for full-time employment. It was also time for fun, at least on Saturdays, Sundays, and sometimes during the week, when we'd play hooky out of town for a day of play. After all, we felt we'd earned it.

We spent many weekends at the family cottage the summer of 1960, swimming, and sunning on sandy beaches of the Lake Michigan shore, water skiing with friends who had boats, and taking all-day hikes in the Dunes State Park. School was over and it was time to enjoy our freedom. Sometimes we'd bring Dolly's youngest sisters, Joy and Lillian to the beach. They were thirteen and eleven at the time. My dad seemed to enjoy showing the girls a good time as they splashed and played happily on our yellow military surplus rubber raft. Lillian often recalled how kind he was to them when they were young girls. I think they really loved my father because he gave them his full adult attention, ensuring they had fun, something they were not used to.

My first attempts at serious photography also took place that summer.

"Okay gorgeous, it's photo time."

"Must we. I'll feel so self-conscious in front of the camera," Dolly said.

"A girl like you? I doubt that. Have you any idea how beautiful you are? So, come on, let's have some fun."

"You make me blush with your compliments, but okay, if you insist." Maybe Dolly acted reluctant because she didn't want to appear vain. It would be just like her not to play the princess. I photographed her using the old black Kodak Brownie Hawkeye box camera I'd been given as a boy. My favorite shot from that day is an upward looking view of Dolly posed on some pier-like pilings that were driven into the sandy beach. Those well-weathered pilings still exist to this day. as does the snapshot I took, dated now by hairstyle and her one-piece bathing suit, but still such a pretty shot of my dream girl. "Point your toes down," I directed. "It will extend your leg line. That's it. Now you look like Marilyn Monroe."

"I'm so sure," she shot back, laughing. I knew she was secretly enjoying this. Girls love attention, especially when they're feeling pretty and the guy taking the photographs is drooling all over his camera at the sight of his subject. I liked to think I had a natural talent for knowing about things such as pointing toes to lengthen the leg line when posing a girl in a swimsuit, and that I had a natural sense of what looked right that seemed to come easily to me. But I'll be honest; in this case I'd seen the famous nude calendar shot of Marilyn Monroe in the barber shop and I remember she had her toes pointed in just that way. Yep, I'm guilty. I'd been influenced by a barbershop calendar picture.

At that time, we were enamored of nearby Michigan City, a classic middle-America town with one Main Street (Franklin) that ran north-south right down to the lakefront ending in Washington Park. In the evenings it was a teenage *drag* as kids drove hot rods, customs, and ragtops up and down, from Eleventh Street to the park, over and over. To see and be seen was the name of the game. It was classic small-town USA, and we joined in the parade some evenings.

On the lake side of the park was a yacht harbor and working lighthouse. A group of small-scale, kids carnival rides existed then, including a little train that let children travel through the park on small-gauge tracks. Vendors sold hot dogs, drinks, and cotton candy. A little zoo was part of the park and was extremely popular with visitors and locals alike.

There was a hotel on Franklin Street in Michigan City, and in the lobby was the barber shop I used. Two movie theaters, the Tivoli and Lido, Sears and Montgomery Ward stores, an old-time hardware store, a tobacconist, men's and women's apparel stores, and many other small shops of all kinds including, of course, a Five and Ten and a Walgreens. This gem had a soda fountain with classic black and chrome stools and a floor made of those little black and white tiles. They made great ice cream sodas. Foolishly, I was a smoker then although never around my parents and a new brand of cigarette had come on the market called *Virginia Slims*. I thought I'd try them, so I went into the tobacconist, and asked for a pack by name. The man looked in a drawer and said,

"Nope. Don't have that brand. I got lots of Trojans though." I laughed, understanding what he assumed I wanted and said,

"No, not condoms, it's a new cigarette brand."

"Well," he barked, "I ain't got those either." I settled for Winston's.

Buses ran from the downtown area east along the beach on Lake Shore Drive (or the *Beach Road,* as we call it) until it ended. Each bus stop was cleverly called a STOP and numbered. Back then and to this day, if someone from Michigan City's beach area is asked where they live, they answer with their "stop" number. Sadly, the buses are long gone, but many people have nostalgic vanity plates on their cars with their stop number on them such as, STOP 37.

In August Dolly and I turned eighteen. At the time Michigan City still possessed much of the idyllic look of the pretty small towns found in the '30s and 40s movies such as the old *Andy Hardy* stories. We were enchanted by the movie set feeling of the place and started to hint to each other how much fun it might be to live there. The word "someday" was not used yet, as married life was still a dream we hadn't discussed. Truth was, I hadn't asked her yet, but I did have a plan.

By mid-summer I'd found a job at a cardboard box factory. For eight hours a day, I stood at the end of a conveyor line and tied a twenty count of folded flat cartons together in a bundle with twine. It was hot, boring, mindless work and I hated it, but it was a good paycheck. I continued to search the job ads and query friends who were working to see if they knew of anyone hiring where the position would at least be interesting.

Dolly found employment at World's Finest Chocolate Company in Chicago. The office and plant were in her neighborhood (the smell of chocolate often filled the air) so she was able to walk to work. Initially hired for the switchboard, one of those old-fashioned ones with wires and plugs, she was soon promoted to the art department as she'd learned a style of calligraphy that the company used to personalize their product labels with people's names. These personalized chocolate bars were often given as gifts, but the biggest part of the business was fundraising for schools and organizations. The art department also designed other collateral material for the company. "I love my new position in the art department," she told me. Then she laughingly added something that made my heart sink. "There are all these young salesmen who are so full of themselves and they're always hanging around where I work trying to chat me up." She thought they were funny and clownish. I thought they were a threat. High school guys were a fair match for me, college grad sales guys with good-paying jobs…that was heavy competition. Would she be tempted by some twenty-five-year-old with a fancy income and nice suit? No, I assured myself. She'd promised me forever and I believed her. And yet there I was, sweating in a factory while those sales guys in posh suits hovered around my girl, flirting with her. I hated them.

I sold my Ford and bought a 1956 Chevy convertible. I only mention it because Dolly liked this car. I imagine that to her; it was classier and more adult-like than my hot rod Ford…and it had no name written on its side. I suppose in this way, and with Dolly always in mind, I was doing my best to grow up. We often went to outdoor movie theaters, both in Chicago and Michigan City, because they were one more place to find privacy. Sometimes we watched the movie, but mostly we just made out. The more time we spent together, the more intimate we became, ultimately leaving little of each other's territory unexplored by greedy hands. In autumn 1960 this led to a much desired and longed-for outcome.

# 6.

"Come slowly Eden! Lips unused to thee.
Bashful, sip thy jasmine as the fainting bee
reaching late his flower, round her chamber hums,
counts his nectars-enters and is lost in balm!"

Emily Dickinson

Dolly's brother Jerry had a small apartment of his own in the lowest level of the family house, and when he was away one weekend, we borrowed his space for an evening to take advantage of the privacy. When the kissing and fondling of overheated lovers reached an energy level powerful enough to light a star, Dolly whispered, "Paul, I want you to make love to me. Neither of us can take this frustration any longer. You've been waiting until I was ready, and at this moment, I'm more than ready."

I admit I'd been begging… "Please can't we— just a little?" But the decision had to come from Dolly. My desire for her had long ago taken control of my brain and overridden all objections, but I waited, albeit impatiently. It appeared the time had finally come at last, and my pulse rate increased in anticipation.

"We know we love each other and will never part," she said. "To join our bodies is the natural thing to do and we both want it. But we've got to be careful and not get pregnant until we're married, so you'll have to stop before you…well, you know." And so, she took my hand and led me across that final bridge. At eighteen years old we were still virgins, but only for a few minutes more.

According to the church teaching of our youth, we were expected to wait until marriage, but we didn't believe physical loving was a sin. We were meant to love one another, and so we did; it was that simple. No guilt, just pure joy. Nothing else mattered, as we were fully committed to each other so this couldn't possibly be wrong. To us it was an expression of our love which was pure and fine in every way. Words said in a marriage ceremony do put a public and legal declaration on a marriage promise. But love based on deep commitment like ours doesn't require a public ceremony to make it true and beautiful.

I had never seen Dolly completely nude before, so as I watched her boldly but slowly undress in front of me, the reality of her perfection nearly made my heart stop. Michelangelo would have had to work hard to sculpt a more stunning body. She knew well how lovely she was and so enjoyed seeing my reaction to her beauty. She was flawless; five feet and one hundred pounds of curves, hills and valleys that were clearly created by the gods of love. This was no ordinary girl standing before me; this was one of natures perfect creations and I was about to know her in the most intimate way possible between two people.

We played for a time as lovers do, getting so excited we couldn't wait, not for even one second longer. Yet we had to go slowly as neither of us was experienced. Still, we managed to work it out, anxiously but without haste, passionately yet gently, and every move done with grace and beauty. There was no reason to rush this melding of our bodies, this passionate expression of our love for one another.

To finally know her intimately was to experience true ultimate bliss. In the joining of female and male, yin, and yang, it became apparent to me that Dolly was the part of me I'd been missing; she was the final piece of the puzzle. For the first time I felt complete. I suppose for people truly in love, this is a portion of what love is; we complete each other. In this holy union Dolly and

Paul become what Aristotle had so wisely described love to be; *one soul occupying two bodies*, but bodies that for a few moments in time had just found the meaning of life and the love that existed between them as they gifted themselves to each other.

Neither of us wanted to leave that room, ever. We made love a second time and then I slowly attempted to kiss every beautiful part of her, and she allowed me all the time I wanted and all that I desired to know and experience of her. I could conceive of nothing to equal the glorious experience of loving Dolly. What could possibly be better? Absolutely nothing, for I had found my Nirvana, my heaven on earth, and she was sublime and a perfect completion of me.

Autumn surrendered her pallet of russet hues to the bitter wind and cold of another Chicago winter. It came as ever, costumed in crystalline white and ice. On Christmas Eve 1960, at my parents' house in Chicago, we at last found time alone in front of the Christmas tree. Dolly was wearing an A line dress (my favorite) in a cream color with a little sparkly Christmas tree pin and a silk scarf of green for seasonal color. High heels finished the Christmas package. "Doll, I have a special gift for you," I announced. A look of anticipation appeared on her lovely face and once again I had the feeling this quick, bright girl was reading my every intention.

Pine fragrance permeated the room as I took her left hand in mine, knelt on one knee and said, "My one true love, I offer you this ring as a symbol and a promise of my total life commitment to you. I know we must wait a while longer, but my beautiful precious girl, please say you'll marry me. I promise to love you forever, take care of you, and as long as I live, I will be there to watch over you." Dolly's eyes glistened in the colored lights of the tree as she said, "Yes Paul, my answer is yes, of course I'll marry you." But then she added sweetly with a little wink, *"You only had to ask, you know."*

It seemed this laughing girl had guessed what was coming, so she'd decided to add a touch of fun to the proceedings. I decided to continue her game by asking,

"What makes you so sure you want to marry me anyway? I don't even have a career yet."

"That's easy," she said. "I like your last name and knew almost from the day we met that one day it would be mine. It does sound pretty, doesn't it? *Dolly Marshall!* I just love it."

The tintinnabulation of her laughter followed, sounding to me like church bells softly ringing. There was no winning with this girl (or maybe it was all winning). She seemed to have an answer for everything, and of course she was right; Dolly Marshall did sound pretty. I wondered if our life together would always be this playful. Not quite nineteen, we were still aware that life had a way of sending rain and even storms. I knew in my heart it wouldn't all be smooth sailing on the passage we'd committed to. That's impossible. But to marry an angel I was willing to suffer through anything, just as long as we struggled together.

When we announced our engagement, my family were surprised, even shocked, as we were still teens. But happily, no one said, "you're too young," at least not out loud, though I'm sure my mom was thinking it. We were congratulated while my grandma just smiled. Some grandmothers possess the wisdom of old age; I believe mine did. She knew I'd made a wise decision. I will never forget the words she'd spoken in her kitchen: "She is the one for you, Paul, and you will be happy with her all the days of your life."

We then drove over and shared our engagement with Dolly's mom and dad. Her mother was thrilled. "I saw this coming," she said. Her dad just shrugged his big, hardworking shoulders. Not an articulate man, I sensed he was struggling to think of words to say. Finally, he gave his daughter a long hug as if he didn't want to let her go, kissed her on the forehead, then reluctantly shook my hand. His paw felt like a worn-out leather work glove. I'm sure that to this hulk of a man, no punk kid would ever be good enough for his princess daughter.

"You be kind to my girl," he finally growled. "She's a special one, so be damn sure you take good care of her." This big, gruff man had tears running down his unshaven cheeks. He knew just how special his daughter was. I gave him my promise, repeating his own words back to him: "I'll be *damn sure and take care of her* sir," I said. "I give you my word." I think my use of his words elicited the rare hint of a smile on that whiskery mug of his.

Though we saw ourselves as adults, I'm sure our parents still saw us as kids, and both views were correct. We were precocious, and not frivolous in our thinking as some our age were. We admittedly lacked years of experience, and didn't have all the answers, but we were confident in what we wanted, and that was each other and a happy loving life. The rest, well, we'd just have to figure it out as we went along.

We were planning to purchase our wedding bands when we chanced to have dinner with my sister Ann, home from Iowa. She had a male friend in tow. I remember the evening well, even what the restaurant looked like inside, cozy, with dark wood that framed in semi-enclosed private booths, a very romantic ambiance. When we discovered her friend was a Latin teacher, we asked him if he would tell us how to write *Our Love Is Eternal* in that language.

He wrote it for us on a napkin, and that's what we had engraved inside the wedding bands we purchased at C.D. Peacock: *Amor Nostra Aeterna*.

Now that we were engaged, I had to seriously consider finding a career. Still with no idea what I wanted to do; I realized the time had come to *find myself.* I continued to hold what I called temporary jobs while I considered my future, one position being as an "Overs, Shorts and Damaged" clerk in the office of a trucking company. It paid well, but for me would not be the beginning of a career in transportation. By 1962, I'd already worked at various jobs, the last with a finance company chasing deadbeats to encourage payment on their debt. People being what they are, it was a potentially dangerous job, so I didn't last long at that training position. I wasn't being paid enough to risk bodily harm. Debt does not cause people to feel kindly toward some kid in a suit asking them to pay up. I continued to struggle with career.

I purchased a red 1960 Austin-Healey 3000 two-seat British sports car. I'd fallen in love with an earlier version of the Healey as a young boy when I saw one up close parked outside a restaurant my family was entering. Now I had my own and immediately joined an organization called the Midwestern Council of Sports Car

Clubs. At its meetings I discovered an educated, professional, and polished class of sports car enthusiasts and instantly wanted to become one of them. They were my idea of what civilized should look like. I was, at the time, working for a tire store so soon the Healey was shod with race tires, not really the best choice for driving on the street but I didn't care. I just had to be careful when it rained as they became slick. With guidance and training from the club, I worked toward a competition license and eventually raced the Healey. Dolly never came to see me drive in races, not even once. Although I discovered I had a talent for race driving (I was young, invincible (in my mind) and willing to push my car to the edge, Dolly didn't approve. "It's too dangerous, Paul," she told me. "I'm so afraid you'll get hurt, or worse." But as it happened, our lives were moving forward at a pace more rapid then any car race.

Increasingly serious worldly concerns were pressing on us every night via the six-o'clock news, where our government was obviously divided on what was really going on in a place called Vietnam. Some said we would have a quick victory while others argued the situation there was quickly deteriorating. Washington denied we had soldiers in combat in Vietnam. Many Americans believed otherwise, and they were right. I had 1A draft status, and the specter of the escalating conflict in Southeast Asia was a sobering fact of life for me and all young men my age. Still unsure of a career, I got the idea to investigate joining the military reserves. I don't remember why I didn't consider quickly entering college. Active students were given a pass at that time, at least for a while. But the reserves is what I focused on and there was logic in my thinking, as this was early in the days of an as-yet undeclared war and I thought, as did many others, that if I joined the reserves, I might avoid getting drafted and could continue seeking a career. Dolly thought it was a reasonable plan, so off to the recruiting office I went. The recruiters laughed at me. "Reserves!" said the recruiting sergeant. "Right. You and a million other guys. Why don't you just test for the regulars?"

"Not interested," I said.

"Hey, it doesn't cost a dime and there's no commitment," he said. "You just take tests to see where you might fit. What branch would you choose if you were interested?"

"Air Force," I answered, thinking instantly that in that branch it would be technical work rather than carrying a gun, which was something I had no desire to do, not out of fear or cowardice, but because it was not in my nature to kill people. I couldn't even kill a rabbit let alone a man. In the end I took their tests out of curiosity, which proved a bad idea because I scored in the top tier of three of the four categories with the fourth, math, being on the weak side.

"Wow," said the sergeant with great enthusiasm, as he held the piece of paper containing my test scores. "With these grades, you're in the top percentile man, and almost guaranteed one of your job choices." *Hmmm, I thought. Maybe this is not as bad as I thought. There may be some positives here.*

"If I make the decision to join," I said, "and understand, I'm still undecided, my goal is to learn some useful occupation that I can use in civilian life. I want nothing to do with guns, radio or radar."

"No problem," he said. "You have the grades. You should get a job you'll like."

At that time, the military did not guarantee job choice, but recruiters didn't exactly spell this out for you, a fact I didn't know. Instead, the sales guys basically shaded the truth like mad to get you to sign on the line, and they certainly fooled me. I wondered if they were paid a commission for every kid that got to sing up? I also told the recruiter (probably a used car salesman in civilian life), "I have plans to get married soon, so what are my chances of getting stationed where I can have my wife with me?"

"Oh, really good," the smiling recruiter said. "We even have bases in southern Illinois, Indiana, and other nearby places. It would probably work out for you." There was a lot of "probably" and "almost guaranteed" in the pitch. I should have listened more carefully and asked hard questions. I was swayed, but I didn't sign myself away right then and there. I went home to talk it through with Dolly.

"So, what do you think, Doll? Should I join?" I asked her. "At least I might learn something I can use in life. It's a long commitment, but let's face it, I'm 1A and certain to be drafted into the Army soon, where I'll be another gun-toting soldier with a reduced life expectancy."

"Gee Paul, I don't know," she said. "You're right, it is a long commitment. But at least what you'll do in the Air Force should be technical. And if we thought of it as a job with a steady paycheck where you can learn something useful…well, maybe it wouldn't be so bad. The risk is we could end up apart for long periods if you don't get lucky about assignments."

"The recruitment guy told me I'd only do five weeks of boot camp in Texas instead of the usual eight because my good test scores guarantee I'll get into a tech school to learn whatever job they give me. They also said that after schooling, I would get a few weeks' leave before reporting to my assignment." This was the only bright spot Dolly could find in all of this, so she sighed, took my hand tenderly in hers and bravely said,

"We can get married when you're on leave and just pray that you get a good assignment. If we're lucky, I can come where you're stationed and find a job." I could hear the doubt in her voice, and I swear this strong girl was on the verge of tears when she added,

"I'll be honest, this all scares me." Two fat tears finally rolled down her cheeks, breaking my heart. "I hate this war in Vietnam," she said.

This became the dream plan, emphasis on the word *dream.* I wanted to get married as soon as possible so most of my Air Force pay would go to Dolly. I sold our Austin Healey. Dolly didn't drive so I saw no point keeping the car. The proceeds went into a saving account we'd opened for our future, I signed on the line, raised my right hand agreeing to "protect America from foreign enemies" (who, me?) and went off to do five weeks of boot camp in Texas. Leaving Dolly at the airport was heart breaking; our immediate future looked bleak indeed.

Boot camp was time spent in hell because everyone yelled constantly, shouting orders at you, and obedience was the theme of each day. The two main goals the Air Force had for new recruits seemed to be getting us physically fit and grinding down personality until it disappeared, and you've become just another tooth in a gear; one who jumps when someone of higher rank tells you to. I made up my mind to give the Air Force my best effort, but it would never become my career.

After boot camp the ugly facts of my assignment were revealed. The Air

Force needed radio operators in Vietnam, so I was shipped off by train to Kessler Air Force Base to spend six months being turned into a radio operator. My cursed good grades and ability to identify dots from dashes on a hearing test made me a good candidate. It was exactly the kind of military job I didn't want, as it would be of no use to me later in life. I was already regretting my decision to join, as it was now clear that I'd been sold a story that wasn't quite true. My good test scores had not gained me any special status at all. What the Air Force needed the Air Force got, and what I'd gotten was myself into another fine mess. But there was some comfort in the fact that at least I wouldn't be carrying a gun.

Compared to basic training in Texas, Kessler was a treat. It was on the Gulf of Mexico in Biloxi, Mississippi, at that time a sleepy Southern coastal town an hour from New Orleans. The deep South was an entirely new experience for me, with radically different weather, plants, accents, smells, and food. I enjoyed the change finding it interesting. The Air Force began treating us as adults, allowing more freedom. School was a job we went to each day. Boot camp abuse was a thing of the past, although we still stood inspections and had to do physical workouts and some fancy parade marching. I made new friends, and my group began classes in Morse Code and radio voice procedure. Many months were devoted to mastering Morse Code, which I'd never use. I would ultimately be assigned to a tactical control group with the Air Force, where we were in support of aircraft. After tech school I'd spend the next year and a half taking with planes and never once use Morse code.

Dolly and I wrote letters daily. For two young people in love, separation was painful. Still, I thought it might test our ability to endure. Time apart only proved to make our commitment stronger. All those letters baring our souls didn't hurt either. We were able to be more thoughtful and serious on paper, getting to know one another more deeply while a thousand miles apart.

A serendipitous thing occurred one day. I was down the hall from my room, visiting another airman, when I noticed photo enlargements of his girlfriend hanging in his locker. They were only 8x10s but looked huge to me, as I was only familiar with snapshot-sized prints.

"Where did you get those big prints of your girlfriend?" I asked.

"Made 'em myself in the photo hobby shop here on base," he said. It was a simple exchange of words, but it set the stage for something that would be important to my future. I began spending my spare time shooting pictures and taking lessons from the civilians who ran the hobby shop, learning how to develop film and make prints. The darkroom was a magical place; I never tired of watching prints appear like ghosts coming to life in the developer tray. I'd found something I really liked and started teaching myself more about the art and craft of photography from books and publications. I'd always enjoyed taking pictures and had a half-decent Argus 35mm camera that my dad had given me when I left for the Air Force. I was now able to put it to good use. I wrote to Dolly and said, "I've discovered I like photography… a lot, and maybe even as a career." She was very encouraging. The word "career" sounded like I'd finally found my passion, a reason for her to rejoice.

The civilians who taught me said I had a natural eye for composition and an obvious talent for photography. Their encouragement would change my life and give me, at long last, a sense of direction. The field of photography contains many different sub-specialties; my love of beauty found me perusing fashion magazines and intensely studying photography as used in advertising.

At home, Dolly was taking evening art classes at a local college. "I just love my teacher," she wrote. "His name's Vincent and he's quite handsome, but I promise I'm not swooning too much and am learning a lot." Oh great, I thought, just what I wanted to hear. Jealousy is a curse. He could spend time with my Doll, and I was stuck on this Air Force base a thousand miles from home. So, how did I feel about Vincent the teacher, you ask? That's easy… I hated him.

After being at Kessler nearly five months (an eternity to a young man in love with a girl out of reach), I managed to get a long weekend pass arranged. Dolly and I made plans for her to fly down and visit me in New Orleans, a mini vacation for her. After a little research I booked a room in a classic hotel called the *Monteleone* in the French Quarter. The trip would mark Dolly's first time on a commercial airplane.

Meeting her at the airport, seeing and holding her again, was heaven. I wore my Air Force dress blues, she was wearing a trench coat and colorful French scarf, lavender cashmere sweater, straight skirt, and heels…very European. I could have eaten her up right in the airport. She seemed even more lovely then I remembered.

It was the beginning of a glorious reunion. Though we'd been intimate whenever possible before I'd left, we'd been apart for five months. Not having discussed the sleeping arrangements with Dolly, in the cab on the way to the hotel, I whispered, "I've only reserved one room, and by the way, you're my wife as we're booked as a married couple."

"I should hope so," she replied. "And I trust it only has one bed."

"Yes, my beauty, only one bed."

"Good," she whispered in my ear, "because I plan to make up for lost time. And by the way, I'm on the pill for now." I wanted to ask the cab driver to drive faster but controlled myself. It wasn't easy.

We closed the door to our room, dropped bags, and between kisses, began tearing off clothes with anxious fingers, pulling blankets down, and beginning exactly where we'd left off, in total ecstasy once more, but this time in a hotel room in the Big Easy.

To drift off to sleep holding Dolly, feeling her warm skin against mine, our limbs tangled together all night…it was indescribable. "Did you pack any of those baby doll pajamas that I like so much?" I asked. Dolly just grinned and said,

"Whatever for?" Silly me. Of course. What was I thinking?

I was sitting on the edge of the bed when she came from her bath wrapped in a white towel which she let fall to the floor as she approached.

"How did you learn to be so sexy," I asked?

"Instinct. Simple feminine instinct." She was so overwhelmingly perfect, it hurt to look at her.

"Paul, once when we were first going together you told me I had 'beautiful everything,' at least everything you could see…you said you had to dream about the rest. Well, you don't have to dream anymore. Now you get to see every bit of me any time you want. So….how do you like me now?" She was teasing me of course and as she rose on her toes she raised her hands to her hair and slowly rotated artfully to let me study her as if she were a marble sculpture. I reached for her warm, fragrant body and kissed her everywhere as I whispered, "Doll, I fear the gods may strike me blind for having been allowed to see you like this." Our insatiable loving continued.

New Orleans marked the first time we slept in a bed all night without fearing interruption. In the past, loving had always taken place in stolen moments and borrowed rooms, so this was something we'd longed for.

Our days were full as we sampled Creole food, listened to live jazz, and walked everywhere or rode streetcars, absorbing the quarter called the *Vieux Carre* ("Old Square" in French). New Orleans has ordinances that don't allow changes to original buildings; even the exterior colors are controlled, adding to the feeling you've stepped back in time.

Before departure we reviewed plans for our wedding. Too soon our perfect long weekend came to an emotionally—and physically—painful end. To leave her at the airport was so difficult it gave me chest pains. I held her tight before she boarded her flight to the Windy City.

"Doll, I don't think I can let you go again." With tearful eyes she said, "We have no choice, but remember, it's only a matter of weeks and you'll be back in Chicago in no time, and we'll be getting married. Focus on that." It was a dark and lonely bus ride back to base that night.

A little less than a month went by after Dolly's visit before we received assignments. Nearly my entire class was being sent to Clark Air Base in the Philippines, there to await final orders for Vietnam. Tour length would be a year and a half. Dreams of a base in southern Illinois or Indiana had been crushed by events in Vietnam. At the time we were only supposed to be advisors, but those weren't the true facts, as there was shooting going on and boys were dying. Now, I too was Southeast Asia bound, heading toward an undeclared war many didn't want or understand, one taking place in a country we'd never heard of.

At least I'd be able to go home for four weeks, get married and honeymoon with my bride before shipping out. Miraculously I'd been given extra leave.

It had to do with names on a boarding list and room on a plane that filled just before my name was reached. One group, including some of my classmates from radio school, were going over after a three-week leave. When that aircraft filled, it shifted my name to another plane a week later, giving me and a few friends an additional week. I had no idea just how propitious that full plane and an extra week of leave would prove to be to my life, but I can tell you this… it was significant.

# 7.

"She's beautiful, and therefore to be wooed.
She's a woman, and therefore to be won."

Wm. Shakespeare

"I think of love and you and my heart goes
full and warm, and my breath stands still."

Emily Dickinson

On April 25, 1964, at St. Simon Catholic Church in Chicago, during a high mass ceremony with music I'm not sure I heard, I married the girl I'd been in love with for five years. Our wedding rings were unadorned wide gold bands, elegant in their simplicity, engraved inside with the Latin words my sister's friend had scrawled for us on a restaurant napkin: *Amor Nostra Aeterna...* Our love is eternal. This we believed; it was our promise. Dolly had so much faith in me that I feared my ability to live up to her trust. But I vowed I would work hard to be the man she believed in. We were blissfully happy on our wedding day, full of confidence and the belief we'd live "Happily Ever After." Perhaps there is a certain naivety in lovers as they marry, a shield from worry about what the future holds, allowing them to live in that euphoric moment when they gift each other their hearts. Dolly and I were filled with joy, wonder, and love, so whatever it is that protected us from concern, I'm glad of it. There would be abundant time to deal with the challenges to come and the truth that during our life together, we would know sorrow and pain, as well as joy. One cannot live without experiencing rainy days as well as sunshine.

Dolly looked beautiful as always, her dress classically simple with no unnecessary adornment. Her head piece had a flower shape formed of fabric and faux pearls above her forehead from which her vail emerged. Her maids wore, what else but pale lavender dresses which were elegant and not over designed or flouncy. Dolly had a sense of style about most things and for her, simple and tasteful were nearly always best. My groomsmen, drawn from among my friends and a cousin of Dolly's, wore black tie with grey vests, again the classic approach. Her bridesmaids were chosen from among her friends and sisters. If I had to choose two words to describe our church wedding, they would be classic and elegant.

On that breezy April day of sunny, intensely blue skies, when we said, "Take this ring," and "I will," and "until death," we meant every word. I would never make a more solemn promise. I looked into those golden eyes and saw, "this is forever," and in my heart I answered, "yes my love, forever."

Our wedding reception was a late afternoon into evening affair. We were chauffeured to the restaurant ballroom in Dolly's Uncle Bill's Cadillac, one of those cars of the period with quad headlights, masses of chrome, and huge tail fins. Gaudy certainly, but considered hot stuff in that era, and it was a Cadillac, so a good substitute for a pumpkin carriage.

After Dolly's months of careful planning, the celebration flew by in a misty haze. Guests enjoyed music provided by our good friend, bassist Wayne Roepke and his jazz trio. As a surprise, when we walked into the reception, the trio burst into what else but "Hello, Dolly!"

Our first dance was to a song handpicked by the two of us, *All the Things You Are,* with poetic lyrics that for me suggested Dolly was *the angel that lights the stars.* As we moved about the floor, I asked my bride if she was happy? She looked at me with great tenderness and affection, held me even closer and assured me that happy was not a strong enough word to express her feelings. "Today we vowed to love each other until death. I've chosen you and am over the moon with my choice. So yes, my sweet lover, I'm far beyond happy to a state of bliss."

We were the center of attention, photographed every few minutes, trying to greet and thank all our guests, squeezing a dance in here and there, eating a meal we didn't remember, cutting cake and finally making toasts. When it was my turn, I stood and made the toast I'd written myself:

"Dolly is my golden girl. When we first met, I suddenly found I believed in angels. She was a star that seemed to burn too bright for this world, as though Venus had kissed her on her brow and there she was, in all her perfection. I adored her instantly. And now, for some unfathomable reason, she's chosen me to spend her life with. How blessed can one man be? I've waited five years for this day and now I can spend a lifetime showing her how much I love her. So, dear family and friends, please raise your glasses and drink to the girl who's made every dream I've ever dreamt come true. To my beloved Dolly!"

The celebration flew by in a blink; soon it was metaphorically midnight, and the ball over. All the planning and preparation was gone like Cinderella's pumpkin carriage, and what was left was to take the glass slipper, place it on her tiny foot, and take her home for the first time as my princess bride. And so, I did.

My grandfather had gone into hospital just prior to our wedding for a simple operation that should have been uncomplicated. He'd never been in a hospital overnight in his life. Dolly and I had visited him after the procedure and just prior to our wedding. He was lying in bed doing arm exercises when we walked in. A tough old bird, he was not about to let himself grow weak in the hospital. We had a soft spot for him because he had been our chaperone when we'd spent weekends at the summer cottage. Some chaperone he proved to be. He went to bed at 8:30 every night, wink, wink. He was very fond of Dolly and she of him. At the hospital, he took her young hand in his old paw, looked at me and said, "Haven't you married this beautiful girl yet?"

"Just two more days, Grandpa."

"Well, hurry up because when I get out of here, I may just ask her myself." Dolly winked at him and said, "Grandpa, you're just an old flirt, and besides, you're already married."

Sadly, Grandpa never left the hospital. He died there on April 28, three days after our wedding, from a stroke caused by blood clot. We returned from our honeymoon to attend his wake and funeral, saying our farewells to the chaperone we no longer required. His work and life were done, ours was just beginning. Newly married, we were twenty-one years old, and to us, our cup was charged with potential and full to the brim with life's promise.

Our honeymoon was spent at my family's summer cottage, a house Dolly had come to love as much as I did, and as it was near, none of my precious leave time would be wasted in travel. We'd known many happy weekends there in Michiana Shores, and liked to think of it as our personal hideaway in the dunes. The village had a rustic, almost magical feeling, roads winding this way and that, seemingly without plan as they followed the shape of the hills. The effect was very charming. Houses were an eclectic mix that ranged from modest cottages and log cabins to posh lakefront homes. There were also endless sandy beaches and spectacular sunsets over Lake Michigan.

Our honeymoon hide-a-way was only a short stroll to the beach and placed atop a medium-sized hill in a forest near the end of a dead-end road called Sunset Trail. In those days there were no houses nearby, so it was secluded and private enough to allow me fantasies of chasing my beautiful new bride naked through the forest like an erotic fairytale come true. In my dream she'd be crying out: "Leave me alone you big bad wolf!" Sadly, the dream never happened. It wasn't warm enough for such games anyway.

The main room had a lofted cathedral ceiling with exposed beams vaulting to twenty-two feet at the peak. Walls of varnished knotty pine glowed with the warm golden color of rich honey. There was a wood-burning fireplace and windows looking out on a forest of oaks, maples, and sassafras, just now beginning to turn green. Old furniture had become welcoming and comfortable through many years of use. It was a snug cottage, cozy, private and made for lovers; a very romantic place to idle away our precious few days together.

The master bedroom was an open balcony overlooking the main room. We'd lie in bed listening to logs singing their warming song in the hearth while light from the flames danced a flickering waltz across the ceiling above our bed. Heat from the fire rose into the loft, making it an inviting and toasty space. Though it was only the end of April, we were fortunate to have balmy spring temperatures as the house had no heat beyond fireplaces. It was a perfect love nest. We dressed in slacks, sweaters and light jackets, casual comfort clothes to relax in. Of course, lots of time was spent wearing nothing at all, doing what lovers do. We took many long walks, talking and dreaming of our future life together.

Meals we prepared at home were kept simple, or we dined out at a little restaurant in town that offered good home-cooked fare in a friendly, quiet atmosphere. The small staff got to know us… "the newlyweds are here," the waitress would cry out to the chef, which was a nice touch.

It was sweet time we spent together, walking the long pier out to the lighthouse or along the shores of Lake Michigan, leaving footprints in the wet sand, then watching the waves wash them away, reminding the amateur philosopher who lives inside of me that a footprint is like life; neither is permanent. One day we too would disappear like our impressions in the sand. My doubts about the reality of life after death made the present time even more priceless to me.

I loved Dolly's almost childlike footprints; there was something tender about their small size. She'd stand at the water's edge, the still cold waves making their swooshing sound as they rushed back into the lake. Slacks rolled up but still getting splashed, she'd laugh happily as she bent to capture a piece of beach glass worn smooth by years in the water. Shouting above the roar of the waves, she'd sing out, "I'm saving this one as a memory of this day and before the lake can take it back." Putting it in her pocket, like a little girl saving a treasure she'd skip along, looking for more gifts from the sea. I've never known anyone who embraced life so completely, turning everything into an adventure. To this day, I can still see her in her yellow slacks, a little matching scarf on her head, her *joie de vivre* contagious. I couldn't help myself; I completely adored her; my love for her so intense it sometimes hurt.

What would I do if I lost her? I couldn't even let myself imagine as it would instantly drive me to dark despair.

In the evening, while staring into the fire, we planned and dreamt of our life to come. Sipping tea and laughing playfully, we'd feed each other leftover wedding cake, then make love to soft jazz ballads and love songs by Johnny Mathis. It seemed we couldn't get enough of each other, as if we were storing up the feel, touch, taste, and fragrance of the other, saving intimacies in memory for the long months of separation that loomed ahead. The reality of parting would soon be upon us. I was trying to avoid dwelling on the depressing fact that in not too many days I'd be leaving my beloved girl to spend a year and a half in Southeast Asia.

One evening, while cuddled together on the couch under a blanket watching the six o'clock TV news, it was announced that an Air Force C-135 personnel transport plane had crashed while attempting a landing in a tropical storm at Clark Air Base in the Philippines. All lives were lost. Dolly turned pale. "Do you suppose that might be the plane some of your friends are on? The same one you could have been on?" There was no way for us to know at the time, but the possibility was sobering. Having been given that cruel reminder of how fragile life can be, we held each other more tightly that night.

Departure day arrive, dark clouds threatening rain. Dolly and my parents had accompanied me to O'Hare Airport in Chicago. I knew that to leave her after our beautiful love-filled honeymoon was going to be painful. My folks said their goodbyes and left us alone for our last few minutes together. Waiting for my flight to board, Dolly said,

"Well, my lovely, brown-eyed boy, this day matches my mood exactly; dark, gloomy, and without sunshine." I could feel her pain and perhaps some fear too, of what lay ahead. I knew I needn't worry about her. For all her gentleness, Dolly was tough and could rise above almost any challenge. Even so, I put my arms around her and bent to whisper in her ear, "While I'm gone, know that I will see you in every sunset, every rising moon, and in the glow of the first star in the night sky. You will always be in my mind and heart… always, and I will come back to you. I promise." I left her standing in the airport weeping just a little, breaking my heart. I would not put my arms around her again for a year and a half.

The plane I boarded was a commercial flight to San Francisco. I then took a cab to Travis Air Force Base and climbed aboard an Air Force transport plane for the remainder of the trip. We would make stops in Hawaii, Guam and finally Clark Air Base in the Philippines. Starting from Chicago, total time in the air would, as I recall, be about twenty-two hours. Due to a tropical storm in Guam (our fuel stop), we were grounded in Hawaii for two days. Required to report in at eight a.m. each morning, if it was no-go, we had freedom for the rest of the day and night. My friends and I swam, body surfed Waikiki Beach, rented a car, and explored some of the island, having a good time. It helped soften the pain of leaving Dolly just a bit.

Finally, we were able to take off, and fourteen hours later, after a quick fuel stop on Guam, we landed at Clark. Passing through the door of the C-135 into the pounding sunshine felt like stepping into a blast furnace. Was it my imagination, or was this place hotter and more humid than anywhere I'd ever been? Dolly was half a world away and my new home seemed to be a tropical hell. What had I done to us?

Once at Clark, I learned the plane that crashed had indeed been the very one I'd avoided, only because the last seat was taken by someone whose name happened to fall before mine on a list. It was a fatal roll of the dice for him, incredible luck for me. Serendipity. I felt real sorrow for my friends from radio school and all the men who had been on board that fated plane, and for those they'd left behind. Still, I was obviously thankful I hadn't been on that flight. I'd be less than honest if I claimed otherwise. The pilot made a fatal error in poor visibility, one of those random occurrences we call accidents that can happen in life. Chance had favored me. There was no other way to view it. I had escaped death; was it simply luck? I certainly didn't believe it was part of some grand plan. But to come this close to perishing and survive is a sobering thing that makes a young man think. Would I prove, in years to come, worthy of this gift life had just handed me?

I spent a lonely year and a half overseas, and even though I was intended for Vietnam, luck once again led me to secure a job at the ground/air radio station at Clark Air Base. The officer who ran the station took a liking to me and kept me there, and although my work was a part of the war effort in Vietnam, I never set foot in that country . My job was in support of our air effort and entailed keeping track of military airplanes flying in that part of the Pacific and the Red China Sea. I did my work and apparently did it well enough.

I liked my job, and it had its perks. For example, my workspace was air-conditioned (a plus in the relentless heat) as the radio equipment must be kept cool. I took hourly position reports from planes in the air, coming and going from Saigon and other points in Vietnam, Guam, and Okinawa. Once they left air traffic control after departure, they were required to report to me every hour with their position and the status of the plane. It was, I think, important work. I was, in my small way, responsible for knowing where those planes were at any given time during their flight. I felt that I was making a real contribution, an amazing rush for a kid who'd only recently become old enough to drink legally. Thousands of times I'd heard the following words come over my earphones:

"Hello Clark, Clark, this is Air Force 1234 on 67…do you copy?" I would reply: "Air Force 1234, this is Clark… Go ahead." "So how is it down where you are, buddy?" *Air Force radio operators didn't always follow proper voice procedure.* A position report included informing me of issues with their plane and if they had one, I'd ask for a breakdown and type out all the problems with the plane for the record…it might even include a feathered down engine. I'd ask if they were in trouble and the usual answer would come back," Nah, no sweat Clark. We're good. Brave young guys and most of them not much more than kids…like me.

To say missing Dolly was painful would be the understatement of all time. We wrote nearly every day. Sometimes we'd share a kind of intimate lovemaking, using words to describe what we wished we could do to each other if only we were together. This was a delicious treat, but hell at the same time. She'd send me snapshots of herself, some normal everyday pictures, but others wearing baby doll pajamas to tease me. One time she sent a picture of her posing on a bed in a half-slip barely covering her breasts. All these sexy pictures were taken by her friend Mariann. Though torture, these photos helped me cope with endless months apart. Letters became a crucial survival tool for both of us. Imagine the elation I felt receiving a letter smelling faintly of Hypnotique and containing a photo of Dolly wearing almost nothing. It was like heaven-sent oxygen that kept me alive.

My skills as a photographer and darkroom tech were also being honed, as this base had a state-of-the-art photo hobby shop. I can't say I enjoyed military life. In fact, I didn't like it at all. We lived by rules and regulations. One's life was completely controlled by the Air Force. As my mom would say, "It's not my cup of tea." I suppose if Dolly were with me, I might have felt differently. It wasn't the work I disliked; I enjoyed my job. It was the separation that was emotionally painful for a young and romantic man in love, newly married and then kept apart from his wife for such a long period of time. I had a new appreciation for soldiers in other wars, as many were away for years. And in my case, I wasn't in any real danger on Clark.

I made a handful of new friends but many of the men I had to live with were crude, young, mentally adolescent guys who, once free of parental influence, only wanted to drink and shack up with the young prostitutes off base. Many came down with venereal disease. Most had little interest in anything but party time, so I just avoided them, did a lot of reading, and relaxed with new friends who came from various places in the U.S., and possessed functioning brains. In fairness to those guys bound for Nam, perhaps they needed to cut loose. I can understand so shouldn't judge.

I spent time shooting with the new Nikon I'd purchased at the PX. I had always been a bit of a loner so was comfortable spending time alone, concentrating on making photographs. My friend Byron from Fort Lauderdale worked a different shift and would let me use his Honda motorcycle so I could run around the huge base finding subjects for pictures. More than once I had film taken from my camera and exposed to light by the Air Police. It was not allowed to take photos of fighter jets armed with ordnance or body boxes being unloaded from Vietnam. After all, according to our government we were just "advisors," not direct participants. Hmmm, really?

After I'd been at Clark about fifteen months, I began seeing doctors at the base hospital with medical issues having to do with digestive problems that had become somewhat debilitating and too distasteful to describe here. Thus, began an extensive battery of diagnostic tests.

Also, at this time I got a letter from my mother saying, "Dad and I are thinking of selling the cottage. You kids are all grown, living your own lives, and I think your Dad's getting tired of working on it." *Opportunity* was screaming at me, the words being, Call Dolly! Late that night (which was daytime in the USA) I made an overseas phone call (no satellite cell phones then) to Dolly and explained my parents' thoughts about the house. The words, "Do you want to buy the cottage?" …had barely left my lips when she exclaimed, "Yes! Are you kidding? Our honeymoon cottage? Yes, yes, yes!" I then phoned my mom, a nice surprise for her and a comforting sound of home for me, just hearing my mother's voice. After a short chat I said, "Let's talk business. Dolly and I want to buy the cottage."

"Well, I'll have to see if your brother or sisters have any interest." They didn't, and within a few weeks we made a deal, and the house was ours.

Neither my mother and father nor Dolly and I fully realized that this transaction would alter our lives in so many ways. The unfinished house would require lots of work over a long period and a fair amount of expense. It amazes me today to think how quickly and casually the young make such serious, life-changing decisions. We'd purchased an unfinished house without heat or hot water, in a rural area with no thought to occupation or how living there might affect our lives. We plowed ahead because we wanted to live in a small town in the country in our honeymoon cottage. Romantic people like us sometimes do things first, without considering all the issues, then work it out later. Dreaming and romantic thinking came naturally to us.

Doctors at the base hospital continued to search for a reason for my ongoing medical issue. After many tests and then visits with a psychologist where I was asked lots of questions about Dolly, my new marriage, did I feel lonely and how did I feel about being apart from her. "How do you think I feel doc, it's hell so of course I'm lonely...*sir*". It was decided my problem didn't have a physiological basis but was probably more psychological. The diagnosis was that I might be mildly depressed, and this was causing my physical problems. My Air Force work record was examined and found without issue, and I had never had any disciplinary problems, so the recommendation was that I be honorably discharged at the end of my overseas tour. I'd never shirked responsibility and had given the Air Force my best effort. I'd done my work well at the radio station and in my free time had continued to teach myself photography in the photo hobby shop. I had served for two years and two months, but this was the decision, so soon I'd be on my way home with an honorable discharge in my pocket.

I was ecstatic, of course, knowing I'd soon be seeing my true love again. I'd been separated from Dolly for more than two years while serving in the Air Force and I never wanted to be parted from her again. For whatever reason, I was incomplete without her. I have no idea how other people's lives linked or didn't link together. I only know I needed Dolly in my life. She was an integral part of me now, and I didn't fly quite right without her. Together, we two were one, and that made us stronger. And I know that Dolly relied on me as much as I did her. We were a team. The dance steps of life only seemed to work out well when we danced together, and I wanted that music to keep on playing forever.

# 8.

At home on Sunset Trail

Servicemen in that part of Southeast Asia at the time would say they were going *back to the world* when they were going home. I went *back to the world,* back to my bride, back to living my life my way. No more radio calls that I'd hear in my sleep. Now it was Dolly and Paul, beginning our new life in the cottage on the hill.

There was endless kissing, hugging and other sweet activities at every possible opportunity in my first days home, but also immediate work to be done. We began moving wedding gifts and things Dolly had purchased to Michiana Shores and our new home on Sunset Trail.

Prior to leaving the Philippines, I'd asked Dolly to have her brother Jerry help her find a reliable used car cheap as we would need one right away. When I arrived home, I found we were the owners of a shabby 1960 Ford four-door sedan. It was two-tone in color—yellow and rust—and looked like it had about a million miles on it; about one hundred thousand to be exact, high mileage for a car of that era, and enough for it to be considered worn out. "Couldn't you have found something a little nicer?" I asked as gently as I was able.

"Well, Jerry said it's a good runner," she said defensively. "It also has a trailer hitch and was only $200.00." It seems I hadn't asked gently enough. I had to get used to being married and in an equal partnership.

"Right. It will do," I said. "You've done a great job." In truth I was cringing inside over the purchase. But what's a man to do when he's deeply in love with a girl who is almost certainly part angel? He tells her she's done a wonderful job, that's what he does.

Michiana Shores is on the Indiana/Michigan state line and an hour and a quarter from Chicago when traffic was light, much longer in rush hours. My parents sold us the cottage with everything in it for the cost of their investment. They'd also offered to carry a mortgage at a low interest rate. In this loving and generous way, my mom and dad were helping us get started. Thanks to their kindness, Dolly and I never had to live in a rental. We had, from the very beginning, a home of our own. There was an upside for my mom who genuinely loved her beach house...*it stayed in the family* and that meant a lot to her.

It wasn't a finished house when we moved in. The shell had been built in 1948 on one forty-foot-wide lot, so it was a small cottage with 720 square feet on the main floor, a comfortable 360 square foot loft bedroom and unfinished lower lever, also 720 square feet. My dad had taken on the tasks of wiring, plumbing, and building out the interior himself with occasional help from friends. I was just a little kid at that time but helped by holding the end of the board he was cutting, or he kept me busy straightening bent nails. Dad wasted nothing; even bent nails were salvaged as my parents well-remembered the Great Depression, especially my mom who specialized in squeezing every penny of value from a dollar.

My father had finished the living room in natural pine. It was the most beautiful room in the house, but the floors were still plain speckled vinyl tile covered with throw rugs. The other rooms had varnished quarter-inch plywood walls. These were just *for now* wall coverings, as the house was a work in progress. There were only two bedrooms, one down, plus the master loft which was half the depth and the full width of the cottage. When my parents owned the house, this bedroom contained several beds to sleep extra people when necessary, much like a dormitory. Dolly and I moved out the un-needed beds and kept just one double. This was our cozy hideaway. The main level bedroom had two pairs of built-in bunks totaling four beds, each with its own little square window looking out into the forest.

There was one exceedingly small full bath, tub only, no shower. Dolly disliked its location adjacent to the kitchen. From our bedroom, the bathroom was down a flight of stairs and through the living room, a long trip for that midnight visit. It was not a private location either, being right off the kitchen.

Our new home was, as mentioned, three levels. The lowest would normally be called a basement, but two-and one-half sides were open to ground level outside, so it was a walk out, as the house was built into a hillside. This lower level also had a fireplace and was ripe for finishing as a TV/family room. Dolly would not have television in the living room on the main level.

On her long-term wish list was to build a new bathroom off our bedroom and another in the lowest level, with none on the main floor. She felt that bathrooms should be put in areas of privacy, a civilized idea. The lowest level also contained a laundry area and a primitive "very temporary" toilet enclosure.

First on the list was getting heat. We ordered service from the utility company, and a gas line was brought down our lane and connected so we could install a furnace and hot water heater. One mistake we made was not having air-conditioning installed at the same time to deal with the humid days of summer. The forest can get damp and make a country cottage musty, especially the lowest levels like our TV room. Humidity, we discovered, was no friend to furniture or absorbent books on bookshelves.

Dolly was excited about having hot water. It never seemed an inconvenience that the cottage had no hot water when I was a boy. What did kids care? We went swimming every day anyway. If instructed by Grandma, we'd take a bar of Ivory soap (it floats) to the lake in the evening when no one was around to have a quick bath, which is not exactly a "green" idea by today's thinking. We could also burn some kindling in a little potbelly stove in the basement to warm enough water in a small tank for one bath. Those were the old days. Now, Dolly said we were "civilized at last." To an urban girl, a swim in the lake in the dark of night is for romance and skinny-dipping, but not for a bath. Her reason…no bubbles, of course. A girl needs her bubbles.

Much of the furniture included with the cottage was old and of good quality, some pieces more than one hundred years old so considered antiques. It was a look we called cottage classic and we liked it. We were twenty-three-years old, and *the new folks who lived on the hill,* kept busy "feathering up" our love nest. We felt a great sense of freedom; a feeling that we were in control of our lives for the first time.

We used money we'd saved plus proceeds from the sale of the Austin Healey to fund the initial improvements, which were all paid for with cash. I toiled away happily on other fixing-up jobs. Dolly told me that a visiting friend of hers had heard me whistling while I worked and asked if I was always so cheerful? "If you hear Paul whistling," Dolly told her, "it means he's happy." She was correct. Being back home with Dolly and living on Sunset Trail was what I had dreamt of during my final days in the Philippines. Now a reality, life was good. All I needed was a job to make it perfect.

Bethlehem Steel was putting in a new mill west of us, so I put in an application for the photography department. I didn't really want a job in industrial photography, but it was near home. They said they wouldn't be hiring for some time yet.

Dolly continued to work in the art department of the chocolate company in Chicago. I landed a job locally as a commissioned car salesman, which was to be a temporary thing, as I had my sights set on a career in photography. I don't know how we did the things we did at that time, nor how we found the energy. Dolly didn't drive, so I had to take her to the South Shore commuter train early each morning, and once in Chicago, she took a bus to her office. She would reverse that trip in the evening, arriving in Michigan City after seven, when I would meet her train. It was a grind. "We're practically living on hot dogs, store-bought potpies, and macaroni and cheese," I whined one evening. "When will we be able to eat real food?"

"Perhaps more tea would help, my love," she answered playfully.

"Well, I really had a taste for a steak and a dry martini, but tea will be fine. By the way, how are the gourmet pork and beans coming?" Was it possible for two people to be happy in this situation? Yes, it is possible, and blissfully so.

Sunday morning found us relaxing on a white faux fur rug Dolly had purchased and put in front of the fireplace. I'll leave to your imagination, what the fur rug encouraged on cold nights in front of a cozy fire. I'll just report one fact however, for others who might be so inclined…the side of a naked body that faces the fire is warm, but the side that faces away gets very cold indeed. Let that be a warning. But on this Sunday morning we were properly clothed and oak logs blazed warmly as we enjoyed cups of Jasmine tea. Our gray cat Tyke was purring playfully as she rolled on her back, swatting the *Chicago Tribune* newspaper Dolly was reading.

"Paul, look at this," she said. "There's a number of ads seeking photographer's assistants at commercial studios in Chicago." She handed me the paper so I could have a look. "I've never been in a commercial photography studio in my life," I said stating the obvious, "so I don't exactly know what a photographer's assistant does, but it sounds interesting. I think I'll go into the city with you tomorrow, drop you off at work, and go job shopping."

My first stop was 22 West Hubbard and Kranzten Studios. They specialized in catalog photography. I filled out the application and interviewed with the production manager, who asked if I could start the next day. Pay was $65.00 per week on an hourly basis, "but with all the time and a half overtime you can handle," he said. I was also told that the photographer I would assist wouldn't start until next Monday, but they had a project that would keep me busy until then.

"Of course," I said. "Do you want to see samples of my photography work?"

"That won't be necessary," the manager said. "Let me show you around and give you a little background on what we do and what your job will entail."

$65.00 per week doesn't sound like much, and it wasn't. I used to earn far more when I was employed summers at the plant where my dad worked. But with overtime, our combined take home would keep body and soul together…barely. I was given a tour of the studio and felt I'd entered a photographic dream land. It was summer, yet a Christmas set propped with evergreen trees, fake snow, and a large dollhouse was being photographed with children as models. There were lights everywhere, cables snaking around the edges of the set. I felt I'd landed in photography heaven. This was what I wanted and where I belonged. This felt like home.

Kranzten primarily did photography for the major catalogs and many small, specialized catalogs. Items for summer were being shot in the winter and winter things in summer. Each photographer had their own shooting "bay," and different shooters had different specialties. Some did furniture, some food, some soft goods or household items like pots and pans. One man seemed to do most of the model photography. I was told the man I was to assist would also be doing model work. I was thrilled to be working in photography and couldn't wait to pick Dolly up and share the good news.

She proved as excited as I was. "Wow, a job in photography!" she exclaimed, "Just what you wanted and a paycheck too." We splurged that night, grilling a couple of inexpensive chuck steaks topped off with a bottle of Mateus wine to toast our good fortune. (The wine was chosen for the pretty bottle, as we knew nothing of wines.) At last, we could cut back a bit on the hot dogs and mac and cheese diet.

We began to commute into Chicago together in the yellow Ford. I would drop Dolly at the city bus that took her to her job and then head downtown. It was a nicer setup for her; no train, only one bus. And we had more time together commuting, which we thought would be nice. It was... most of the time.

My first four days were spent stacking bricks into a cart, taking them down in the freight elevator, and putting them into a dumpster in the alley. The studio was breaking a hole through a wall to connect two buildings they owned, gaining additional space. That was my glamorous introduction to the photo biz. That night at supper Dolly reminded me, "It's just for a few days and then this new guy will arrive, and you'll be working on real jobs. I'm sure you're going to love it." Ever the optimist, Dolly had no idea just how much.

Monday came and my photographer arrived. The first shoot we did was of a stunning five-foot-nine female model stepping out of a bathtub wrapped only in a towel. We were selling the towel. The set had already been built and painted; all we had to do was light it and shoot. Our model seemed all legs, and beautiful limbs they were. I had no idea models were burnished to such a high level of perfection. Her hands, feet, nails, hair, eyes, and makeup were all perfectly groomed. It seemed the world of photography included girls polished to a degree almost beyond human. I grasped an important fact immediately; in photography, it was all about the details. But photographing perfect models was not too shabby. I could hardly wait to have fun telling Dolly.

That night, once home I finally agreed to describe my day. She'd been begging me to tell her, so I enthusiastically painted a picture of the shoot, especially details about the beautiful model. I left nothing out. Dolly listened; her face scrunched up in an exaggerated but cute little frown. I concluded by imitating Groucho Marx, pretending I was tapping ash from a cigar as I said,

"…and honey, I have found the perfect job for me, and I'm never leaving this business!" I instantly received a punch on the arm.

"Hey…that hurt!"

"Five-foot-nine models, eh?" she said. "You just watch it, Buster." We both laughed, but I'm fairly sure she was serious.

During my life I've known many women I found interesting and whose company I enjoyed, usually in work or creative situations, but I never did anything I shouldn't. As tempting as a smart attractive woman can be, for me they remained friends and no more. A man can be friendly with a woman and not allow himself to get overly involved. Of course, there are those who would challenge my alleged ability to avoid the feeling of natural sexual attraction that is a part of all of us. I didn't avoid it. I could feel it like anyone else; I'm human. It's a matter of self-discipline to refuse to surrender to it. A vow once made to another, should never be broken. Somewhere in all my reading, most likely in a poem, I'd come upon words I remembered, and I took them to heart: *"He sighed at many but loved only one."* It was good advice to follow. In my career in photography the girls were always beautiful, I admired many, had my favorites, but I always went home to the girl I loved. Always.

At least we had two regular paychecks coming in. We could afford meatloaf, pot roast, and potatoes. We were young and in love, but I admit, a bit more income would have helped our happiness. Dolly desperately wanted to carpet the living room and cover the speckled tile we both disliked. However, she wanted a high-grade and quite expensive carpeting ("it will last for years," she'd say) that was far out of our reach monetarily. We'd wait a long time to get the carpet she desired. Other demands always seemed to come first. I wanted to please Dolly in every way and couldn't do it, at least not yet. I felt her pain over unfulfilled dreams even though she didn't press me about them. I wished I had a magic wand I could wave and give her what she desired. And yet looking back from today's perspective, even with financial challenges, we were unbelievably happy in our little cottage on the hill.

We were putting lots of miles on the yellow Ford and after a dangerous and frightening experience we had it was obvious the old car was no longer safe for expressway commuting. We knew we had to get another car because the commute was crucial to our incomes and careers. This was to be one more demand on our meager finances, and another reason for putting off that expensive carpeting. Dolly may not have realized it, but it hurt me to be forced to buy a car instead of the carpeting she wanted, but needs must be met.

We had enough for a small down payment, so bought a brand new two-seat Triumph Spitfire sports car to commute in. The price was reasonable, far less expensive than a regular sized car, and we could just afford it. Also, the car had been in the dealer's showroom for a while and he was anxious to move it, so we got a great deal. It was British racing green, sporty, fun, got amazing gas mileage (it cut fuel expense by more than half) and we could handle the small payment. It was not a completely sensible car because of its small size, but we loved it. The old Ford was kept around for doing local chores that didn't suit the Triumph.

"This commute is exhausting," Dolly said one night as we buzzed down the freeway in our little green Triumph. "More than three hours are spent on the road every day. What were we thinking when we bought a house an hour and a half drive from our jobs?" She became thoughtful for a few moments, then sighed and said, "I wish we could afford a tiny apartment in the city for weekdays. It seems all we do is drive, work, drive, sleep, and not many hours of sleep." I remained silent and kept driving, guessing that, without doing any actual research, an apartment must be out of the question financially.

Even devoted couples, when spending as much time together as we did, are going to lose patience on occasion. Lovers we were, but I'd be avoiding the truth if I said that our life was ideal every moment of every day; that would be impossible. Just the three hours spent commuting in heavy traffic daily, with giant semi-trucks towering over our little sports car, was stress-inducing. On occasion, when worn out, the pressures of our lifestyle could take over and some insignificant little problem would become an argument. Fortunately, we were particularly good at resolving our differences. I couldn't live being at odds with Dolly. To hurt her was to hurt myself, so we never went to bed angry. That was an unbendable rule with us.

The studio decided to let my photographer go; I was never told why. They liked me, however, and as luck would have it, the assistant of the studio's main model shooter was leaving. The photographer's name was Joe Gregorio, nicknamed Greg, and I was assigned to work with him. Once more, fortune smiled on me. Not only was he a skilled photographer, he was also a wonderful teacher; kind, patient, and always willing to take time to show me how and why things were done a certain way. Also, he was a gentleman, so a favorite with models.

After we'd worked together for a while, he allowed me to express some of my own ideas, and we'd sometimes try them out. He also let me direct models and shoot a few sheets of film. My time at Kranzten was photography college, and Greg, my professor and primary mentor. I learned so much working with this patient man and will be forever grateful to him. Other good things happened to me in my first half-year at Kranzten. Dick, the studio stylist/art director and I became friends. He oversaw the way things looked, the props, booking of models, the artistic side of things.

My friendship with this man moved my career forward. He taught me about antiques and furniture periods such as Art Deco, French, English or American. Dick also tutored me about color. He was a man of classical and elegant taste and as I absorbed some of his knowledge, I began to develop an aesthetic I hadn't possessed before, or if I had, his input helped me take it to a higher level. I proved a quick study, both artistically and photographically, so with his encouragement I began doing some fashion and beauty "model tests" on my own time after hours. The studio owner allowed this. Our ride home became even later but this night work was critical to my development. A test is when a model (usually young and new to the business) works free with a photographer to produce sample prints for both their portfolios. Greg let me hang the resulting prints I made in his bay.

Dick watched my skill level grow rapidly so decided I was ready, and he wanted to personally style a shot for me. He brought in one of Chicago's top models who owed him a favor and we did a picture of her wrapped in a real zebra skin, sitting in a throne-like chair holding a high-powered hunting rifle. She looked otherwise nude (she wasn't). A magazine happened to be doing an article about her, and she turned in my photograph along with others for possible use. It was featured, my name got around, and models began calling the studio asking to shoot with me. It seemed I was building a reputation while still only a lowly assistant. I was a bit of a Cinderella story as things were happening for me at a dizzying pace.

The studio got in a Yamaha motorcycle to photograph and for reasons of their own it was suggested that I take it home for the weekend on its trailer to do some shots. I towed it very carefully with our old Ford. Dolly and I rode the cycle around, finding nice locations, and I shot pictures of it using her as a model. The studio showed Yamaha's agent the resulting pictures and they chose one to use in a national ad in multiple magazines. It was my second published picture, and showed Dolly sitting side-saddle on the cycle which was parked under a willow tree. Soon salesmen were coming up to the gallery and asking me if they could take some of my prints out as samples of studio work. I was flattered, so of course, said "absolutely." Apparently, my photography got good feedback from clients of the sales reps because an amazing thing took place.

I was called into the office and informed the studio wanted to "put me on camera," which meant I was being promoted to photographer and would get my own bay and an assistant. In shock, I was told that in the history of the company, only one other assistant was ever moved up this fast. "It's obvious to us you have a natural talent that's being wasted assisting. We'll put you in a bay next to Greg, so when you need help, he'll be there for you. By the way, Greg approves of this advancement." I knew I'd worked hard and done everything possible to improve my skills, but photographer…wow.

When I called Dolly to tell her, she was over the moon. After expressing excitement, her next question was predictable: "OK big shot…how much more money?"

My grandmother died in October of 1965. It was a sad day for my mom, but also for my brother, sisters, and me, as she'd been like a second mother to us. She and my grandfather lived with us in Chicago during our childhoods and spent every summer of our youth watching over us so we could be in Michiana Shores while our parents worked in the city. Up to the time of her death, I'd never known a time when my grandma was not a positive presence in our lives.

Though my siblings and I spent idyllic summers in Michiana, we were required to do our chores for Grandma before going to the beach or to meet our friends. "She'd say, "Each of you take one of these saucepans and go fill it with blueberries before you go to the beach."

"Aw Gramma…. those berries are so small…it takes forever to fill a pot," we'd moan. (We really were whiners.) She'd just reply, "The longer you stand here complaining, the more time you'll waste before you get to the beach." Chores like picking the blueberries that grew wild in our wood, or the blackberries found along the stream on thorny bushes which scratched us viciously, were a part of summer life that we now recall fondly. At the time, however, chores were an interruption of kid fun. Only after we produced would she turn us loose. That sweet lady ruled with a firm hand, but we loved her absolutely.

Grandma made a monetary gift to Dolly and me when she departed. We were wise enough to not spend it on anything frivolous. Rather we bought land, a lot adjoining our property that had come up for sale. I know she would have approved of our use of her gift. We continued to make improvements to the house as we could afford them, mostly things I could do myself to save money. Of necessity I was becoming a half-decent carpenter, utilizing some of the skills I'd learned working on set building. The studio had a full-time carpenter on staff named Fred. Calm, quiet and steady, he was often seen stirring his coffee with his pencil. "There goes Fred, signing his coffee again," someone would always remark. From him I learned how to miter trim, hang doors and other skills. He was a good man who took time to teach and advise.

A favorite project was the bookshelves I built on either side of the fireplace extending around windows to the outer walls. We were owned by many books, (when one acquires a large collection of books, they do seem to own you) and had also collected lots of small art objects, so the shelves filled quickly. We both liked the feel of books around us, plus, for me a home library is very British. Dolly had purchased some beautifully bound classic titles such as *Moby Dick, David Copperfield,* and many others which were finally able to come out of boxes and find a home on the new shelves.

On occasion I'd play a little game with Dolly, keeping out of sight when she was near the end of her bath. As she left the bathroom on her way to our bedroom I'd leap out, snatch her towel off and chase her beautiful naked body through the house and up the stairs to our bedroom, all the while imitating the terrible voice of the Wicked Witch in *The Wizard of Oz.*

"I'm going to get you, my pretty," I'd shriek in that terrible falsetto. Escape was impossible, so between giggles, she'd cry out,

"Leave me alone, you sex fiend!" If these games seem childish, and perhaps they were, they made us happy. We played adult games that no one ever saw. They were for us alone.

"Paul," she said after one of my attacks, "you really must stop chasing me from hiding places. You know how I am; loving begins in my mind. Make love to me with words, gentleness, affection, flowers and song... and of course lots of kissing, but not that crazy growling." Then with a wink she added, "And don't forget that you can never say you love me too often. Romance me first because it's what I like. Then sex becomes about love and not just a physical thing. You can have my body, but it must be with love. That's just the way I am." Then she grinned adding, "but, I suppose attacking me occasionally is actually fun. I guess it doesn't have to be ruled out completely." That was my girl. Compromise. She would have made a great politician. However, it was a good lesson about the art of love I learned from her and I took it to heart. She was telling me in her honest gentle way, *don't use me…love me.* Still, on occasion, I continued to hide and pounce. Yes, being weak, I'm afraid I did. I was like a kid who'd discovered a real live doll in the playpen, one so desirable I had no self-control. None at all.

We continued to enjoy long walks on the beach or through the village, often waving at neighbors I'd known most of my life. Dolly had quickly become a favorite. People skills can be learned, but Dolly possessed a natural talent. Neighbors sensed her friendly, honest interest in them. She wanted to know about their lives and not just talk about herself as so many people do. She listened; it was one of her many gifts. Often, she'd have a joke or anecdote to share and after telling it she'd laugh happily, especially at herself. Everyone loved how she found pleasure in everyday life.

The instrument of my art, a Nikon F, was always present to photograph the subject of my love in various settings. She was so "female" and perfect to me, that I eventually asked if I might photograph her in the nude. She agreed and would even occasionally initiate a session with a creative concept of her own. As for the artistic photographs, she asked that I never show them. "It's not modesty," she said, trying to explain why. "After all, the bikinis I wear to the beach don't cover much up. It's more about privacy, and though I'm not overly modest, I'm very private about personal things like the nude photography. It's only for us."


One day, after spending the afternoon in town with a friend, Dolly came home in a state of excitement. "There's an antiques street fair going on downtown," she said, "and I found the most beautiful antique iron and brass bed. I just had to have it for us, so I bought it for $100.00. I wrote a check."

Then, tugging on my shirtfront and bouncing up and down like a little girl, she said, "That's okay isn't it, daddy?" I knew she was just having fun with me, playing the "I'm your cute little Dolly card." She was so happy; what could I say? I'd learned early that when a man loves a woman, there is only one right answer to questions like that, so I gave it. I was soft clay I her hands, just as I always knew I would be,

"Of course, it's OK, my beauty, and you don't really need to ask me anyway. This fortune we have in the bank," I said, winking, "is ours equally." We went back to the fair in the old yellow Ford, hauled the new acquisition home in pieces (it weighed a ton), and set it up in our bedroom, nearly killing me in the process as I only weighed 140 pounds at that time. We put our mattress and bed linens on, and suddenly it seemed a grand idea to joyfully christen our new bed for good luck by making sweet love. Little did we know that our antique bed was enchanted and had its own plan for us. Soon after the bed became ours, I got a surprise.

"I've got important news, *baby cakes*," Dolly said, (this was a pet name for me she'd begun using...no idea where it came from.) "I've missed my period and I'm fairly sure I'm pregnant. What do you think about that?"

"Are you happy?" I asked, unsure how I wanted to respond to this news.

"I'm excited and a little frightened, but yes, I'm happy."

"Well then, I'm happy too."

I was telling a partial fib. A baby was going to complicate things financially. In eight months, there would be only one income, and the thought struck terror in my wallet. We were barely getting by with two paychecks. I was going to have to beg a big raise, and soon. But a baby? Oh yes, I did like the sound of that. Is it an instinctual thing programmed into us, this desire to have children of our own? One would think two young people having fun just being lovers wouldn't want the responsibility of babies, but curiously, many do. It's in our biological makeup to procreate. And happily, nature made the process of making babies so appealing and pleasurable for us.

However, good fortune turned its back on us because this pregnancy ended in miscarriage after a time. We were disappointed, but at Dolly's insistence, we'd told no one she was pregnant, so that was for the best. Privacy again. Sometime later, the enchanted bed caused the same thing to happen, and once again Dolly was pregnant. I couldn't understand how this kept happening. Was it magic? Was our bed under a spell? Oh, all right, I admit, I held half the responsibility. But it was Dolly's fault too, for being so lovable, so I wasn't completely to blame.

This pregnancy lasted a bit longer but again, she miscarried. "I hope there's nothing seriously wrong with me," she said, true concern in her voice. "Do you think we should be concerned? That's two miscarries?" "Let's wait and see what happens next time," I suggested. While we were suffering concern over those miscarriages, we were blindsided by an even greater tragedy.

Dolly loved her siblings; they shared a genuine closeness. But we all recognized that Joy was special. A pretty girl with a smiling face and turned-up nose, she had a gentle heart overflowing with love, and a kind temperament. In other words, another angel molded from the same stardust as Dolly. Of the four sisters, Dolly and Joy were the most alike. In late spring 1966, Joy was hospitalized after being diagnosed with a kidney disease that was deemed incurable. We visited her in the hospital often, helplessly watching her deteriorate.

On July 3, 1966, Joy died. She was alone at the time as the hospital had given us no warning. She'd just turned eighteen. It seemed so wrong that this loving girl was gone. For me, her death convinced me even more, that life was random and there was no plan for us. It seemed to be the only explanation for why good people like Joy died before they had even had a chance to live. This could not possibly be a part of some plan of a loving deity.

Dolly was inconsolable. It was the single most devastating thing that ever happened to her up to that time. This was far more painful than two miscarriages. "Why?" she would ask me with tears running down her cheeks. "Why Joy. She was the best of us, innocent and genuinely good. Why did she have to die?"

"I don't know," was all I could say. "Sometimes painful things happen in life. A necessary part of Joy's body was broken and couldn't be fixed. Her death wasn't anyone's fault. There is no mysterious reason, and her illness was not part of some great plan made by an unseen God. It's just chance; the risk we accept when we're born." Dolly looked puzzled by my words. Perhaps she was more spiritual or retained more of her Catholic upbringing. She sought a reason for Joy's death, a way to explain or justify it. I, however, accepted that life was full of chance. For Dolly, the pain ran deep. For me, a hard lesson came out of this event; we should love those we care about while we're together on this planet and tell them that we do, because we can't know what's on anyone's dance card.

Back home on Sunset Trail, Dolly continued to suffer the loss of her sister. I could do little more than hold her, sharing her grief as we continued to mourn Joy. Fortunately, in time, the resilient human spirit lets us get on with our lives, as it did for Dolly. There is some truth in the saying, time heals. Bad things can happen in the best of lives, but sometimes a thing that starts out bad can turn out fine, as it did for us one night in October of 1966.

Dolly's senior high school photo

Dolly

Dolly with siblings

A date with Dolly in the park

Senior Prom, Age 17

On State Street, Chicago 1960

Leaving for Air Force basic training

Home on leave – April 1964

Our wedding, April 25th, 1964

Austin Healey - 1962

Dolly dressed Carnaby Street
style, with our Triumph Spitfire.

Dolly modeling for Paul in an ad for Yamaha

Dolly with the hot look in the 1960's

An Angel with her kitten, 1966

Life on Sunset Trail

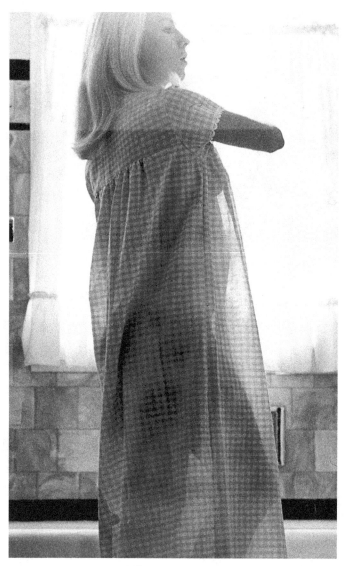

Dolly pregnant with Gabrielle

Dolly and our children

Gabrielle and Tyler

Virgin Islands - 1980

Paul with crew finishing the Mackinac Island Race – 1968

Son Tyler continues the family passion for offshore sailing and racing

The face of an angel

Somewhere in Europe – Photograph by Dolly

Our lifelong love affair

Our Family today

Veronica and Marshall, the next generation

Paul Marshall, 2019 – Portrait by Gabrielle

# 9.

"Luck, be a lady tonight!"

Frank Loesser

Having been in Chicago for a family party, we were driving home in the Triumph two-seater. We'd reached Michigan City after dark and were only fifteen minutes from home. While sitting at a stoplight at a major highway intersection at the edge of town, we were hit from behind. Violently thrown across the intersection to the sound of mangled metal and breaking glass, we came to rest against the wall of a restaurant four traffic lanes and many yards away. I reached over to Dolly in the dark, crying out in fear, "Are you OK?" When I touched her, she was sticky, and my heart began to pound violently

"I think you're bleeding," I shouted as panic burned through me like a cutting torch. I was sure Dolly was seriously hurt. This just couldn't be happening, not now, not to us.

"I'm not bleeding, Paul," she replied calmly. "It's cake." I licked her arm, and indeed, the sticky substance on her skin was frosting and not blood. A large slab of cake we were bringing home had splattered all over her on impact. So, hugging each other in the cramped space, we began to laugh hysterically over the discovery that it was cake, not blood, and we had survived. Luck had been a lady that night, because incredibly, we both walked away without a scratch, suffering only whiplash to neck and back. The Triumph was a total wreck, crumpled from the passenger seats back, the worst of it on Dolly's side.

The man who hit us was driving his ex-wife's station wagon, he was drunk, had no driver's license (already driving on a DUI, of course), and no insurance. But we were alive and for that, most grateful. The police who caught him said they estimated he'd been going about sixty mph on impact and had left the scene. "He'll be going to jail," the trooper said, then added stoically that if there had been any other cars in the intersection, we would be dead. Such a happy thought he'd elected to share with us.

In need of new transportation, I purchased yet another car destined to become a classic, but not our classic. It was a 1957 Corvette with hard and soft tops, black and silver in color with a red interior. I'd always wanted one and the price was very modest, less than the money we received from insurance for the Triumph. I liked the Corvette. Dolly hated it. It creaked in the cold (early fiberglass), rode hard, and did not get great gas mileage like our Triumph. If I had kept it and put it in storage it would be worth a fortune today, but we were not buying cars to collect. Though I didn't know it, I had a genuine talent for owning cars that would ultimately become classics. Years later Dolly would say, "If you had kept some of those collector cars you had, we could have retired today by selling them." I had to remind her that at the time, we were poor little mice and not collectors. "My darling girl, we were driving those future classics to work every day. They were our transportation and not yet collectables."

My photographic skills continued to improve. I was shooting lots of model work, rounding that out with some product photography. In addition, the studio was breaking me in on location shooting, which meant travel. I continued to compile a book, or sample portfolio, and started doing some side jobs on weekends for a small ad agency in Indiana. I earned good rates doing freelance work and we needed the money desperately. These higher-paying jobs made me start to think about having my own business one day.

One morning, Dick, our stylist at Kranzten, confided to me privately that Chicago's most famous fashion, beauty, and celebrity photographer was looking for a new assistant.

"I can get you an interview; his studio manager is a friend of mine. This would be a great opportunity for your career, Paul. You should take the meeting." I did, and it went so well that I was offered the position of assistant and twice the money per week I was earning at Kranzten. There was a catch, however. "Please understand," he said, "this position is for a professional assistant. You won't be doing any shooting for yourself. You'll be doing light setups, darkroom, camera, and equipment care—in other words, all the work an assistant does, but no shooting at any time. You'll also be required to travel to Europe with me for the fashion shows." It all sounded great... for someone who only wanted to assist a big name. But I wanted to shoot. In fact, I already was shooting and doing well, except for the money part. As I was about to leave on a week-long shoot in Florida, I asked if I could tell him what my decision would be when I got back, explaining this was a big decision for my wife and me. He agreed.

Dolly and I talked it over before I left for the South. She was in favor; I was torn. It was, without doubt, a great opportunity. I would learn how a successful small studio functioned. He was shooting assignments for international cosmetic companies, movie star portraits, fashion, all the things I'd dreamed of when I got into the business. That didn't alter the fact that I would always be the well-paid assistant, the guy in the background... the invisible man who went for coffee. On returning from Florida I told him, "Thank you for considering me, I'm honored, and I love your work, but I must say no. The truth is I want to shoot, not assist. I'd be lying if I said otherwise." He said he understood and appreciated my honesty. I told Dolly what I'd said, and of his assurance that he understood.

"Well, I *don't* understand," she said, incredulous. "Are you crazy!" She was quite capable of speaking her mind forcefully when she felt it appropriate. "This is the opportunity of a lifetime. To work with a man like that would take your career to a whole new level. He's the top guy in Chicago, world famous, with a huge reputation. You couldn't do any better. You'd rather keep shooting catalog?"

"I'd rather be shooting, period," I responded with a little anger in my voice. "This is my career and you're challenging my decision as to what's best for me. I'd be carrying his equipment cases through airports and loading cameras while he did the shooting. And where would I eventually set up shop once I knew the ropes? New York or L.A.? Remember, Chicago is not a fashion/beauty town, it's a food, product, catalog shooters town. He's an exception who's somehow made it work for him." She continued to look at me like I needed to have my head examined.

"Doll, I love where we live, I love this house, and I'm beginning to think maybe I don't want that upper stratosphere kind of lifestyle. I don't think I'm emotionally cut out for fame or the big city scene. What I want most of all is not to spend half my life commuting to Chicago every day. I want to live in the beach house we love and make babies with you." She did manage a smile at that.

"Well, lover," she said, "I have always trusted you and I still do. But gee, Paul…what an opportunity, and twice the money." Though she accepted my decision, Dolly always felt I'd made a big career mistake. If we hadn't owned a house we loved and weren't shaping a life we enjoyed, I might have felt differently. Dolly saw her dreams of a finished family room, a bathroom off our bedroom, carpeting, all of it disappearing, or at least being put off again. It hurt me to disappoint her, but I knew it was important that I become the kind of photographer I wanted to be and to live the life I wanted to live.

I didn't want work to rule my life. Career was important to me but so was my wife and the family we hoped to have and the lifestyle we were creating for ourselves. In truth, I had doubts about my decision. I wondered if, when I grew old, I'd look back and wish I'd stayed in the city. I also knew that once Dolly had a baby she would stop working. She had already informed me that being a mom would be her full-time gig until her children were in school, so supporting our family would fall to me. It scared me, yet facing fear is a part of living.

There was another facet to this decision-making process, and it was the biggest one of all. I questioned whether once I went out on my own, I would have the temperament to be in a high-visibility position. I knew I had the talent for the work. I hadn't risen as fast as I had because I was mediocre. But there were times I questioned my ability to handle success and its responsibilities. I didn't want to admit this to Dolly. I knew that someone in that position would be expected to entertain and create a certain kind of image…to *play the game*. That didn't appeal to me. Maintaining the constant front of "here I am, folks, the hot 'name' photographer" held no major attraction for me. I liked being admired for my work, but I didn't feel the need to be a megastar.

I should have shared those fears with Dolly, discussing them, working through them… but I didn't. I wanted her to see me as one of philosopher Friedrich Nietzsche's Supermen; described as "strong and beyond fear, a man who lived by his own code and not that of anyone else." But deep down, I knew I was no superman. I was pushing myself to reach a level of success that if achieved, was a little scary. It was a terrible conundrum. Admitting to this weakness, this lack of confidence to myself was not easy. Revealing to Dolly that I had a latent fear of success because of the pressures put on the "celebrity star" meant telling her I was not as confident as I pretended to be… and that was unthinkable. She was the heroine of my life, and I wanted to be her hero. So, I decided to leave the illusion of a supremely confident Paul at status quo. In retrospect, she may have understood my concerns, perhaps better than I. She was an unusually perceptive girl.

In April of 1967 Dolly took me to see an Andrew Wyeth exhibit at the Art Institute of Chicago. I'd never seen Wyeth's work before, and it had a profound influence on me.

"You're quiet," Dolly observed as I stood staring. "Don't you like the paintings?"

"Just the opposite." I said. "I've never seen pictures like these. They speak to me, deep inside, and the colors have an unusual, muted feeling I like."

"It's partly because he uses tempera paint, which he mixes himself using raw egg yolk, vinegar, water and powdered mineral pigments," she said. "He's a master of the medium." How, I wondered, did Dolly know all this? She never ceased to amaze me with her knowledge of art.

"I also love his subject matter," I said. "It makes me wonder about what he's saying. There's a loneliness or bleakness there and yet his human subjects, though ordinary country folk, are in possession of such beauty, dignity, and power of personality. They're a portrait of rural life and intrepid people."

"Well," Dolly said, "I guess you really are thinking about what you've seen.

I'm impressed and happy you like his work so much." From that day onward, I developed a new way of seeing, and my personal noncommercial art photography began to have a new kind of focus, a look. I researched Wyeth, collecting books about him, and admiring the way he saw beauty in common settings

In early summer of that year I sold the Corvette, much to Dolly's relief, and bought my dream car, a black 1964 Jaguar E-Type convertible, a car I never believed I'd own. Before I go any further, I'm certain some readers will wonder why I bought a Jag when Dolly wanted carpeting, expensive carpeting. Fair question, and there were two justifying reasons: We did not require carpeting to live but we did need a reliable car in which to commute to our jobs; our careers depended on it. Second, I'd cut a great deal on the Jag and had not gone crazy and bought something we couldn't afford. The price I'd negotiated was ridiculously low as the American car dealer didn't want a British car on the lot. I was able to pay cash for much of it with proceeds from the Corvette, a car I'd turned a nice profit on when I sold. So, in truth, it was not an imprudent purchase. It was good value and it placed us in sports car heaven. It came replete with wool carpeting, the smell of highest quality leather, a wooden steering wheel, and sexy gauges and switches. The E-Type Jag was, without question, the most beautiful car to ever leave England. Its shape was a cross between a running cat and a reclining woman's nude body; in other words, it was all smooth, sensual curves. To a British car nut, it was automotive nirvana, and, in this case, Dolly also liked it. Besides, an up and coming young photographer needs his image so he can make his game. Day by day we were growing up, learning how to keep the music playing as we danced to a complex tune called career building and early married life. Obstacles are a part of even the best marriage, but we coped well. I'm certain that a large part of what made things work for us was that we were crazy about each other. We also supported one another and were stronger together than alone. Love truly is the answer to many of life's problems. It certainly worked for us.

Things were good in 1967: We continued to live in a house we loved in sand dune country along the shores of Lake Michigan. We were, I admit, sixty-five miles from Chicago and had to commute to the city and our jobs daily. And even though, in many ways, we were poor as mice in a church basement, we traveled in style and comfort in a Jaguar convertible. I had the primo parking space in the lot behind the studio because the parking guys loved my car. I had a handsome and hip African-America assistant named Lance and we worked happily and well together. My wife was a lovely, vivacious graphic artist whom many men admired too damned much for my comfort. I got to travel to some nice places and often photograph beautiful girls and handsome boys for a living. Sound glamorous? I suppose it was, or at least it looked that way. But here's the balance of facts...

Not having been in the business that long, I was still paying my dues, so my weekly take-home pay was far from impressive. I was shooting important jobs, but not being paid like the other photographers and was not mature enough in business matters to negotiate for more money, which I deserved based on my work. Our house in Michiana Shores was unfinished. We were tired all the time from the pace we kept and couldn't afford to make improvements to our cottage as fast as we liked, and Dolly was thus far unable to carry a baby to term. We were twenty-five years old.


Dolly wanted to learn to drive (at last) so I tried to give her lessons in the Jaguar, so she'd learn on a manual gearbox, as we owned sports cars. It made complete sense but turned out to be a big mistake. Only five feet tall, she was barely able to reach the pedals in the Jag and seemed unable to get the rhythm of easing out the clutch while applying a bit of gas with the accelerator. The poor car would jerk, buck and she'd kill the engine. It seems I was not the most patient of teachers, so there may have been times when I raised my voice just a wee little bit, which was why she eventually shouted, "That's it, Buster. We're done. I want someone much calmer and not so in love with his car to teach me. I also want to start out in an automatic." She then informed me she'd seen an ad for Sears driving school, and so off she went, got lessons, and learned to drive. She was right again; it was a much better solution. And honestly… I really don't think I raised my voice all that much. No…seriously!

Too small to drive the Jag, Dolly had to make do with the Ford, but soon, from a friend of Dolly's, we were able to make an inexpensive purchase of a nice little two-door hatchback with an automatic transmission. Freedom for Dolly had arrived at last. I also recognized that shopping trips would no doubt increase, along with new treasures for the nest. Oh well, I thought. It's only money.

That same summer we took a short vacation trip to Mackinac Island at the northern end of Lake Michigan. On the way up, we traveled on a beautifully paved road through forest that, at the time, had no traffic on it in either direction. I turned to Dolly and said, "Let's see what this Jaguar can do."

I backed off at somewhere around one hundred forty miles per hour. Dolly's knuckles were white on the grab handle, her hair in disarray, but she was grinning ear to ear. All she said was, "Wow, that was something." Our Jaguar was a rocket. It was fun but we never did it again. The passenger on board was too precious to put at risk. That speed test had been dumb male bravado on my part. Thinking back, I should have known better.

Visiting the island was like going back in time. There are no cars allowed, only bicycles, and horse-drawn buggies and wagons. The Mackinac sailboat race from Chicago was just finishing. Upon arrival on the mainland just off the island, we parked the Jag in a safe place and found a guy with a motorboat who was about to take a group of people to the island. He managed to fit us on for a fee. After the crossing, we arrived at a pier and one of the dock hands helping us tie up casually mentioned there had been a cancellation of a room booking at the Iroquois Hotel. As I now had an inkling it might be difficult to get accommodation at any hotel at race time and others on the boat seemed to have come to the same realization, I jumped out of the boat, yelled, "watch our bags" to Dolly and sprinted for the hotel, which was right on the main street. I got the room.

Once inside, Dolly flopped onto the bed, laughing, and said, "My hero!" We were told later that it was in fact nearly impossible to find a room during race week, something we had been unaware of, so serendipity again. A second-floor front, the charming period room had a rounded turret corner with windows facing the street, and through those windows, we could hear voices and the happy laughter of people on the street below out walking or biking and the clip-clop of horse's hoofs. It was a lovely trip; we bicycled around the island, fed each other lots of the fudge the place is famous for, and looked at all the boats that had finished the race. We were young, carefree, without the responsibility of a family, and feeling particularly good about life.

"I just don't know if it can get any better than this," Dolly said.

"I have a feeling we are going to have lots of times like this," I replied, "even better times, but your right, this one is pretty special." We were having a fine time being married because we didn't have the responsibilities of a family yet. Money was on the lean side, but if we were careful, we could do most anything we wanted if we could pay for it. It occurred to me this was a good thing. It allowed us to spend time focused on each other as lovers before the serious days of raising children began. We were free to enjoy a bit of glamorous lifestyle, all without the responsibilities of the life that lay ahead. It gave us time to grow even closer as a couple.

Back home again, the Jag developed a dead battery. As we still had the old yellow Ford I said to Dolly, "Will you help me get the Jag started, please? I can't find the darn jumper cables, so we'll have to do a tow start."

"Are you sure? I'm not good at that kind of thing," she said. "You know I'm not."

"Well, I don't have anyone else," I said, "so you're it." I coached her carefully on how she would pull me up our street with the Ford, a rope attached to the back of the tow car and to the central portion of the Jag's dainty front bumper. "Once rolling," I said, "I'll ease the clutch out, you'll hear the Jag start and when you do, gently stop the Ford and I'll stop the black car. Okay? Got it?" I asked.

"I think so…maybe."

"Are you sure?"

"I think so."

Well, Murphy's law stepped in, and things didn't quite work out the way I'd planned. I don't know why I thought they would. Momentary madness? My precious girl got overly excited, and hitting the gas on the Ford too hard, pulled away too fast, ripping the bumper right off the front of the Jag. It was a rather delicate little chrome, tubular steel bumper, more for looks than serious protection, so it didn't take much to do this. I climbed slowly out of the Jag, picked up the sad, bent-up little bumper with the rope still dangling from it, and stood in the middle of the street shaking my head and muttering, "I don't know why I ask you to help me with these things. I just don't know what possesses me." Dolly thought the scene hilarious and over the years, told the story many times. It made for great cocktail party conversation. It really was funny… sort of, and she did tell the story awfully well, the little devil. I hung that bit of bent bumper over the washtubs in our laundry area as a reminder of the pain she'd caused me and my precious Jaguar. It was there for years, a private joke between us.

During the long days of summer, if we arrived home from the city early enough after work, we'd eat, then go to the beach, launch the sailboat we'd recently purchased for a song from a neighbor, and sail out to enjoy the sunset. There was another couple, good looking, tall, with foreign accents, who had a slightly smaller sailboat. They'd often go sailing at the same hour and we got to know them as we'd help each other beach our boats…ours was very heavy. Their names were Lothar (pronounced Low tar) and Brigitte; they were probably ten years older than we were, and German, but had been living in the US for some time. He was tall, rangy, handsome, and worked as a design engineer. She was also tall, willowy, and elegant. One evening after we'd put the boats up, they invited us to join them for a cocktail at their cottage, which was right at the beach. The drink offered was the gin martini, and Lothar volunteered to show me how he made these lethal bombs.

"It's simple really," he said. "First, you fill a tumbler with ice, then pour in the gin and here's the real secret." He then showed me how he had pierced a small hole in the tin cap of the dry vermouth bottle, and through this little hole he shook out about two or three drops into each glass, then stirred the mixture gently.

"Vermouth is chemically important as it 'softens gin,'" he said, "but never use too much or it will spoil the flavor of the gin. Add a nice large olive, and now you know how to make a proper martini."

Not being used to gin, Dolly and I quickly got buzzed. In conversation, it was revealed that we were the owners of the beautiful black Jaguar E-Type seen around the village. Lothar started to laugh. "At last! I finally get to meet the crazy man I saw trying to teach his wife to drive in that beautiful car, and obviously having no success whatever." The night ended with the four of us marching around their living room to the choral movement of Beethoven's Ninth Symphony, a classic example of the power of gin to make friends and remove inhibition…or should I say, common sense?

Lothar, it turned out, was the navigator on a thirty-six-foot racing sailboat named *Gung Ho* and he invited us to go pleasure sailing the next Sunday. We met the owner, Joe Oran, and cast off the mooring lines. As a large sailboat is basically a bigger version of a small sailboat, I began to help a bit with the lines and sails. Joe noticed and said, "You know something about sailboats, I see."

"I have zero experience on big boats but do know how to handle my sixteen-footer," I told him.

"Why don't you come out with us next Sunday for a local race?" he said. "We're short a crewman who went back to college. You can lend a hand."

When I showed up at the dock that Sunday, it was blowing a gale and big waves were running. It looked like it was going to be baptism by fire. I prayed I wouldn't puke. I didn't, the day went well, and I was welcomed aboard as a new crew member.

I crewed on the Tri State race aboard *Gung Ho* that Labor Day weekend. It's called the Tri State because each of the race's three legs finishes in a different state: the boats start in Chicago on Friday evening a little before sunset, and race at night, finishing in St Joe, Michigan, usually in the early hours of Saturday morning, and sometimes still in the dark. It's about seventy-five miles. The boats then lay over on Saturday for big parties with impressive imbibing of spirits, loud music, and mad dancing. Then on Sunday morning, the fleet races down to Michigan City. I remember attending the pancake breakfast that Sunday morning, and being able to hear waves out on the lake. I took a Dramamine with my coffee, just in case. Back in Michigan City it was party again, this time, with Dolly joining in.

"Hey, sailor boy. What's on the agenda for your first mate?" No one loves a party more than my Doll, and she didn't require drink to enjoy as good a time as everyone else. On Labor Day morning we raced back to Chicago, finishing in Illinois, the third state. We bagged a trophy as our boat almost always finished among the top three in our class and was often first.

I loved sailing on offshore races. It was a rush to be crewing aboard a boat with a reputation for winning. It gave me dock cred when sailors found out I crewed on *Gung Ho*. I rarely felt fear on the boat, even in bad weather, but I did have a phobia about getting seasick. Slight nausea did occur on occasion, but thankfully I never got sick. That would have been a sign of weakness as it seemed no one else on the crew had any problem with motion. The way I appeared to others was a crippling hang-up of mine. I seemed to expect perfection from myself.

After the Tri State race was over, my time was devoted to Dolly and the needs of home. This did not concern me as I loved working on our house, often to the point where Dolly would come out in the failing light of nightfall to talk me into stopping whatever I was doing and come in. There's something rewarding about working on a house you own. I imagine primitive men felt that way about their caves. It's a powerful feeling, this sense of home and place.

In time we realized we needed a car that would fit both our needs as homeowners and for moving photography equipment on location, so with *great* reluctance, sadness, and a broken heart (take one of my limbs, but don't mess with my Jaguar), I sold the black beauty. It was replaced with a big Plymouth station wagon we called the *Queen Mother*. Dolly hated the color which was maroon. As a bonus, and to appease our soul (remember, we only had one that we shared!) I acquired a lovely little 1953 MGTD sports car. Dolly loved it, dubbing it "CUTE." I couldn't pass up the low price, but it did need a little work. Once I'd rewired part of the car (electrical gremlins) it was reliable, albeit old-fashioned, and by modern standards, an antique. Still, it was lots of fun; a little toy car with abundant character from the past that we kept around for pleasure. In the movie *Love Story*, Ryan O'Neal and the beautiful Ali McGraw drove a similar MG. Ours would become a classic collectible one day, but not our collectable. We never kept them long enough. With the appearance of the MG and the Queen Mother, the yellow Ford went to its final resting place. Dolly still had her hatch back.

A fashion look that mirrored the influence of the Beatles and other British rock groups was the rage in the sixties and seventies. We both had fun with that *look* on weekends, each wearing bell bottom jeans or outrageous stripped pants and other Carnaby Street fashions. Dolly was so cute in her *rock* attire including hip huggers that revealed her pretty navel, tops worn without bra; it was all so sexy. I had taken a photo of her leaning against our Triumph Spitfire dressed in *the style*; when it first appeared, her hair done the way hot models of the time wore theirs. She did it very well. But at her job she avoided the *look*. In the photography business, anything was accepted, even expected, but not at the chocolate company. It was a freewheeling crazy time. We embraced the fun parts but avoided others such as the common use of marijuana. I tried it a few times, had one less than fun experience, so that was the end for me. I barely drank at that time and never touched any sort of illegal drugs again.

The commute was getting to us, so, at last, we rented an apartment in Chicago that had become available in our friend Senn's building to cut down on the need for daily travel. This change also allowed me to work more overtime. The rent was a surprise, so ridiculously low we could afford it, and the apartment came furnished. This required taking our cat Tyke back and forth to the city, which led to some interesting Monday mornings. That darned cat could sense we were leaving, and she'd hide. Running late one morning, I'd found myself chasing her around the house, under beds, and behind furniture. The chase made me crazed. In frustration, I threw a small lamp at the beast and missed. It was apparent Tyke did not think much of riding in cars. When I finally got into the station wagon with the cat, Dolly asked, "So, what was the holdup?"

"Your damn cat, of course." In truth I was fond of the cat too, so it was really *our* cat, but I was pretending to be angry, making a big deal out of it for fun. Dolly laughed at my anger saying, "Poor Paul, she's only a cat and understandably afraid of cars. Give her a break." Well, I thought to myself, I think I'm going to have fun with this situation. "You're laughing at me," I said testily as we drove through our village. "It's not nice to laugh at me. Do you know what happens to naughty little girls who are rude to their husbands? They get a spanking on their pretty little bottoms, that's what happens. So, I'm thinking that tonight, when were in our little love nest apartment you're going to have to accept your punishment?"

Dolly was still laughing hysterically as we pulled out onto the highway. Finally, she wiped away a few tears and managed to gasp out, "In your dreams big boy. I'm not into pain."

Oh well, I tried. It seemed a fun idea to me, considering how lovely her derriere was. And after all, I would have been gentle. Perhaps, I thought, on some other night I might get lucky? A guy can only hope. Why did she have to be so incredibly sexy anyway? It just wasn't fair.


In October 1967 Dolly was again with child. This time the doctor said he was going to keep an even closer eye on her throughout her time. We followed all his instructions exactly while I watched over her as if she were made of Waterford Crystal. Dolly continued to work in the beginning, but in her fifth month, she decided to stay at home. It was the longest Dolly had carried a baby thus far. We had to give up the apartment in the city to my recently married brother John and his wife Penny. They used it while sorting out their life plans, then turned it over to John's friend Vince. As I said, it was crazy cheap.

In January of 1968, Dolly's dad was in hospital, dying from a bleeding ulcer and complications. "I'd like to drive in and see him," she said. "He's not in good shape." "Of course, we will. He's your father," I said. We were able to visit several times before he died. Dolly was grateful for having that time with him. The cause of death was listed as pneumonia, but it was the hard life he'd lived that had taken its toll. He was fifty-eight years old but looked nearer to eighty. Once again, Dolly had to cope with loss, this time, during a pregnancy. I don't know how she managed the stress, but somehow, she did.

We were both excited that she'd reached the seventh month of her pregnancy, but soon she was not feeling quite herself, so I took vacation time to be at home with her. On the third day of the seventh month, she started to spot, and then bleed a bit. I immediately called her doctor. "Get her down here as fast as you can," he said. "I'll be waiting." We lived fifteen minutes from the hospital. I made it in ten. The doctor examined her and said, "Your baby's still alive. I want to do an emergency C-section right now before we lose it."

I was panicky and visibly shaking. Dolly looked at me in her calm way and said, "It will be fine, Paul. Don't worry." I'm sure she could see the panic in my eyes. How she remained calm, I don't know. Though a petite woman, she was also fearless. I was terrified. This situation was beyond my control, so I had to put faith in the hands of people I didn't know who were about to cut her open. Those experienced in this procedure know that a cesarean section is generally quite safe, but to me, it was frightening. Did they understand what she meant to me, and how much I depended on and needed her? Then I realized how selfish my thoughts were. I was making this about me, and not Dolly. She was the one going through heavy weather.

Dolly was whisked into surgery. It didn't take long before Doctor Jack came out, his scrubs spattered with Dolly's blood, to tell me she was fine. "Dolly's stable, and you have a little girl who weighed in at four pounds ten ounces." My heart pounded, excited that we had a baby at last and that Dolly was fine. "She's small," he said, "but seems to be strong and is doing well in an incubator, where you can see her now," The problem, he explained, was that the placenta was tearing, causing Dolly to bleed internally, which would have quickly drowned the baby in blood.

Our little girl was tiny, and not the picture-perfect pink baby of the movies, having just been snatched, in most traumatic fashion from Dolly, her warm human chrysalis. She looked so vulnerable, with many tubes and things connected to her. We'd already picked out a name if our baby proved to be a girl, so on Wednesday, the third of April 1968, we became the parents of a tiny little person we called Gabrielle. We first encountered the name in a book on the life of French composer Claude Debussy, who had a mistress of that name. We loved the sound of it and assumed it was a variation of Gabriel, the arc-angels name.


I couldn't celebrate with Dolly, who was still in recovery, so I started phoning everyone I could think of with the news that we were now a Mom and Dad! Gabrielle's parents were twenty-six years old at her birth.

# 10.

Gabrielle's birth though joyful was also the arrival of the day that caused me so much worry and concern. Dolly had warned me the first time she'd been pregnant: "I'm going to be a stay-at-home mom. I will live on hot dogs if necessary, but I'll be raising our children myself, at least until they go to school. Gabrielle will know exactly who her mother is. She will know my smell, my voice, and how it feels when I hold her. She will know how much I love her every minute. This is important to me and I prefer it not be open to discussion."

That was Dolly as I'd always known her. She knew exactly what she wanted, and her vision was clear regarding her intended path. She was going to be a mother, and that was how it would be. There must have been some deep motivation behind her insistence on being a stay-at-home mom, but I never asked what it was. She also took some of the pressure from me when she said she'd arranged to do work for the chocolate company at home in the busy holiday seasons or on larger projects, so she would still be contributing financially after all. I was proud of how she managed these things with logic and organization. That said, I would still be the prime breadwinner. "The main support of our family is now up to you, my love. Are you ready?" she asked.

"I promised I'd watch over you, and I will, and Gabrielle too," I said with a confidence I hoped to live up to.

Buddha stated: "Love is not what you say, love is what you do." For me, it was showtime, and I had miles to go and promises to keep. The loss of half our income caused me sleepless nights. I'd just have to go out and find more freelance jobs, and maybe raise my fees. I'd also ask for a raise at the studio for reasons I hoped would be obvious to them.

Unfortunately, our house at the time wasn't exactly in the ideal shape to receive mother and baby. I had a bad habit, you see. I'd often begin large house projects such as the remodeling of a room at the most inopportune times. In my defense, I could not have foreseen that Dolly would give birth early. We should have had a couple of months to go before baby time. She had not been feeling well during the last stage of pregnancy, and wanting to cheer her up, I'd suggested we order the new kitchen cabinets we'd been saving for. Remodeling the kitchen was high priority, so this suddenly seemed a good time to get the project underway. Off we went and placed an order, custom designed to fit our space, of beautiful cherry wood cabinets, new counters, and sink, all from a custom kitchen cabinet store. Dolly was thrilled. Then nature slapped us with an early special delivery...a baby.

Dolly came home from the hospital (without Gabrielle, who was still in the ICU) to find the cabinets had been delivered and were stacked in our living room. She also found that in her absence my dad and I had torn out the old kitchen with the intention of surprising her with a beautifully finished new one when she came home. The only surprise she got was to discover she had no kitchen at all because we hadn't finished the job yet.

When I look back and recall the things I did to that poor girl, even with the best intentions, I'm amazed she didn't leave me for some normal guy with a steady income, a lawyer maybe. Then again, Dolly would never marry a lawyer because most were not artistic or romantic enough for her. Our life was unorthodox and therefore exciting. A normal person would say, "Come look, we had our kitchen remodeled." But in our peculiar household. the occasional foray into madness was legend: "When I came home from the hospital, my crazy husband and his equally looney dad had completely destroyed my kitchen and…." Well, you get the idea. After all, anyone can lead a normal life. We, however, were living a life of happy misadventures that made for great stories.

At first, the new mom was barely able to move about due to her sore tummy. Our baby was still at the hospital in an incubator, as she had to reach a certain target weight before they'd let us bring her home. My sister Leona arrived to help, and after seeing the mess and bedlam, asked,

"And exactly where do you expect me to do dishes?" I shrugged my shoulders and said,

"The bathtub? And we'll temporarily hook up the stove. Will that do?"

"I suppose it will have to," she said, mumbling something I didn't hear…probably just as well.

The weather was good in April 1968, so Leona would plant Dolly in the yard on a lounge with lots of pillows. Out of the construction zone, she could enjoy the show the daffodils were putting on and let the sunshine touch the scar on her belly. She believed the sun would heal her faster.

"Paul, my scar is so ugly. It's makes me sad that you have to look at it." I came to her, and kneeling, gently kissed her scar. "My darling girl," I said, "it doesn't bother me, not even a little bit. You are so much more to me than that insignificant mark. And we have a daughter, so what could be better?" I don't think we ever spoke of the scar again, though I often kissed her belly, offering reassurance I hope she felt. I'd told her the truth: it really didn't matter to me, and she was still my angel. After the C-section, Dolly took to wearing one-piece bathing suits to the beach for a time, but soon went back to bikinis, boldly letting her scar show. I found this behavior courageous and sexy. Perhaps she just decided to tell the world, "I have a daughter who makes me happy, and this scar is a small price to pay for her." She was a brave, strong woman, and more beautiful to me than ever.

One bright sunny morning while Dolly was still recovering, Leona suggested, "Let's take all the books off the shelves in the living room and freshen them up" and so she did, with Dolly looking on. There were hundreds of them, so no small task. She'd take them outside to dust, then bring them back where Dolly, now occupying the couch, could direct their placement.

They were having fun and I could hear Dolly saying, "Please don't make me laugh. It hurts." Then they would laugh some more while rebuilding the library.

Leona stayed two or three weeks. When she left, my mother came to take over. We couldn't have managed without their help. I believe Gabrielle finally came home about eighteen days after she'd joined us in this world. Dolly couldn't do much, and she certainly wasn't comfortable picking up the baby yet, but my mother was in her element with baby Gabrielle to care for. Leona and Mom were angels when we needed them. Perhaps the angels of our imagination aren't spirits at all, but the caring humans around us who come to our rescue when called, not by prayer but with a phone call and some pleading.

Meanwhile, Dad and I continued to work on the kitchen. He was always happy doing things for his family. He had wired and plumbed, teaching me along the way. I did much of the carpentry. Together we had hung the cabinets and tiled the kitchen floor and breakfast area in a dark red and deeply textured raised brick vinyl tile. It looked rich and old, like it had always been there. When the kitchen was finished, we had Dolly wait in another room while we polished it up, complete with fresh flowers in a vase and scented candles burning, then invited her in to inspect. She looked at her new kitchen, and then at us.

"It's just beautiful," she said. "I can't thank you all enough. I can hardly wait to start cooking for you! It was definitely worth the wait." Dad just beamed. Me too.

While all this was going on, I'd been doing side jobs for an ad agency in Michigan City. The man who owned it had been encouraging me to consider opening a studio in town. I told him I was in no financial position to go out on my own yet. His latest enticement was offering to be a silent partner, putting up half the money needed. He had recently purchased an old church and school building and suggested I rent, at reasonable cost, the 4,000-square foot upper floor for a studio. It was formerly an auditorium with a large stage.

He also said he'd pay me the going rate for any work I did to improve his building. This would be a plus and extra income beyond my studio paycheck. We would need that extra income while getting the business going. Of course, his agency would feed me jobs. I would then have to go out and sell myself to other ad agencies, design firms, and companies. I gave the concept serious consideration.

"Doll, I know this is madness," I told her one evening. "We have a new baby, and an unfinished house, but I'm not sure I would get another opportunity to have someone else fund part of a business I think I'd like to own. I'd be able to stop commuting to Chicago, which would save us gas money, time, and maybe even me. If you agree, I want to take the chance."

As always, she expressed her belief in me. "I have trusted you to do what's best for us," she said, "and if this is what you want, you should go for it. But remember, you'll be leaving a big established studio that loves your work and keeps giving you raises. There's a lot of security in that." She was right, of course, so her comments added additional fear to my own. But as mad and risky as it seemed, in a moment of youthful optimism, we decided to go forward with the scheme.

I gave notice at Kranzten. They were disappointed, but understood, as this is often the track of young shooters with talent and a little madness. I was brought up to be loyal, so felt guilty doing this to a company that had been good to me. Kranzten had been more than just a job; it had been photography college. But this was our life, and I had to do what I thought was best for us. I only hoped I was making the right decision.

It's not unusual to worry we won't ever achieve the goals and dreams we set for ourselves. And sometimes we become fearful when we do. I lived with both those emotions, but kept pushing forward, with no way to know how the story would unfold. My old friend, the voice in my head kept saying, *Boy, it's possible this move suggests you might be in need of a good shrink.* and I probably did.

I discovered very quickly, to my dismay, that my new business partner, an older man set in his ways, was very controlling. He insisted I use his bookkeeper, for example, so every time I wanted a check written I had to walk over to his office, which was a big nuisance. All billing had to go through his office also, and every expenditure needed to be approved. I was certain there was no dishonesty in these practices. He just liked feeling in control of what he'd invested in. He also liked to have endless meetings, often on weekends, another nuisance and often the sign of a lonely man with nothing better to do. I became unhappy with the arrangement. I felt like little more than a picture-making puppet.

On the other hand, I was having success selling myself. I had an impressive portfolio made up of my own personal work and work I'd done for the clients of Kranzten, much of it on large format transparency film in mounts. While most photographers' books in the area were shot on small format or at most 4x5, my work looked impressive on 8x10 film. It didn't hurt that I was from Chicago, which carried the cachet of being the big time.

I'd secured an appointment with a prominent ad agency in South Bend, home of Notre Dame University and numerous large corporations, to see the production manager. We sat down in the conference room and he went through only four or five samples of my work before he said: "I'll be right back." He returned with another man who turned out to be a brother, and after introductions, they looked at my work together. Then they spoke to each other in private and returned with a layout of a musical instrument. They asked what I would charge to shoot the ad. I estimated quickly and gave them a price on the spot (something I stopped doing as I gained experience and knew better), and they handed me a flute in a case, a layout and purchase order, and said, "Go do it." I was astonished. They went on to say, "We don't want to be entertained. We don't need fancy promotions or Christmas presents. We want good work delivered on time and we will pay you... on time."

I shot the flute as per the layout, but also did a second shot of my own creation in which I placed a Monarch butterfly (dead but looking very much alive) on the keys of the flute. The agency's client was so excited about that picture they had it made into big mural-size prints for trade shows. And that is how I won my client's trust; by giving them an award winner, and more than they had asked for.

I also started shooting for the recreational vehicle and manufactured housing industries. In the beginning, selling seemed easy and I thought I had it made. Then I discovered that a client may love my work, but being in a smaller market, might only have something to shoot on occasion, which made the workflow spotty. Consequently, I started to experience anxiety about my ability to support my family and the studio overhead.

Some people deal easily with business stress; I was not one of them. I was feeling overwhelmed and began to wonder if I had what it takes to be a business owner. Perhaps I'd been hasty in leaving a secure position in Chicago. There, I only had to shoot; there was no bookkeeping, no sales, not even darkroom work. I wondered if they would take me back if I failed. I suppose it was always an option. I did like working there, they liked me, and I probably had a job for life at Kranzten, if I wanted one. But it was the commute I dreaded, and so much time away from home.

I kept my fears from Dolly and tried to move forward. Not sharing my concerns with her was a mistake. She was my life partner, and I should have sought her wisdom, practical common sense, and encouragement. Instead, I closed the door on the one person I needed to trust most of all. It turned out to be a foolish decision.

I'd only been in business a short time when I got a call from a fellow photographer, one I'd worked with at Kranzten. Walt was an excellent product photographer. "Well, I've left Kranzten," he said. "I never did get along with that production manager. I'm in Indiana today visiting my wife's family in Valparaiso."

"Hey," I said, "Why don't you run over to Michigan City and see what I'm up to?"

"Sounds good," he said. "Is today inconvenient? I gave him the address of my studio. When he arrived, we took the full tour. He liked what he saw, one thing led to another until he asked, "Would you be interested in joining forces? I soon convinced my silent partner that it would be a wise move on our part to acquire this excellent product photographer by letting him become another partner.

There was comfort in sharing responsibilities with someone, but two salaries were a strain. After a time, we went to our partner and told him we wanted to buy him out and go it on our own. We met with resistance at first, but eventually realizing he had no choice, he caved in. We continued to rent from him but also arranged to have a wonderful new studio put together about six blocks away in a former brewery owned by an architect. He was willing to build out the space to our requirements.

We made the move, took on the ten-year lease, which concerned me, and were truly on our own. It was a fantastic studio with an open balcony office overlooking the shooting area, accessed via a spiral staircase inside what had been an industrial chimney for the brewery. The architect had renovated and lighted it inside, topped with a bubble skylight. It was all exciting but taking on the additional responsibility was stressful for me. Our combined portfolios gave our studio a more diversified look, and soon we picked up some new product clients. It also turned out that Walt had knowledge of bookkeeping and I did not. We split tasks, with me doing sales, and Walt doing the office and billing.

On paper, things were looking good, but deep down I had a nagging fear of the big overhead that, in our enthusiasm and desire, we had committed to. Fools rush in and all that. We kept pushing forward, but I was not comfortable knowing we had such a large overhead to cover each month that included much more expensive rent, two salaries, and all the other expenses associated with running a growing new business. My anxiety level was rising.

At home Gabrielle were doing well and Dolly was loving being a mom. The two of them were adorable together...my two little women. I did not share my business concerns with my wife. I should have, just so she'd be informed of the state of things. It was unfair of me, I know.

Meanwhile, I was still crewing aboard *Gung Ho* and the Mackinac Island race was coming up. We were competing in Chicago most weekends and winning or placing much of the time, putting us at or near the top of the *Chicago Tribune* Boat of the Year rankings. The downside of all this sailing was that I was leaving Dolly alone with a new baby and that did bother me. Every time we raced in the city, we had to cross Lake Michigan from Michigan City to Chicago and back home again, a five-hour trip each way.

Occasionally the trip home would only be the owner and one or two crew. We would cross the finish line of a race, and some crew would jump off onto other boats to go ashore and pick up the cars they'd left there.

After one of those races in Chicago, it was only Joe and I who turned *Gung Ho* east, setting a course for Michigan City. Part way across he left the boat in my charge and went below to nap. It was a good feeling to be alone and in control of this beautiful little ship as we rode the waves eastward. I knew that down below he'd be checking up on me periodically with the compass he had mounted in his bunk. *Gung Ho* would charge along happily, like the beautiful girl she was, the wind singing a sailing chantey in the rigging. Her tiller would kick in my hand, reminding me that a sailboat is in many ways a living thing, and she was sending messages if I weren't steering her properly. Like a good horse, she knew her way home and was reminding me to pay attention.

After a couple of hours, we slipped silently past the Michigan City lighthouse into our home harbor in fading afterglow, safely returned and ready to put our faithful girl to bed. Boats are always called "she" and perceived as feminine. Sometimes they are named for the woman the skipper loves. *Gung Ho*'s owner had not done this. His wife shared a name with mine, and if he had named his boat after her, she would have been called the *Dolly*. However, unlike my Dolly who loved sailing, (she'd go out with us while pregnant and watch us practice spin sets), his Dolly did not love sailing as she suffered *mal di mare*.

Men often have a romance with their boat, or in my case, the one they crew on. She becomes like a lover, beautiful, challenging, and endlessly exciting, just like the woman who was waiting for me at home. As we tied up, I could imagine hearing my lover calling my name, so it was time to shoulder the sea bag, abandon my mistress of the sea, and join my true love and our little baby girl.

Gabrielle too, was like a sailboat; demanding attention, and always "right now." She wanted what she wanted when she wanted it. Since the trauma of her birth, she had grown more beautiful to us every day, and exhibited a healthy pair of lungs. It was fortunate we had no nearby neighbors. As for Dolly, she glowed about the house in a contented way, always smiling like she knew a secret I didn't. It had to be motherhood. The loss of her sister and the trials of her failed pregnancies had made Gabrielle even more precious to her. I was surprised Dolly never suggested Joy as a middle name (Gabrielle has none), as we both would have liked that choice. We were proud and happy to be parents, and speaking for myself, having a child finally made me feel like a grown-up.

There was, however, a slight downside to this fatherhood thing: the responsibility part. I found myself sitting around calculating how many jobs I'd have to shoot to keep that little result of our love in formula and diapers, to say nothing of little frilly dresses and patent leather shoes that I knew would come soon enough. But what proud mom and dad don't like dressing up their baby?

I was busy refinishing the crib that my siblings and I had all slept in as children. It was a beautiful, well-made classic crib, quite old. I found it a little frightening to suddenly realize I was responsible for a tiny human being who was completely helpless, yet it didn't seem to worry Dolly in the least. She was meant to be a mother, that was apparent. Would I be playing second fiddle with Dolly now that she had our twinkling little star to treasure and occupy her attention? What happened was that Gabrielle drew Dolly and Paul even closer. Interesting.

"Paul, would you be willing to stop sailing after the Tri State race?" Dolly said one late summer day. "Gabrielle is very demanding right now, and I need help and a little more sleep than I've been getting." I had noticed that the choppy hours were hard on Dolly and I was feeling guilty about it. "Absolutely," I said. "I'll leave the boat after the Tri State. Joe's selling *Gung Ho* anyway, as he and his wife are moving to Colorado." Dolly was relieved. I understood that having a child was the responsibility of both parents. I would miss the boat and crew, but my family was more important. I'd had two years of racing and we would still have our beach boats. I refused to be one of those men who expect children to be the work of wives alone. We were in this together and I liked caring for our little girl.

Lake Michigan is not really a lake at all. It is, in fact, an *inland sea*. Weather is unpredictable and racing here can be a serious challenge, particularly in the middle and upper parts of the lake. It's possible, though not common, for waves to reach twenty-five to thirty feet offshore, and winds of ninety-plus mph can occur in a squall.

The 1968 Mackinac Island race (The Mac) dealt us lots of wind, coming for a large part of the race from behind, so we carried Spinnaker (a large parachute-like sail) for the first half of the race. Sadly, we blew out, i.e., ripped to shreds—that heavy air sail in spectacular fashion off the coast of upper Michigan, potentially damaging our chances for a win. We pressed on regardless, running downwind under main and two jibs set wing and wing. We experienced lots of rocking and rolling with this setup, giving helmsmen a real workout, but speed was good. The Coast Guard reported winds of forty to fifty knots and more at times. The seas that came up from behind out of the dark looked frighteningly large, demonstrating the power of the sea and reminding me that I had made a conscious choice to be out here in the dark of night battling high winds and seas. At the same time, I also had responsibilities on shore, a wife and child. I had chosen a hobby that, although possessing a good safety record, was also potentially dangerous. Why are men drawn to these activities? Perhaps we have something to prove to ourselves. But on that dark night I had a revelation: As a young father, I had responsibilities and should be weighing risk more carefully in future.

It was a fast race, *Gung Ho* covering the 330 miles quickly, finishing on Monday afternoon, placing second in our class and twelfth overall, handicap corrected.

I wrote an article in 1971 about my Mac experience in 1968, which I was able to sell, with pictures, to the *Chicago Tribune Magazine*. It was published as a cover story. In it I related what it was like racing aboard *Gung Ho* on the Mackinac Race, the longest freshwater race in the world. I received a very nice check for my efforts. This was like manna from heaven and thrilled Dolly, who was finally able to purchase the carpeting she desired!

I felt proud that my writing had contributed to her happiness by providing the means to acquire what she had waited so patiently for. The carpeted room looked warm and cozy, as she knew it would.

Several readers wrote comments on my article in the *Letters to the Editor* page of the *Tribune Magazine.* One said, "I've seen the boats starting that race and thought, *toy sailors.* Then I read Paul Marshall's piece on racing to Mackinac. I was glad to learn there are still iron men who go down to the sea in small ships." I could have kissed the guy. Who knew I was able to communicate my experiences to others, and with my words? Writing and publishing was a thrill, but one that got shelved as my time was occupied with building a photography business and supporting our young family. It would be years before I'd publish again.

# 11.

"Sometimes my brave, strong girl would go for hours without tears.
then they would begin again, and no matter how hard I tried,
I could never dry them all."

Paul Marshall

In October of 1968, Dolly was once again, pregnant. She carried this baby full term, but when her due date was nearly upon us, she started bleeding at home again. Although we rushed to the hospital and her doctor performed another emergency C-section, we were too late. Our baby was dead, caused by the same internal bleeding problem as in the past. It was the 4th of July 1969, one calendar day apart from the death of Dolly's eighteen-year-old sister Joy on July 3rd, 1966.

Our baby was a girl. My mom joined us at the hospital for what should have been a happy occasion but turned out to be anything but. Mom and I were directed to the hospital morgue where the tiny body of the baby had been taken. They asked for a name for the death certificate. If we had a girl, we'd planned to name her Sabrina. As Dolly was still sedated and could not make her choice known, my mother suggested the name be Mary, "just for document purposes." I was feeling such despair, I don't think I really cared what name was on a piece of paper, so Mary Marshall she became.

I forced myself to look at our perfect little girl and it was heartbreaking. She would never know life and our love for her, and Gabrielle would not have a new sister. The thought of Dolly coming out of anesthesia wanting to see her new baby and being told she was dead was causing me profound anguish. I could not imagine the misery and sorrow she would have to suffer after having carried her baby in her body for nine months, already loving this new life, anticipating how exciting it was going to be to hold a new member of our family in her arms.

My rage needed venting. I wanted to scream or strike out at something, blame someone. Where was the God of Love when we needed Him? I was a decent person and Dolly nearly an angel, so why did this bad thing happen to us? I never wanted to hear, "these trials are sent to make us stronger," or any other meaningless platitudes and cliché's people offer, even with the best of intentions.

I was beyond angry because the kindest, most loving person I knew was going to have to endure the greatest suffering of her life, the loss of her child. It was too painful to think about. I will never be free of the image of our little girl, already turning pale blue in a stainless-steel sink in the hospital morgue as they prepared to wrap her up. It was heart-rending, but nothing compared to the sadness I knew Dolly would suffer. She didn't deserve this, and I didn't know how I was going to help her.

Many members of my family have been interred at a Catholic cemetery in Chicago. Baby Mary (Sabrina) was buried in a tiny newborn baby-sized coffin on top of my grandmother. As the little box went into the ground, it contained not only the body of our child, but the broken fragments of the religion I was taught to believe in. In this tragedy, faith had proven cold comfort and of no use to me. Faith, if I still had any left, was fading fast.

My mother's recommendation of the name Mary was suggested for a reason; she knew it was not the name Dolly intended, which would help distance her from her loss. Also, being a religious woman, my mom felt the name of the mother of Jesus was the right choice and would somehow protect little Mary's infant soul. I was never clear why her soul needed protection as she was an innocent. This was an example of the peace of mind truly religious people like my mother derive from their faith, and I suppose that's not a bad thing. Even if, in my opinion, it's likely based in illusion, it does help many to cope. As for Dolly and me, we were not strict as Catholics go, but if Dolly found comfort in spending an hour at mass on Sunday (she called it her spiritual time), I gladly attended with her, although I was growing increasingly convinced there was no God and we are on our own in this life. The loss of our child would prove hardest for Dolly but was also an additional weight I too would now carry.

I had no experience dealing with the depression and grief of a mother who has just lost her child. What could I possibly say to give solace? I tried to dry her tears and offer my love, holding her close and whispering, "It will eventually be all right, my love." I said this knowing it would never be all right, not really. But these words of comfort, truthful or not, are all we have. In her sadness, she would ask me through tears of pain and despair, "Paul, what really matters in life? Do pretty clothes and fancy cars or vacations matter? Does anything matter when compared to our baby dying?" The most stable person I knew was questioning life itself. This was new territory for a woman like Dolly; one normally so stable and strong. She was telling me just how deep the loss of her baby was tearing into her heart. She still had Gabrielle and knowing Dolly, I was sure she would become even closer to her living child, and in time, that proved the case.

Doing my best to care for her, I tried to keep her environment peaceful and restful by disconnecting the bedroom phone and asking people not to call for a while. I tried to fill in by caring for Gabrielle and doing some basic cooking, bringing Dolly her meals in bed. I put off work for a bit and tried to help her struggle through the sadness. She was not only grieving, but healing both soul and body. They were dark days indeed. Later, in a letter to me, she wrote: "I so appreciated your comforting presence, holding me, giving me constant reassurance, drying my tears over and over. You helped me come out of a terrible despondency, and I love you for it."

In time, Dolly was able to put her pain away in some secret place I assume only mothers have, a place where even I was not allowed. When she finally emerged from that intensely blue period, she began to slowly embrace life again. The amazing resilience and strength of character Dolly possessed once more left me in true admiration of her. She was an extraordinarily strong person. But then, I find that women often are.

In the summer of 1970, Dolly was once again pregnant. It may seem madness, but she really wanted another baby, with any luck a boy, so the loss of our baby girl did not deter Dolly. Undaunted and determined as ever, my little girl with the brave heart proved unbendable in her desire for a second child.

At that time, I got involved with the Dunes Arts Foundation, a nonprofit which operated a summer stock community theater. The two people who'd co-founded this organization had been my neighbors in Michiana from the time I was a boy. I became enamored with the romance of theater and got more involved than I should have, becoming a board member and taking on photography and promotion for the group. I was taught how to produce the program book and did the design and creation of posters and ads as well. If that was not enough, I began to try out for, and was cast in shows, accepting acting parts far too large for my inexperience. I even found myself singing and dancing in a musical, in one of the main roles. I was nervous on stage, in fear of forgetting lines. Still, I was told I did a good job, and this unfortunately caused my ego to grow, which was not a good thing. Praise had put stars in my eyes, applause proving addictive. Unfortunately, for me it came with a high price… stress.

Considering that Dolly was again pregnant, my sanity must have slipped its mooring lines. For a guy of my temperament and with responsibilities of work and family, I'd taken on far too much. I didn't recognize my folly and spent lots of time trying to impress people and demonstrate what an amazing guy I was. It was all about image and I was constantly concerned with what others thought of me. On a Sunday night during the run of the play *The Lion in Winter,* in which I had a part, Dolly, Gabrielle, and I were driving home from a family event in Chicago when just before the Michigan City exit from the toll road, I suddenly didn't feel well. One moment I was fine, and the next, a feeling of doom had come over me and I couldn't breathe normally. I pulled the car onto the shoulder of the road, terrified that I was dying, got out and lay down in the grass beside the road, gasping to Dolly, "I think maybe I'm having a heart attack. I can't seem to breathe." In fact, I would eventually learn it was the opposite; I was hyperventilating, breathing too fast, and too shallow.

A man stopped (a doctor? I never knew), looked me over, took my pulse and said, "You're not having a heart attack. You're probably having a panic attack." I'd never heard of such a thing. An ambulance came and took me to our local hospital in town, with Dolly following. Over the next couple of days, doctors did tests and asked me lots of questions about my stress level at work and my lifestyle and concluded that I did indeed have a panic or anxiety attack. They found nothing medically wrong with me and sent me home with some pills. Apparently, I'd gone beyond my ability to cope with obligations, responsibilities, and the demands of my life. Business fears, lack of adequate income, the financial success I sought, the loss of our baby, outside obligations; these things and more caused me to go into overload and blow some internal circuit or other. It was the beginning of some exceedingly difficult challenges for me, and by association, for Dolly, who was innocent of my madness but would now become a partner in the irrational world of anxiety and depression.

Today this malady is a recognized medical condition called Acute Anxiety Disorder. Many types of treatment have been tried but there are numerous forms the problem can take, making treatment difficult. With the help of modern technologies, scientists have been able to learn more about the mystery of the anxious brain, but when I went through this in the early seventies, treating it was hit and miss. I was despondent and beset with feelings of doom. A strong desire to curl up and hide from life had become my daily wish.

Doctors were unable to convince me that nothing was physically wrong. I obsessed over getting panic attacks, which, in fact, causes them to happen. It was a classic case of fearing fear itself. Since I'd had the first one on the highway, I had an additional fear of it happening there again, away from medical help. This led to a travel phobia, and as I was often required to travel for my business, it caused no end of discomfort and stress. I'd become agoraphobic…fearing open places. As I had a family to support, I somehow managed those trips with the help of calming drugs. Obsessed with my pulse rate, I checked it constantly. Suffering painful physical tension in my neck and shoulders when driving on interstates, I was always looking for signs reading, "Hospital, Two Miles." I viewed hospitals as my salvation and seeing those signs made me feel temporarily safe. I was convinced medical science could "save me" from certain death, if only the doctors could discover what was wrong with me. I never actually went to those hospitals two miles away. I just felt comfort knowing they were there. I also avoided social events, becoming a partial recluse, for fear I'd have a panic attack in public. I didn't want people to know of my affliction, but hiding my shame only made it worse.

Thinking back now, it seems so irrational. I should have been able to accept that nothing was going to happen to me, but I couldn't overcome this fear ruling my life. I considered the possibility that my condition had to do with more than just the overload I'd placed on myself. Over time, things deteriorated even further. I wasn't sleeping well and began to feel depressed. Dolly grew increasingly frustrated. She couldn't understand why, when medical professionals kept telling me there was nothing physically wrong, that I couldn't accept the diagnosis and snap out of it. She wanted so much to help but couldn't find a way. I grew angry with her. Carrying the entire responsibility for our finances was weighing on me and I became angry that she wasn't helping me. A fact that I found interesting was that I don't recall ever actually getting an attack on a job. Focused on the job at hand seemed a temporary solution. Still, it was obvious we were having serious problems on several fronts.

"I love you and want to help, but I don't know what to do for you," she'd tell me. I wanted to say, "Get a job, that might help," but that would have been cruel, so I couldn't bring myself to say it. I felt I was failing at my promise to watch over Dolly, Gabrielle, and the baby on the way. I felt guilty and wanted to punish myself for letting them down and for making a mess of our lives. At times I was cool toward Dolly, never considering how this was affecting her; it was always about me. I felt she didn't understand what I was going through. She was such a confident person that my problem made no sense to her. I could do nothing to enlighten her or help her understand how frightening these attacks were and how depressed they made me. She believed the doctors when they said I was physically fine. But I doubted them, certain they didn't know what they were talking about. I continued to love Dolly— nothing could ever change that, not even my madness. And thankfully, she loved me, but neither of us could understand the other. I couldn't understand me either.

I despised myself because as much as I wanted to be successful, I found life defeating me. I became more than familiar with self-pity as I lived with it daily. And the frosting on this crazy cake was the fact that Dolly was pregnant. My troubles were the last thing she needed to be concerned with. Yet she never lost heart, and even when I snapped at her without reason, she was always there for me, most of the time patiently, but not always. Sometimes even my guardian angel wanted to scream in frustration. Sadly, she'd hitched her wagon to a guy who seemed to be going off his nut. And since medical doctors couldn't help this psychological and emotional situation, I finally admitted, to myself and to Dolly, that I needed professional help.

I began therapy with a psychiatrist I knew socially. His fee was a challenge for our purse. He would ask questions, I would talk, and he would listen. We tried different medications, but most just made me sleepy and mentally dull, which was bad because I needed a sharp creative edge for work. Still, pills helped me get by. The talk sessions went on and on. Determined to do anything that would help, we dug deeply into my youth, and he became convinced I was angry with my mother, and if I forgave whatever I felt she'd done wrong, I'd feel better. I was not convinced of this but did realize I harbored feelings that I'd disappointed her which made me feel guilty. Could that be an issue? And yet that was all in the past, and my mom and I got along fine. She was one of the most generous women I would ever know, always helping others, including us. I accepted there were things in my boyhood that made me angry but knew my parents were proud of me now, so I needed to get over the feelings that I had failed and disappointed them.

In February Dolly approached her ninth month of pregnancy. We entered the high-risk zone, as every pregnancy put Dolly and child in danger. As always, she was confident, telling me over and over, "Don't worry. This time it will be good. I know it will." I, on the other hand, was a portrait of raw nerves caused by fear for Dolly's well-being and for my own mental health and the problems that challenged me daily.

# 12.

"THE GREATEST THING A
MAN CAN DO FOR HIS CHILDREN,
*IS TO LOVE THEIR MOTHER.*"

Fr. Theodore Hesburgh/Notre Dame University

"YOU HAVE YOUR BOY!"

Dr. John Luce

On the 31ˢᵗ of March 1971, (Dolly chose the date,) she gave full term C-section birth to a perfect baby boy. We named him Tyler. His middle name was Henry after my dad. Dolly's prediction proved true, as Tyler was her only trouble-free pregnancy; at least, as trouble free as a C-section can be. She'd been pregnant five times, had two miscarriages, three C-sections, and two children, all quite an ordeal for a small girl five feet tall, weighing one hundred pounds, no matter how fearless and strong.

I realize today, I've had the privilege of knowing many highly capable women in my life. Dolly, of course, but also my mother and sisters Ann and Leona, and daughter Gabrielle all leap to mind. All overcame challenging obstacles in their lives, which gave me great respect for them. Women are far from being the weaker sex, and whoever thought that term up should be required to do one half of what most women do on a regular basis, just to learn what it means to be female in our culture.

Tyler's birth was the completion of a dream. We had a girl, and now our boy, at last. Doctor Luce used a rather theatrical method to inform me of the gender of our child. He called me down the hall where our baby was being washed in a shallow stainless-steel sink, and lifting him up a bit by his feet and pointing at his penis with a big smile on his face, he said those wonderful words: "You have your boy." With the ever-present Nikon, I took a few pictures. Doc knew two things; first, that a boy was what we wanted, and second, that Tyler was to be the last baby he would ever deliver for Dolly.

"My professional advice is this," he told us later, "you are done with babies. If you get pregnant again you could seriously endanger yourself. You've had three C-sections and all your pregnancies have been difficult and risky: it's enough. So please, for your own well-being, no more. Unfortunately, the nuns at this Catholic hospital have refused to allow me to tie your tubes, even though I've recommended it to protect your health. So, I'm sorry to advise that you must practice some form of birth control from now on. If you don't, you're putting yourself at greater risk then you have each time you were pregnant."

Ironically, the church calls any form of birth control a sin, so I couldn't see what enforcing this absurd rule of not doing what the doctor ordered had accomplished. Back in the car, I asked Dolly, "What do you want to do about what Doc said about birth control?" She laughed and replied. "We have the two children I've always dreamed of. I'm happy now and no man made, and arbitrary religious rule is going to tell me how I can or cannot love my husband. This body is mine and I decide what's good for it. End of discussion." Her response was one of the many reasons I adored her. Dolly knew her path, and it was always right.

Considering the rough roads Dolly traveled to have them, our children were priceless miracles to us. Gabrielle and Tyler were the survivors, the tough and determined ones. They demanded life and got it. A girl and a boy...our dream was now reality. How did Dolly feel about her little family? One night soon after she'd returned home from the hospital and we were cuddled in bed she said,

"It's all turning out perfectly, isn't it, and just how I dreamed it would be when I imagined my life with you. I have a beautiful man who loves me, two children, a girl, and a boy; we live in our honeymoon cottage on a hill in a forest near the lakeshore and share a good life. It couldn't get much better." She kissed me lovingly and looking into my eyes, said with confidence, "You will soon feel good again—I know you will. You're stronger than you imagine, and you'll beat this problem. Then it will all be perfect. That's what I believe, and I know I'm right. You'll see."

Time passed and still I struggled, but somewhat less as the months flew by. Metaphorically speaking, never once did Dolly let go of my hand. When I was down, I'd tried to train myself not to show it, but she always knew. I loved her even more during that time, for no matter how difficult I was to live on those occasions when I got sullen, moody, or feeling a failure, she remained my faithful healing angel, always reassuring me that all would be well. "You're getting better all the time," she'd say, "I can see it; can you?"

Time ticked on, the kids continued to grow as kids will, and we managed to live a reasonably normal family life. There were days I felt normal and days I was down, but I fought the down days and kept moving. I was great with the kids (Dolly's observation) and we did lots of family things together. Our children were a wonderful distraction for me. Their endless enthusiasm and cheerfulness were uplifting. I don't believe the kids were ever aware of what I was going through. I was just Dad, and they liked to spend time with me. I was happy when I was with them. They didn't challenge my fragile resources. Maybe it was that I didn't have to perform for them or worry about what they thought of me. They accepted me as I was. How can you not love two young faces that get excited for no reason other than you just walked through the door?

Across from our house and through the woods was a little one-lane rutted sand road. It ran alongside a creek called the Mill Stream. We spent lots of time on that rarely used path and in the adjacent woods. The kids loved a children's book entitled *The Dead Tree* that followed the life cycle of a tree.

Down the Mill Stream path was a real dead tree that had rotted out in the middle and fallen. A man could fit into the partially open twelve-foot-tall stump that remained standing. It was a special spot for us. We called it our "Laughing Place," a name borrowed from the Brer Rabbit tales. We also liked to imagine there were trolls hiding under the bridge that crossed the stream further down; trolls who might eat little kids for supper. Fortunately, in our game, children were *always* able to run faster than trolls and escape, scurrying home to safety, laughing all the while.

Our children grew up living a play life that was imaginative and fantastical; much like the adventures in the children's books we read at night. I was just a big kid with a creative imagination, so I could easily join into their playtime. Dolly also did creative things with Gabrielle and Tyler. We often went to the children's library in town, at that time housed in an old Victorian house next door to the adult library and had a magical feeling about it. Young readers would sit in corners, on the floor, or at small tables, slowly turning the pages of picture books while warm golden sunlight streamed through dusty, mullioned windows, illuminating shelves filled chock-a-block with kid's books and lighting the faces of beautiful children. The library had well-worn hardwood floors, smelled of old books and coffee and looked like *Diagon Alley* in the *Harry Potter* movies of today; lots of character and a sprinkle of magic.

Today, when life becomes challenging for my now-adult daughter Gabrielle, she often says, "I wish I could be six or eight again…it was all so wonderful then." She admits to loving her childhood. We did too. For me, spending time with our kids proved my personal happy place. It seems incredible to me now that I could enjoy the hours spent with them, yet still feel anxious and blue at other times. It was as if I had two personalities, a crazy Jekyll and Hyde existence.

I had reached a stage of recovery where I could handle social events well, but travel remained the biggest challenge. I still tried to avoid taking road trips with the family. When Dolly was planning a trip, I'd become sullen and a bit angry knowing she was aware that this was something I'd want to do but would avoid. If I couldn't travel free of anxiety, I didn't want her to go either. This only added to my self-loathing. But if Dolly wanted to take the kids to see Niagara Falls, she was going and taking her friend Emily and her son Lee with her. "I'm taking the kids to see the falls and you're welcome to come," she informed me. "Or you can just sit home and stare at your navel if that's what you want." A determined girl, my wife, and she pulled no punches. This was a Dolly version of tough love. I expected her to take pity on me, and when she wouldn't, I'd sulk like a little kid. So, she would go on her trip and I'd stay home, feeling sorry for myself.

In their absence, I would be constructive and get something done on the house. Work also served to distract me from the mental flagellation I would have otherwise inflicted on myself for not going with them. I always took pleasure in surprising Dolly with improvements. I was like the cat who brings home a mouse hoping for praise. Convinced Dolly would be pleased with me, I'd whistle while I worked. We played a little game in which I'd show her what I'd accomplished while she was gone and then remind her that I'd done the work but now it was time, "Someone must say wonderful," so of course she would, and we'd laugh together at our silly game.

Coldness could occasionally exist between us at times, and it was always my fault. I could even be verbally cruel to her, a woman I loved and respected, but when in a "mood," I saw her as part of the problem. She and the kids were such a financial responsibility. No matter how hard I worked, money remained in short supply and collecting what was owed to me was often a problem. There was the mortgage to pay, sometimes a car payment, and doctor bills. As a self-employed man, I had to save for retirement in an IRA, pay for ever more expensive health insurance for my family, and make 100 percent of my social security payment annually. I also had private school tuition to pay (it was the best school in our area so the right choice). I carried a large life insurance policy on myself and one on Dolly, and for some reason, everyone in our house liked to eat regularly. Creditors expected to be paid on time so I couldn't just stay in bed, even though that was what I often felt like doing. I had no choice but to get up, go out, and do my job, keeping the ship afloat and my slowly growing business alive. Sometimes I'd have to fly, which was another challenge.

Fortunately, I had a talent, was respected in my field, and enjoyed the work. The studio had a reputation in Northern Indiana as the go-to place for good photography, so the business was steadily improving. With a family that loved me and a tranquil place to live with them, I had every reason to be a happy guy and didn't understand why I wasn't. The list of things causing me worry included my share of overhead costs in the business partnership, so in the end I finally sold my interest in the studio and moved to a home office, removing one major item from my list of worries. I believe this change was the right move for me. I was a guy who liked to make his own decisions and to be in control of things that affected his life. I was not good partnership material as I liked to call the shots…right or wrong.

The sale of my half was a bit like selling a stock right before it goes up. Just as things were coming together, I chose to abandon the business I'd created. Some clients followed me, and some went with Walt. We didn't have to concern ourselves with that issue, as it just happened on its own. Walt did well, continuing to grow his business, and I was glad of it. I don't recall specifically, Dolly's reaction to this move. She usually trusted my decisions, but I don't remember how this one affected her. If I were in her position, I might have been thinking about packing my bags and going to live with a sister. She never did that. She stuck it out in the sure knowledge that the madness would end in time. For some reason she still believed in me and the choices I made for us.

I came across an old color slide recently and it reminded me of a day when I'd come home early to find the house empty. Then I remembered it was time for Dolly to meet Gabrielle at the school bus that dropped her off at our beach. Taking my camera, I walked to the bus stop, and standing at the top of the dune, saw Gabrielle running wild and barefoot in the water in her little plaid school uniform, hair flying in the wind like a young pony rejoicing in motion and freedom. Tyler was playing in the sand with shovel, pail and a little truck, and Dolly was standing quietly nearby, her thirty-three-year-old body still beautiful, youthful, and slender in her snug top and shorts, even after five pregnancies and two children. She was at peace with the world, her lovely face raised to the sun. I wondered what thoughts or dreams were occupying that tranquil mind of hers, or if she was simply embracing the beautiful day, living fully in the moment in this idyllic place with her children playing nearby. I often wished I could live in her brain for one day, just to see what it felt like to be sound of mind, confident and at peace with yourself. Without her love and steady hand, where would I be? What a lucky family we were to have this exceptional woman a key part of our lives.

It was such a peaceful scene, a perfect picture of life as we lived it, and for a moment my eyes grew damp. How could I not be joyful every waking moment of my day, knowing all I'd been blessed with? I captured a few images of the scene with the Nikon, then joined them. "Hi Dad," Gabrielle called out, "Isn't this a perfect day?" She was filled with spirit and energy.

"Hey Dad, want to dig with me?" Ty asked.

"How did the shoot go, my darling?" Dolly asked as I started working in the sand with my son. "It went well, and we finished early," I said. "And now, this part is the perfect ending to a good day." She gave my arm a gentle squeeze. No preaching, no 'I told you so,' just a gentle squeeze that spoke volumes. Is it any wonder that scene and day are burned into my memory forever? I'd been so fortunate in life. Now if only I could shake off the bad parts and embrace fully, the wonderful life and relationship we had.

We got our first dog, a German Shepherd/Labrador mix puppy from a friend of Dolly's. We named her Betsy, and as she grew, she became very protective of her new family, patrolling the perimeter of our property like a Marine. How she knew the boundaries of the land that belonged to us was a mystery, but it seemed she did. Wonderful with both kids, she felt it her job to watch over Tyler, who was still quite young. They were always together. We should have named that dog *Bodyguard*, for that's what she was.

At around that time, I started doing something that worried me a bit. I'm embarrassed to admit this because it sounds like the classic crutch and I'm afraid it was, but I developed the habit of enjoying a couple of cocktails at the end of the workday. In retrospect, I was almost certainly medicating myself. Never a "stop at the bar" kind of guy, my cocktail hour was always at home. I found that a drink or two relaxed me, and I enjoyed the feeling of dissipating tension. Over time I formed a dependence on that release and looked forward to it too much. The use of alcohol was an issue for some members of my family, and I reminded myself to be careful and remain in control.

I'm ashamed to say I wasn't completely successful at this, as over time the daily drink became two and then three. Usually, I downed the first one kind of fast. Once Dolly said quietly, "Well, you certainly inhaled that one." I got the message. Fortunately, drink did not make me angry, rather the opposite. I got relaxed and mellow. I never considered myself alcoholic as I never drank during the day, and I didn't hide bottles like some do. My drinking happened at home in the evening, or at social events. Still, that little voice of common sense kept reminding me, *Be careful. It could become a problem.*

I continued to fight my reluctance to travel and finally forced myself to take a road trip with the family. We drove to Louisville, Kentucky to visit Dolly's Aunt Lil and Uncle Bill, relatives we both really liked. I was determined to travel, even though it was a challenge. On the highway, my neck muscles would get so tense I could barely turn my head, which caused me vicious headaches. I continued to watch for those hospital signs. Still, I was not going to continue sending Dolly off to travel alone with the kids. My psychiatrist, Dr. B., had taught me the simple technique of wearing a wide rubber band around my wrist, and if I started feeling anxious, to keep snapping it hard against my skin. I don't know why, but this distraction seemed to work. I began to accept that things were improving for me, even if only a little at a time. Could it be that therapy was working? I lived in hope.

We built a studio onto the house by refinancing our mortgage. I needed a decent place to work. The cost would be a modest monthly increase to our mortgage, as we would spread it out over years. This time, I would own my space, rather than pay rent to someone else. As property values in our area were always going up, it seemed a good investment, and time would prove it to be just that.

About the time my new home studio was nearly complete, a man knocked on my door one day looking for a job in photography. He learned of me because the company his wife worked for was an occasional client. He was tall and imposing standing in my doorway. His name was Jeff Ackil. While chatting I learned he was of Lebanese decent, giving him a dramatic and handsome face in the way of an Arab character in the film *Lawrence of Arabia*. I took an instant liking to him but told him truthfully that I could not afford to pay a salary. "What I can do is give you a try," I told him, "if you're willing to be paid as a freelance assistant with a day rate, and only when I can add your fee to jobs as crew. Also, money is always tight around here, so I can only pay you when the client pays me and that can take a month, or sometimes even more. You'd be getting paid the same way I do when the client pays us. It's not the best, but all I can offer."

I was surprised when he agreed to these terms. Jeff's background was in motion pictures, a medium he loved, but the work was spotty He wanted to work in photography because they were related. He didn't want to be a photographer. He was happy to be crew, just as he was on films. He belonged to the union and would occasionally land a film shoot such as *Backdraft*, which was shot in Chicago. At those times I'd lose him for the duration. Then he'd come back to me.

Ours was a mutually beneficial relationship as he worked more for me than on motion pictures, so it filled out his income flow a bit. I benefited because he was a fantastic assistant. He learned fast, was reliable, highly organized, creative and detail oriented. It felt good to have someone to share the workload and to travel with. I was always grateful for his friendship, companionship, and his contributions to the success of the business. Best of all, we liked each other, became great friends, and always had fun working together. I loved him like family, as did Dolly and the kids. He became famous in my house the day a homemade Christmas ornament of Santa had lost an arm and Jeff, with his offbeat sense of humor, fashioned a new one with a *hook* instead of a hand, and of course the kids loved it. Without him knowing it, Jeff's presence also helped me with my anxiety issues. Having him with me was confidence building. I wasn't alone and it made a huge difference. We were a team and it felt good. I owe him so much.

Tyler entered private school in 1977. Once both kids were in school, Dolly was able to get involved in outside activities. She joined the school board at

Notre Dame School and volunteered to help with or spearhead various school activities. Later, she began to lecture in public grade schools about art and artists. It was rewarding and meaningful work for her. The kids called her *The Art Lady*. She was back in the art world she loved. It was unpaid work, but I was happy that she was happy. I was surprised that Dolly hadn't taken up painting, or some other art form that was hands-on. She'd always seemed headed in that direction. Instead, as a volunteer she was becoming more of a teacher about art and artists to kids when the schools stopped offering such classes in cutbacks. She felt children needed her because "all kids deserve some knowledge of the arts." I was proud of her determination to live her beliefs.

# 13.

"If there can be only one holiday, let it be Christmas."

Paul Marshall

Christmas on Sunset Trail. A favorite time of year at the house on the hill. We hosted many holidays, but this was our favorite. Our families and friends knew Paul and Dolly did not leave home at Christmas. The holiday was always celebrated in Michiana Shores, and all were invited. The house itself was a big part of why. It was, to us, the ideal setting. The cathedral ceiling allowed for oversized Christmas trees, logs in the fireplace added warmth and firelight. Candles and decorations contributed to a "Christmas Past" atmosphere. Every nook and cranny said traditional Christmas; there would be no flocked Christmas trees for us. Our décor for the season was never modern, always classical, and right out of Charles Dickens, the true father of the Christmas as we celebrate it today.

The holiday began with a search for the perfect tree, undertaken at a hundred-acre woodland owned by a friend whose property was dense with long-needle fir trees. On occasion, Dolly would join us in the search, but mostly this adventure was accomplished by our kids and their dad. We'd spend an hour walking through rows and rows of trees, looking for just the right one, always keeping in mind that we would have to drag the green giant to our vehicle. To say these trees were heavy would be understating the problem, as they were always so large, they'd have provide a workout for two grown men. Big, however, was the name of our game, so young voices would cry out, "No, not that one, Dad. It's not full enough. This one has a better shape. Oh wait, check this one out over here. If we just take the top part, it will be perfect!" And on it went. Our kids were expert Christmas tree junkies. Being a photographer, I would capture a record of the cutting down of the tree. The kids would take turns whacking away on the trunk with a hatchet until they grew tired, and the job would be completed with a good sharp tree saw.

We tried various methods for moving trees through the snow and out of the forest to our vehicle. It was always a challenge. One year we took a toboggan with us and hauled our saw and ax in on it. Then we attempted to use the sled to help drag the tree out to the car. The tree proved too big, however, and the toboggan too small. It was exhausting work for one dad and two young children, but we soldiered on every season, dragging these monsters out a few feet at a time.

A pretty baby blue Dodge convertible we owned for a while was put into service one year, to haul a tree home. We put the top down, draped blankets on the trunk to protect the paint work, and dragged the tree over the passenger area, the trunk finally jutting out over the windshield and hood with many feet of tree hanging out the back. We three sat in the front seat peering through branches for the drive home. Luck was with us and no police car pulled us over. It was an unusual sight that pulled into our driveway on Sunset Trail. "Mom!" the kids called as they crawled out of the car through the branches. "Come and see how we got the tree home."

Dolly came down to the drive, stifled a grin and shook her head. "You do realize that all three of you are crazy?" she said. We laughed because every year, without fail, the long-suffering house elf that lived in the cottage on the hill would say the same thing; "It won't fit through the door!" We'd have been disappointed if she didn't say it, for it was tradition and part of the fun. And every year, the kids would cry out, "Wanna bet?" And then we'd drag our outrageously large Christmas tree up the hill and prepare to squeeze it through the thirty-two-inch sliding door opening. At the door, Dolly would continue: "You've gone completely mad this time? You can't possibly get that tree inside this house." Not only were these trees tall (thirteen to fifteen feet) but extremely full, with thick branches that did not bend easily. These were wild grown unpruned trees, not skinny little "tree lot" examples, and would take up a large piece of living room real estate.

Dolly was always close to right in her assessment, but we never once failed to get one inside.

We'd heave and shove the trees through the doorway, and sometimes we'd tie the branches in with rope to make the tree thinner. Once in the kitchen, we had to make a left turn through another opening to get into the living room. This would cause the top of the tree to sweep right through the cooking area of the kitchen, and Dolly would express her annual (softened) outrage about the mess and damage to woodwork that would have to be repaired later. Realizing we needed some sort of plan to keep the peace, one year, my faithful conspirators, Gabrielle and Tyler, came up with an idea: "Dad. We have it figured out" they offered in unison.

"Let's just make sure Mom is out of the house shopping when we bring the tree in," Tyler said. "Then we can clean up the mess before she comes home," chimed in Gabrielle.

"Brilliant, kids," I said, and that is what we did. We'd wait for her to go out, and then get the tree inside standing upright, with holes drilled into the tree trunk to add additional branches if we had sparse spots. This was a trick I had learned from my dad and passed along to our kids. Then we Hoovered like mad to clean up needles and sawdust. When Dolly got home, she would find us stringing lights and putting on ornaments to the sound of Johnny Mathis singing Christmas carols. She'd only witness the house-friendly part of the job. Still, nothing escaped her keen eye. She'd put her hands on her hips, look around, tilt her head, make a scrunched-up cute angry face at us and announce, "You three are not fooling anybody, you know. I get your game."

We'd look as innocent as possible and say, "What game, Mommy?" She was so adorable and patient with us. I knew that once the trees were decorated, she secretly loved them as much as we did and took pleasure when people would walk into her living room, suck in a deep breath and say, "Oh my lord, Dolly. Your tree is huge! It's even bigger than last year, isn't it?"

Eventually, I installed a pair of beautiful mullioned French doors in the living room that led onto the outside deck. They replaced two windows, creating a six-foot opening with no center obstruction. The doors looked fabulous, gave more ventilation in summer, added additional classic looks to the room, and made bringing in our big trees a simple task at last, much to Dolly's relief.

Most Christmases at Sunset Trail were about the same production wise, but I think it was Christmas, 1978 that stands out in memory for a special reason. We had everything in perfect order for our annual Christmas Eve open house. These parties were well attended by our friends, neighbors, and some family which included Senn and our Aunt Leona, who was almost always there as she lived nearby. Many people showed up every year, some for a quick visit before rushing back home, others off to other celebrations, but then there were those who seemed like they'd never go home. I think our event was a social must-do on many a calendar for years.

Days, even weeks of preparation went into this night and Christmas Day. These included the stacking of firewood just outside the door on the deck, decorations on the house, and all white Italian lights hung in many of the trees on our property with the help of my most enthusiastic assistants, Gabrielle and Tyler, aka, the Christmas Kids. Our hill was a beautiful sight, looking like a fairyland on a snowy night as you came down our lane in the dark, and especially if there were flakes falling of the large fluffy kind. Live wreaths purchased from the Boy Scouts were on the doors and over the fireplace, and the house was fragrant with the smell of fresh tree and the burning pine logs saved from last year's tree trunk.

Wonderful smells from the kitchen had been filling the house for days, as cooking and hors d'oeuvre preparation seemed never-ending. Dolly was an excellent cook who worked magic in the kitchen, and best of all, loved doing it. Many batches of cookies were baked, with the overly enthusiastic help of the kids. Inevitably, white flour decorated them, the kitchen, and the cats and dog. A traditional wassail bowl created from a recipe found in a Charles Dickens

Christmas book added to the preparation. The cocktail bar was set up, wine chilled, and glassware and silver polished. Then there was cleaning and more cleaning, right up to the last minute when it all had to stop because it was time to get dressed. During all this preparation, music played on and on. We owned enough tapes and records to play carols for days without repeating. We even had jazz versions of Christmas songs, which I loved. For some musical reason, many Christmas songs lend themselves to jazz arrangements.

When the kids were young, they loved to play with the little manger under the tree, endlessly resetting the arrangement of animals, Joseph, Mary, baby Jesus, and of course, angels, kings, and shepherds. It was, according to the kids, never quite perfect, and needed their constant attention.

In a picture of Dolly taken that special year, she's dressed festively and most elegantly, wearing a floor-length red wool skirt with brass buttons down the front and a white blouse with a large bow at the neck. The final touch was a red and black Scottish plaid vest, making her the perfect Celtic Christmas hostess. After I took a photo of her, the kids and I left to get dressed while Dolly stood admiring the tree. Suddenly, I heard her shout,

"Paul! Help! The tree—" It had fallen, and the very top part had landed on her. Although she'd tried to back away, she hadn't escaped a few upper branches as it came down. We found her partly buried under a jumble of greenery and tinsel, with ornaments everywhere, and inevitably, she had tangled with the treetop angel. The kids and I started laughing. I wanted to say, "Wait, let's get a picture," but I thought better of it, realizing it might not go over well. Laughing and a picture, I thought, would be the wrong thing to do. "Get me out of here, you maniac!" Dolly shouted. "You and your giant trees!" It was not, I might add, said sweetly with love and humor. We got her up, and thankfully, when she saw how hard we were trying to control our giggles, she finally saw the humor of the situation, and joined us in laughing. I fetched some wire and screw eyes from my workshop, and with everyone helping, we got the tree standing again, and safely wired to the walls behind it. Decorations were scattered everywhere. We began to "fluff" everything up again just as the first guests began to arrive. The story of the falling tree was laughingly repeated over and over that evening, much to Dolly's chagrin.

Early guests pitched in to finish the final repairs to the tree. It's a pity I don't have a picture of that farce. It was right out of P.G. Wodehouse. Even though we had a massive iron tree stand made by my dad, we safety wired all tree to the walls after that experience.

We allowed the kids a few hours at the party, then tucked them snuggly in their beds where they had visions of toys and goodies dancing in their heads. But for their parents, it was a long night ahead. One o'clock in the morning would find us cleaning up the party mess in preparation for Christmas day, and then putting out presents for kids from Santa, which often required us to assemble some new toy. Gabrielle and Tyler each were assigned their own wingback chair beside the fireplace on which we would arrange their gifts from Santa, unwrapped presents spilling out onto the floor, especially if Santa had had a good year. Dolly saved all year in a Christmas Club account for these celebrations. Stockings hanging on the fireplace were stuffed with more goodies. Our gifts to each other were already wrapped and placed under the tree, not to be opened until Christmas morning, a practice that evolved because wrapped presents under the tree looked so picture perfect at the Christmas Eve open house.

We kept the birth of Jesus tradition much alive as part of our Christmas celebrations. But when the children were small, we also kept the Santa tradition. One year the kids finally revealed to us that they had long before figured out that there was no Santa, just Mom and Dad. They confessed they knew our hiding places and had inspected some of their presents beforehand. They hadn't told us previously because they just didn't want to spoil our fun, as we seemed to enjoy the illusion so much! *Wait a minute—who's in charge here?* I wondered.

I was sad that we could stop pretending. It was so much more fun when they were little and believed in magic. Children should have a little magic in their lives...grown-ups too. To me, Christmas on Sunset Trail was a season and holiday of family, friends, sharing, gift giving, and most of all, love...especially love. And isn't that what the man Jesus taught? "Love one another." Christmas is to celebrate his birth and his joyful message of love.

Dolly and I would finally get to bed at some obscene hour. We'd share an innocent little goodnight kiss which would become more serious until finally, she'd say, "Should we, or shouldn't we?" Usually, it was, "We should." One year, with her last bit of energy Dolly whispered, "All right then, Santa Boy, lets recharge our batteries." She was always the best Christmas present of all, We still slept in our antique standard double bed (no queen or king for us) and eventually, we would arrange our limbs and bodies in the tangled-up way we slept together and allow exhaustion to carry us off for a few hours of dreaming about wrapping paper, ornaments, and discovered hiding places.

When one hasn't had adequate rest, it's painful to be awakened at six a.m., by the laughter and squealing of children playing with new toys on Christmas day. I can see and hear those mornings of childhood joy to this day. Our bedroom was still mostly open to the living room below so had no door to stop the happy sounds. We'd shake ourselves awake, put on warm robes and slippers, and with a fire blazing in the hearth, and cups of strong English tea or black coffee in hand, watch the delight of children in that euphoric state that only Santa's visit can bring. There is nothing like it. "Mom…look at this!" "Dad, can you figure out how to make this work?"

Then came breakfast and off to church. Afterward preparation efforts would begin again as we got ready to host Christmas Day for as many of the family as were able to join us. Great effort went into these celebrations, but it was always worth it. I was never happier than during the Christmas season. Troubles? Anxiety? During the holidays, they just seemed to melt away like snow in spring.

# 14.

"Love one another."

Jesus of Nazareth

"Being deeply loved gives you strength,
loving deeply gives you courage."

Lao Tzu

Salvation is possible and a soul can be delivered from confusion and despair with love and the gentle caring of a patient, understanding and compassionate wife and the unconditional love of one's children and family. A good psychiatrist or skilled therapist doesn't hurt either. I know from experience; these things are true.

Dolly had suffered my illness with me. She had to cope with my fears, depression, and the panic attacks she didn't understand. They seemed to have no source that she could deal with. How does one defeat an invisible enemy? She feared that in my despondency I might give up and choose a permanent way to end the pain. The word for that outcome was never mentioned by either of us, but I knew the specter of it lived in her heart. Even in the blackest times I never once considered ending my life as an option. I was bad, but never that bad. Fortunately for me, Dolly was a sound person with an abundance of life skills. And yet, even as she was being tested by my illness, her patience with me remained nothing short of heroic. Did

I cause her pain and worry? Of course, but she never faltered when seeing me through those dark years. She had taken the promise, "in sickness and in health" seriously.

I was improving…slowly, but I was improving. I was not quite there yet when Dolly discovered a program designed to help couples communicate more openly with each other while guiding their relationships back to a loving place. It was called "Marriage Encounter." We decided to sign up for their weekend program. Dolly made me promise to give it my total commitment, as would she. During our time there we were encouraged to be open, honest, and loving with each other. This we did, through the letters we were directed to share with each other on a specific theme after each presentation given by trained presenters. I have the letters Dolly wrote to me which she saved .Only a few of mine survived the years. Here are a few excerpts.

**Dolly to P.** "I like everything about you. I like how generous you are to all of us; how kind and thoughtful, always remembering our anniversary with beautiful personal letters to me instead of store cards. How you remember I love pussy willows and find them in the woods and bring them to me each spring. How much you love your children, what a good father you are, and the fact that you make time to be with them. I love that you think seriously about things. You've always wanted to understand, seeking answers to hard questions. I feel happy that I'm married to you, that it's you that's the father of my children. It makes me warm inside to know I have you in this life. I would never, ever leave you,"

**Dolly to P.** "When I look at you, I feel such love. That time you came back from two weeks of shooting in Florida and when I arrived home to our apartment in the city, I found you lying nude on our bed taking a nap. I remember how beautiful you looked just lying there, tanned, and lean. I thought, look at this incredible handsome man, and he's all mine. I remember feeling beautiful myself and thinking how lucky we were to be us. You woke while I was sitting on the bed looking at you, and suddenly, I was in your arms. I felt so loved and warm. You welcomed me readily as I did you."

**Dolly to P.** "I felt very close to you when our baby died. Not right away, but later, when I got depressed. I began to think, who cares about vacations, clothes, houses, or anything at all when the real things that count in life can die. Sitting next to me on the bed where I'd been hiding from life, you put your arms around me, and holding me close, told me things would be okay in time…not to let the bad feelings take over, that life will still be worthwhile, and reminding me that we were truly blessed with a beautiful daughter sleeping downstairs. You said things that helped me. You were kind, considerate, cared how I felt and shared my pain. Because you cared, I could live again. You gave me reasons to go on when I was sad and didn't want to. I was so hurt and angry to lose our baby, but you loved all the cares and sad feelings away. I needed you and you were there. When it matters most, you are always there for me.

You helped me when Joy died, sharing my sadness. When she was dying, you were with me every step, comforting me. After she was gone, you gently forced me to move on, to play, to live and to see that life was still worthwhile. I felt so close to you during those times. I needed your love, and you were there to give it. Thank you for those days of reassurance."

**Dolly to P.** "Perhaps your real problem is you can't see how good you are. There has always been that trait in you. You seem to feel you've failed at everything. If only you could see what a good man, you are. It makes me sad and lonely, as if you're in a glass cage and your falling. I can see you, but can't help you because you won't open the door and let me in. I'm so afraid."

**Dolly to P.** "I feel I have a vocation in life to be married to you, and to show to others that marriage does work, and we are happy. We've experienced some difficult times ourselves and have witnessed so many divorces in our families, in our friends and neighbors. How can so many marriages fail? That option was never mentioned by us. It's not who we are. We're too much a part of one another, always one heart, always lovers."

Dolly's letters opened my eyes. I saw that she loved me without judgment and had more faith in me than I had in myself. She'd put down on paper that she would never leave me; not ever. This knowledge filled me with fresh confidence and helped my recovery take a giant leap forward.

Here's a portion of a letter I wrote to Dolly, one she saved:

**Paul to D.** "I always have hope. Hope that the future will be good. I want to find joy in life again, with you. When we were a young married couple and I was making $65.00 a week, how incredibly happy we were. We had each other and the belief that life for us really was going to be Happy Ever After. Love was all we needed then, and faith in each other. More and more I'm convinced love is everything in this life. We are still together because of love. It has kept us in its embrace for 18 years, nearly 13 of them married, during good times and the difficult ones. I believe love is the greatest gift of all, and without it, something wonderful would be missing in life. Without love, the heart becomes a lonely place."

Letter writing seemed such a simple technique, and yet it proved to be an excellent exercise. It opened a door I had closed to Dolly when we were still teens; the door that hid my doubts and fears. I had always been afraid of losing Dolly if ever she saw through me. Thanks to Marriage Encounter, she convinced me she would love me without judgment, *no matter my fears and insecurities*. She told me she wanted to share my problems so we could deal with them together. This was an awakening and a relief.

I came away from that weekend determined, more than ever, to change; to open the door and share my problems and fears with her. I began to see recovery as possible. Marriage Encounter and Dolly had convinced me that I was going to be okay and helped me walk a step further on the path home.

Of all the things Dolly wrote to me during Marriage Encounter, the following words are the ones I treasure most, because they say so much about the women she was:

*"I feel I have a vocation in life to be married to you."*

I've often described Dolly as an intelligent woman, and she was, but her greatest gift was that she understood life, love, and emotions. Her gifts were not magical nor the product of higher education. They were somehow in her makeup. Perhaps it was simply what we used to call common sense. She possessed a heightened ability to listen and observe and could often see the mistakes others were making that hurt them. Insight and compassion were additional skills. Nonjudgmental and kind, others recognized her wisdom and came to her for advice. Sadly, one person didn't always take advantage of her abilities... me. I didn't believe her when she told me, "You're a better man than you think you are." Dolly had recognized when we were teens that I had trouble believing in myself. Even as I experienced career success, I still doubted. I became expert at trying to hide problems so even she couldn't find them ...until now.

It took a long time before she got me back on track again. I was a hard case, but in the end she succeeded. It's hard to ignore someone who refuses to give up on you. She often said, "You will beat this problem and be happy again." She was slowly able to convince me that I was, in fact, a good person who deserved happiness.

I recall the day she firmly told me, "You're honest, fair, a good husband, father, friend, neighbor, and a gifted photographer." And then she smiled and added, "Did I mention you're also handsome and a great lover?" It became impossible to doubt that sweet, honest face.

I owe getting my life back to Dolly and her resolute faith in me, and to the good work of my psychiatrist, Dr. M. Berkson. He treated my symptoms with medication, helping me to manage anxiety, and allowing me to cope with my work life. Then together we had slowly peeled away issues I had been harboring. I learned from Dr. B., that the more I buried fears, anger, and internal conflicts, the stronger they became. When I pushed them deep, I was planting them in an environment where they flourished. The more I dragged them into the light, exposing and facing them honestly with Dolly and with myself, the weaker they became. Between Dolly, Dr. B., and the gift of Marriage Encounter, there was a rainbow coming through my window, and I was seeing the light again.

The deepest and most challenging part of my illness lasted around five years. Full recovery required more time, but normal function improved daily, life getting better all the time.

Winter of '78 flexed her muscles by dumping four or five feet of lake-effect snow in Michiana Shores and the surrounding region. We were again reminded of the challenges of country living.

"Doll, I'm going out to shovel the driveway," I told her one morning.

"Okay, but don't do too much. That's a huge amount of snow out there. Take it slow." It took several sessions and many aching muscles before accomplishing the snow removal, leaving walls of the white stuff on either side of the drive that were taller than the kids and, in some areas, higher than their dad.

We were snowed in for days without electrical power. We had no lights and the furnace blower required electricity, so could not send heat into the house. Oil lanterns, candles, and flashlights supplied light, while two fireplaces, sweaters, and blankets kept us warm. We were also able to cook as gas continued to flow to the stove, keeping the kitchen warm. "Are you kids concerned that we're isolated?" I asked them.

"Not a chance, Dad. And best of all, no school," Tyler replied. Gabrielle nodded, adding, "This is plain old fun." Ah, to be a kid again. We shoveled by day, even the roofs, to get the weight off them and avoid ice buildup, which would create leaks. Firewood was stacked on the side deck for easy access. At night, wrapped in blankets, we'd play Clue in front of the fireplace, and then hasten to bed to save candles and lamp oil. Because heat rises, the fireplace kept our loft bedroom somewhat cozy. Blizzards aren't all that bad, not if you have a warm, soft playmate. There are many creative ways to keep warm in a storm, so thank you snow, I owe you.

Once things got back to normal winter, we had fun cross-country skiing. Each of us had skis, as one of my clients was an importer from the Netherlands, and after I'd photographed the skis for their catalog and advertising, they said, "Just keep them." We would also ice skate on nearby Lake Claire or build snowmen and women in our yard. The snowwomen were given breasts, which caused lots of giggles. "Well, why shouldn't our snow ladies have them? It's nothing to laugh about," I told the kids. "All females do, even you will, Gabrielle, one of these days."

"DAAAAD!" she cried, "You're embarrassing me."

Lake Michigan freezes over most winters, forming ice sculptures and snow hills shaped by nature. These are natural protection for the beaches from spring storms…until they melt. In the heart of winter, we often went for walks down to the beach at sunset. The warm backlight of the late winter sun painted beautiful splashes of color over and through ice forms made by freezing waves. I still have visions of Dolly, the kids, and our dog Betsy, sliding down the hills like bundled-up snow people. The world looked like a fairyland. I have a creative imagination, one that wouldn't have been surprised to find a little emerald green door leading into a house of ice. Inside, fairies lived and would be happy to share a lovely fire that magically warmed without melting their icehouse made of frozen water.

We were fortunate to reside in this wonderland. I was grateful to my grandmother for being the one to find this little kingdom on the lake, to my mom and dad for building a cottage there and selling it to us, and my great aunts and grandmother for helping us to buy more land. When I thought of these blessings, I wondered how I could ever have been unhappy with my lot. Perhaps it takes reaching an emotional low to ferret out the cause and find a solution. I now saw value in my life and knew I was worthy of happiness. Getting a second chance was a great gift.

In the final days of winter, the crocuses popped their brave heads through the last of the snow on our hill. This was the first sign of approaching spring and a reminder our special place was coming back to life. Soon it would be Easter, and there would be new dresses, Easter bonnets, visits from family and friends, and a release from the burdens of cold and snow. My happy family took walks to the beach to see how the shore had survived the winter now that the ice hills were melting, and to check on how our boat, which was tied down in dune grass, had weathered the winter storms. Our dog was free to run once more without sinking in deep snow, and the cat was restlessly slinking around the house, looking for a safe hiding place, as she was expecting kittens. The kids were out making discoveries and creating games in the woods and at the creek. In other words, everything in our earthly world was exactly as it should be… idyllic. For me, after living through such a long, dark period, life seemed to glow even more brightly than before.

Spring and summer arrived on time. Tyler took up the violin, so we had lessons to attend and practice time to organize. Dolly and I celebrated our fourteenth anniversary with a party at Senn's in Chicago. The kids and I planted an evergreen tree for Dolly on Mother's Day, and we spent lots of summertime sailing. My sister Leona got married at our house on Sunset Trail that year, the ceremony itself taking place on the banks of the Mill Stream across our road. It was a lovely affair and day, adding to a busy season.

In a blink, autumn was again upon us and with so many trees gracing our property, dealing with falling leaves was an ongoing task. The kids loved raking because it led to jumping in the leaf piles, something they never tired of. At dusk we'd burn leaves (it's what we used to do pre-global warming), enjoying that annual autumn smell and hating to go inside while there were still embers glowing in the encroaching dark. Dolly would join us with warm apple cider, a treat the result of our annual trip to orchard country, where we searched for all things apple.

We'd discovered a favorite farm and returned there every year. They had a wonderful pumpkin patch and farm stand, and we'd arrive back home with apples, jugs of fresh apple cider made on site, dried corn stalks, and, after much deliberation, the perfect pumpkins to create jack 'o' lanterns. Always an eagerly anticipated family outing, we'd revel in nature's watercolor of autumnal shades and tones, the haze from burning leaves conjuring the feel of Native American campfires in the misty failing light. That's how autumn was in orchard country; simply perfect. There was a crispness in the air now, a sign that soon snow would be filling our woods. But first, it was jack 'o' lantern time.

The carving of pumpkins was an event that the kids of the house looked forward to, and that included me. We did the carving at the newspaper-covered kitchen table after supper. Because knives were involved, I supervised and once the messy part and the carving was over, we'd place real candles inside, never electric lights. Ancient tradition must be followed.

Our most successful efforts went on our fireplace mantle and into the two windows that faced the front of the house, although, as we lived on a dead-end street, not many people got to see them, but we did! On Halloween night we'd have jack 'o' lanterns on the stairs that climbed to the top of our hill. Occasionally some brave kids came down our unlighted lane trick or treating, but not often. A house in a spooky wood was probably too frightening for little kids and too far to go to beg at just one house. This had an upside because it gave us time to trick or treat ourselves, usually in costumes we'd created ourselves. In our small village, most everyone knew the Marshall children, so they found themselves welcome everywhere.

After Halloween, we'd place the jack 'o' lanterns in favorite spots on our property; on top of the wood pile, leaning against the base of an oak tree, or sitting on a stump in the woods. We loved to watch the carved faces sag with cold and frost, taking on all kinds of wonderful scary looks. I'd photograph our sagging jack 'o' lanterns every year—traditions, always traditions. Gabrielle, a lover of holidays, has kept them alive as an adult, passing on our traditional ways to her kids. We may not have realized it at the time, but the activities we shared with our kids were seeds being planted in their memories.

One brisk fall night, shoulders wrapped in a warm blanket, I sat out on our deck staring into the dark forest. Dolly was inside reading, and I found myself in a philosophical mood, pondering my life as it was now evolving. Poet Robert Frost said: "In three words I can sum up all I've learned about life: *It goes on.*" He was right; life just goes on. I had foolishly spent years in fear I might lose my beloved if she discovered the part of me, I'd been hiding. I was so wrong, not trusting in her total devotion, and I'd suffered for it. In the film *Zorba the Greek*, he states: "A man needs a little madness; otherwise he will always be afraid to cut the rope and be free." I'd suffered a little madness, and now the time had come to cut the rope of fear and doubt and at last be free.

The next morning on awakening, I gazed quietly at the lovely girl with sleep tousled blond hair still dreaming next to me and asked myself how I ever got so lucky. This exceptional, and loving woman is my wife and a part of me. She chose me over all others knowing she could have had anyone she fancied and yet it was me she singled out. The *why* will remain a mystery to me. She has proven to be everything I ever wanted, and more than I had any right to ask for. I shook my head in wonder and asked the other question I'd pondered so many times before; what did I ever do to deserve her? I suppose I'll never know the answer, but I rejoice in the knowledge that, for reasons of her own, she plucked me from the tree and never regretted her choice. I was a fortunate man.

Blessed in life with a talent that supported my family, sometimes in the early years with difficulty I admit, but I also had a wife I loved who loved me just as I was which was a great gift. We had two beautiful, happy children and lived in a place that often felt enchanted. I was finally able to believe in myself; to believe that I was worthy of happiness, that I was, in fact, a good father, husband, and a good man. I thought back to the time in the Air Force when I had escaped death by chance. I questioned then if I would be worthy of the gift of longer life I'd received. Now I knew I was. I'd just do my best as life moved along and that was all I could ask of myself. In that moment of clarity, I knew I was on the road to recovery. The fears that had caused me so much doubt and anxiety were being swept away in the light of truth, love, and sharing. I'd been lost but I'd found my true course again, and I was going to be okay. It was a great feeling.

Out over the lake, the sun had moved deep into the southern sky. Days grew short as we waited for the first snows to blanket our little world. The calendar, once again in December, had marked yet another year in our charmed life in the house on the hill on Sunset Trail. As Old Blue Eyes once crooned, "It was a very good year."

# 15.

"My bounty is as boundless as the seas,
my soul as deep; the more I give to thee,
the more I have, for both are infinite."

William Shakespeare

The dark clouds that once filled my mind had finally scattered, so in 1980 we traveled to the US Virgin Islands with our friend Bryan Dunigan, our first major trip since my problems had appeared. I'd been required to fly for business during the dark days, but I'd had to "dope up" on tranquilizers to get through the flights. On this trip, however, I flew without issue. All right, I'll be honest… If you looked closely, you'd have noticed this grown man was holding his wife's hand during takeoff. Still, I'd already come a long way from phobia and leaving my sweating fingerprints pressed firmly into airplane armrests.

Betsy, our much loved and faithful dog, had to be sent to pet heaven as old age had caught up with her. Soon, Dolly took a trip with the kids to Wisconsin to the place where Betsy had come from. They picked out another Labrador-German Shepherd mix, just like Betsy. We named her Rosy, and she grew quickly into a huge dog so was not allowed on the main floor during parties; at over ninety pounds she was just too big. One year at Christmastime

I entered the living room to find Rosy, lying sheepishly by the fire with a guilty look on her face. "Who let that dog up here?" Then, I wrongly accused my son, saying, "Tyler, I know it was it you."

"No Dad, honest," he said. "She sneaked up on her own."

Rosy must have silently crept in on her belly like a Marine stealth dog. We'd seen her do it before. The kids begged that she stay. "It's Christmas, Dad! Come on, please?" Rosy remained until the kids went to bed.

Life continued to unfold for us in many ways. Gabrielle joined the local YMCA swim team at age eleven. She loved swimming and learned racing stroke technique quickly. "I belong here," she informed us. "This will be my other home." We began to think she was part fish, as water proved her element.

In 1981 Notre Dame University was playing Georgia in the Sugar Bowl and alum Bryan Dunigan was going down to New Orleans to see the game. So were many of his ND classmates, people we had come to know, so we decided to join them. It was a great short vacation and a homecoming for us, as we'd spent such a memorable long weekend in the Big Easy before we married. Unfortunately, we could not get a room in our special hotel as it was already booked solid.

In addition to the game, the trip proved to be a weekend-long party. "Paul let's do something just for us today," Dolly said. We spent time, just the two of us, doing things we liked such as a coffee at Cafe Du Monde on Decatur Street, enjoying their famous beignets, and then wandering the French Quarter taking pictures. The old section of New Orleans, with its iron balconies and faded pastel colors, was so appealing that I said to Dolly, "I'd love to live here, wouldn't you?"

She looked at me with that knowing smile and said, "Here we go again. You're a hopeless romantic, and I love you for it, but you always say you want to live every nice place we go." She was right…I do always say that.

ND did not win the game, a crushing blow for our friend Bryan, who has only missed one ND home game in South Bend since 1963. I told him I was sorry about the score but even the Irish can't win them all.

More years passed, dates on a calendar racing by. I was fully recovered but could still recall just how bad it had been for a time. I suppose it's a bit like giving birth…it's painful when it's happening but the pain is set aside with the joy of the baby. You remember it hurt but it doesn't stop you wanting another child. I was trying to forget those hard times and focus forward. Our family was now enjoying life to the fullest. Gabrielle graduated from Catholic grade school and entered public high school. She was immediately accepted on the swim team and began a stellar swim career. Our little premature baby was MVP three of four years during her high school career and team captain as a senior. The smell of chlorine was like Chanel No. 5 to her. I try to forget the times we got up at four a.m. to drive through winter storms to watch her compete in two or three events that lasted only seconds. And yet, in truth, we loved it and were proud of her. Those swim years were a good time in our lives. To this day, Gabrielle can step into a hotel lobby, sniff the air, and announce, "POOL."

Ty was deeply involved in scouting with Boy Scout Troop 2, in Long Beach, Indiana. This was not your average scout troop. They called themselves *The All-Weather Troop,* and they were, tenting summer and winter. Ty took to scouting very seriously, learning skills to be used in the wilderness pursuits that became a lifelong passion for him.

In 1983 Dolly and I made the decision to open a studio in Chicago. My newfound confidence had given me a desire to get back into what I perceived as the "big time." Dolly was in favor because it meant more of what she called "concrete time." In less cryptic language, she meant getting her "city fix," and being able to spend more time with her friend Senn and her family. We would still service our Indiana clients and hopefully find new ones in the city. We rented a studio in a very arty rehabbed loft building at 117 North Jefferson in the Hay Market District. Our studio was a small but hip loft, with high ceilings, sandblasted brick walls, sanded and varnished wood floors, and track lighting. It served our needs while we tested the water in the big pond. Business was good and money no longer the issue it once was.

Dolly became my sales rep in Chicago, calling on potential clients with my portfolio. She'd bring in jobs such as point of purchase displays for beer and liquor accounts, photographic illustration for use on billboards, couples ecstatically happy using their new coffee maker, anything with people. In total we spent nine years in Chicago, eventually moving to a larger space across the street from the Merchandise Mart. I built in simple living accommodation; a mini kitchen, bath with shower and a bedroom so Dolly and I could spend a night or two in the city every week, attending Lyric Opera productions or frequenting jazz clubs. We felt the kids were old enough to fend for themselves and we hoped they'd be trustworthy, although I'm quite certain parties sometimes took place on those nights we stayed in Chicago.

For us it was a happy time. We were having fun in the city, pushing the business to new successes. Most of all, we were still wildly in love, having a ball, (as we used to say) and enjoying our marriage to the fullest. Life was good.

In the spring of 1986, Gabrielle graduated from high school and in the fall entered the School of the Art Institute of Chicago. After one semester she decided to transfer to Indiana State University as that school had a foundry for sculpture, which was her interest at the time. Later, her sculpture professor at ISU told me she was the hardest-working woman he'd ever taught. He also said she was fearless in the foundry. Fearless? No surprise there, she sounds like her mother.

As driving and travel were no longer a problem (I'd now developed a passion for travel), I took several exciting camping trips with Tyler's scout troop and began to think of myself as an expert tent camper. So, when Dolly and I were scheduled to make a trip to Florida on photo assignment for a travel agency, we decided not to fly, but to drive down and camp in the Smoky Mountains on the way. It would be her first tent camping experience. The weather was perfect, pleasantly cool with falling leaves in a full autumnal spectacle of color. My goal was to have her enjoy camping. I told her I'd do everything and all she had to do was have fun. I made the campfire, set up our tent, did the cooking and cleaning up after our meal, making her comfortable and happy in every way. I also discovered something new about camping. It revealed itself after dark had settled in the woods. "OK, Davy Crockett," Dolly said. "Let's see what kind of mischief we can get up to in this tent of yours, shall we?" I guarantee things like this never happened on boy scout trips.

Dolly took to this lifestyle with enthusiasm, so we continued to camp extensively in our travels in America, not to avoid the expense of motels, but rather to be outdoors in spectacular natural settings. Dolly loved wild places and I... well, I loved my wild Dolly in wild places. Happily, some things never changed.

In 1989 our twenty-fifth wedding anniversary was approaching. I asked Dolly what she would like to do to celebrate. She said, "Oh, let's not plan anything. Surely someone will throw us a party." Sadly, no one did. Men accept these things, but to a woman, they're important. I felt her disappointment; she deserved much more. All those years she spent putting up with me, supporting me when I was a problem. Her faithful belief in me and her unbending trust that I would recover, this level of support deserved recognition. I'd have to find a way to show her how important her faith in me was. It would take almost five more years before the perfect way to show her my appreciation would reveal itself.

My father died in 1991. He had just turned seventy-six, had some dementia and was diabetic, but his ultimate decline was caused by falling and breaking his hip. During his hospital stay I thought about my parent's marriage. I knew they had known ups and downs, and yet they remained together for fifty-four years, raising a family of four children and in the process, showed us so many good examples of how to behave and be good people in life. We learned a work ethic from both, again by example. It was a long marriage and my mother never left his side when dementia took over some of his behaviors. I suddenly realized just how much I had learned about how to live from these solid people. I was my parent's child, as were my siblings. I doubt any parents are perfect, but ours had directed us on a straight path, and always by example.

Serious medical complications ensued for my dad that I won't detail here. When it became clear we were only keeping him alive with artificial life support, we had it stopped. It was what Dad wanted. I know because he told me so on the morning of June fifth. Jeff and I were on our way to Chicago for a photo shoot. It was not visiting hours at the hospital, but the nurses let me come up to see my dad. I had the opportunity to tell him that I loved him and what a great dad he had been to all of us, thanking him for the life he'd given us. As I prepared to leave, he grabbed my wrist and pulling me close said, "No machines Paul, no machines."

"It's okay Dad, we've already told them." He sighed, satisfied. They were the last words we would ever share. He died that afternoon. My mom and sister Leona were with him. That night I cried alone, as Dolly was out of town. I grieved for him of course, but I now know grief has many pain levels. Saying farewell to my dad was hard but not crippling. It surprised me, but I was able to cope with the loss and get on with life.

After about nine years Dolly and I decided to close the Chicago studio. At the time the business climate was changing, and we were making the larger part of our income doing location work, so we decided to shed the overhead of the studio and rent shooting space on an as-need basis. By this time, my old home studio had been converted to beautiful living space but as I had a heated, drywalled garage, I was able to use it on occasion for small tabletop product shots.

One of my last city assignments provided a great send-off. I'd received a call from a magazine asking if I was available to go to one of the big Chicago hotels and follow actress Audrey Hepburn around the ballroom shooting candid pictures. She was in the city raising money for UNICEF. Being assigned to photograph one of the great film stars and beauties of the era was a thrill. I never spoke to her beyond the usual hello's at introduction, as when doing that kind of work, you're expected to be invisible and not interfere. Still, just being close enough to touch her was a kick. Hepburn was older, but still amazingly sleek and beautiful. The man who had dressed her in life and so many movies, the very tall (6'5") and elegant Hubert de Givenchy, was also present. The magazine took all the film unprocessed as they had a publication deadline, so I never got to keep any outtakes. I wish I had. Who would believe that a not particularly famous Paul Marshall from Michiana Shores, Indiana had photographed Audrey Hepburn? I'd come a long way and felt proud of all I'd accomplished. I could never have done it without Dolly's constant love and support. She was my strength and the keeper of the wisdom of life.

When we left the city, Dolly accepted a sales position with Newcomb Printing Company based in Michigan City, which was owned by friends of ours. She worked for them in sales for a time but eventually decided to go it on her own as: DOLLY MARSHALL, GRAPHIC RESOURCE. This enabled her to continue representing Newcomb Printing as a freelancer, but also go after bigger projects requiring larger presses. This she did, landing some large projects for major clients.

But our life wasn't just about working. Both our kids were living with friends now, so we were free to come and go at whim. Our friends Doug and Senn bought a new Catalina 42 sailboat. They asked us to accompany them in picking it up at the dealer in Wisconsin. Doug retained a stretch limo to take us up and, on the way, we sipped champagne. Dolly, looking at home in this luxurious situation, suddenly announced a great truth about herself: "I like high living." We laughed at her pronouncement. It wouldn't be the last time she'd use these words. She must have liked the sound of them.

Sailing their new boat down to Chicago presented no problems. That boat they had named *Ragtime*, and our dear friends would afford us many happy times, lots of long sunny summer days and balmy nights in various ports up and down the eastern shore of Lake Michigan. It must have rained sometimes, but what I remember is ideal weather with lots of "sundowners" consumed on deck (too many at times I fear but we did have fun.) in various harbors at sunset. It's good to have generous friends who like to share their wonderful toys, and it was good to be approaching a time in life when we could enjoy the perks of our labors and those of our friends.

In 1993 Doug and Senn decided to bareboat charter a sailboat in Antigua and asked us to go along. Bareboat charter means you rent a boat and sail it yourself, no captain. They arrived before us, took care of the formalities, and had the boat ready when we joined them for cocktails at sunset on board. It was a dream week, sailing the French-built thirty-six-foot ocean-capable sailboat with a beautiful interior of warm varnished wood. On an ideal tropical evening, we dropped anchor in the beautiful remote bay of a small island with a few other boats as company. That same evening another boat came in, arriving from France with one thirty-something couple aboard. Next morning Senn said, "You boys better check out the French boat next to us." Looking out of our companionway, Doug and I saw a beautiful French girl standing on her deck having a shower from a water-filled shower bag. She was dressed as nature had made her; no clothing at all. Doug and I agreed—she was an extremely healthy example of French womanhood. No wonder we liked sailing so much. You encounter such pretty people, and some have no inhibitions at all.

That night, after cocktails and grilled steaks and wine (we had a small charcoal grill attached to the stern rail) we were winding down for the night. Dolly and I had stayed on deck a little longer to enjoy the star show when she whispered, "Meet me in our cabin in about ten minutes, sailor, and you'll find something nice." I did, and it was obvious my Doll did not intend to be outdone by some thirty-year-old French girl. Warm breezes, the scent of tropical flowers from the land, and a gently rocking boat can encourage romance to bloom like a flawless orchid, and it did.

"So, sailor, what did you think of that hot French girl?" she asked as I climbed into our bunk.

"French girl? What French girl?" It was exactly the right answer, so I was rewarded, as promised, with something nice, until we sailed off to dreamland. It was 1993. We were both fifty-one years old, had put on some pounds (the price of the good life, success, and age), gained a few wrinkles (earned), and Dolly was, as always, the cream in my tea. We'd both left behind the sharp edge of youthful looks, yet were still as in love as ever, continuing to behave like teenagers. My Doll remained as adorable to me as ever she was.


I'd never forgotten Dolly's disappointment at the lack of celebration for our twenty-fifth wedding anniversary, so as our thirtieth anniversary approached, I decided to give her a surprise party, planning it to the last detail. I reserved the large ballroom of the Holiday Inn and Leona, Gabrielle and I prepared a dual projector slide show with images of our married life during the first thirty years. Music was recorded, including versions of "Hello, Dolly!" on tape. I'd purchased a diamond cocktail ring to present to her and a complete party outfit she could change into after she'd been surprised… from lingerie to evening dress, shoes, perfume, earrings, hose, and a gardenia. Nothing was missing. Invitations went out, and as it was a surprise, guests were instructed to arrive early. I told Dolly we were meeting our friends in the cocktail lounge at the inn for drinks before going out to dinner. We were dressed nicely but not in fancy party clothes.

On course for the cocktail lounge, we came to the ballroom door and I pushed her through it as "Hello, Dolly!" began to play and friends and family crowded around to greet us. My family, who'd all pitched in during planning and preparation, had helped me pull off an amazing feat that could have been spoiled by one small slip along the way. The surprise was a complete success, and worth the stress.

It was Dolly's day, and my intent was that the stage be hers. After all the greetings, hugs and kisses were delivered from the crowd of family, relatives, and longtime friends, I took her to our reserved room where she discovered the garments, I'd purchased for her. Looking them over she shook her head, came to me, put her arms around my neck, and kissed me deeply.

"My darling Paul, I am overwhelmed that you've done all this for me, including these beautiful party clothes. And they look like they'll fit! You are one special guy."

"I wanted to do this for you for all you've given me, remaining so steadfast during all I've put you through. You never doubted me. There was a time when my greatest fear was that I'd lose you if you saw through me or could no longer cope with my problem. But you never gave up. You saw something in me that I had been unable to see; that I was a good man."

She looked at me thoughtfully for a moment and said, "Sit down, Paul. I want to say something." We sat on the edge of the bed and she took my hand in hers.

"When I was young, and before we ever met, I used to dream of you. What

194

I mean is, I imagined meeting someone just like you. Then one day, there you were, a boy not yet a man, but a boy I was sure wanted to love me for a lifetime. I believed you to be my destiny and time has shown I was right. So no, Paul, you need never doubt I love you." Then, squeezing my hand, she added, "you will never lose me… not ever."

A shiver ran through me, as if her words were an omen. It chilled me for a moment, but then the sensation was gone. We almost didn't return to our own party as passion overruled good manners, but eventually we managed to get dressed, Dolly into her black sequined evening attire and I into black tie. We returned to a celebration in full swing and hadn't even been missed.

We had photography and video covered. A microphone was hooked into the sound system, so after the party settled down, I spoke a bit about what a joy and privilege it had been to be married to Dolly for thirty years. I presented her with the cocktail ring, which was one large diamond surrounded by small ones clustered in circular rows around it. When Dolly took the floor, I picked up the mic and offered it to her. She refused, saying with a laugh that she didn't need it.

"I'm overwhelmed," she announced, "and I hope Paul has won the lottery to pay for all this." This was greeted by lots of laughter. "For the first time in my life I'm speechless" (more laughs), "and I didn't have to organize a thing for this party. For once I'm not in control of anything, not even myself." (Even more laughs, as everyone knew Dolly was the great planner and always in complete control). She put her arm in mine and said,

"This is one great guy I have here, and I love him dearly. I've loved him from the moment we first met, and it's only gotten better over the years." Raising the microphone, I asked her, "Will you promise me another thirty years?" She looked at me, then at the gathered group and said, "Keep doing things like this and you can have all the years you want." More laughter and applause.

The slide show was a hit, a portrait of our first 30 years. Dolly rejoiced in our anniversary party and I couldn't have been happier. I loved giving her this small thing as a gift for all she'd given me over the years. Our marriage had been tested, suffering through challenging times. Not only did we endure, but we also emerged stronger each time, the bond between us seemingly indestructible. That kind of love and commitment deserved celebration. Could what we'd begun in June 1959, and consummated with rings and promises on April 25, 1964, last forever? That was the dream we kept living.

Gabrielle was married in the winter of 1995. Mike, her intended, was not Catholic, so the ceremony was held in a beautiful turn of the century non-denominational church, and performed by our neighbor Reverend George Bowie, who had known Gabrielle since she was born. Friends with trained operatic voices sang during the service, and music included organ, piano, and strings. Gabrielle had asked us to choose the music, so father and daughter did something few brides have ever done; walk down the aisle to the Puccini aria, "O Mio Bambino Caro," (Oh My Dear Papa) sung in Italian. Dolly and I loved doing things out of the ordinary and with panache.

The reception was held at a separate venue one block away, so we walked between the locations led by a bagpiper we'd retained. Gabrielle wore a white satin cape with a hood that Dolly had sewn herself. The banquet room was like the great hall of a castle. Tables were decorated in medieval style with holly and ivy arrangements and tall silver candlesticks of varying heights at every table. Our wish for Gabrielle's marriage was that it be as good as ours. Could they find that something special we had? Marriage is a sometimes-capricious thing. In the end, all parents can do is send their kids off hoping that day by day they'll figure it out. I wasn't exactly sure what made Dolly and Paul one voice singing the same song. We just were and had been from the beginning. For Gabrielle and Mike, we could only wish them well.

# 16.

I was awarded the perfect photo assignment from an ad agency that liked my personal landscape work. It was completely open-ended. My mission: "Go out West and shoot landscapes, any you want, and lots of them." The concept was to use powerful images of wild places in advertising for a steel company. Tyler would accompany me, so we spent a couple of weeks in South Dakota and Wyoming, just roaming around making photographs and camping along the way. It was a trip I will always treasure, a fun creative adventure that also gave me lots of one-on-one time with my son. We camped and photographed in Yellowstone, the Grand Tetons, and many other sites along the way. Our client was pleased with our work.

That summer Gabrielle gave birth to our first grandchild, a girl she and Mike named Veronica. We were now grandparents, a job that Dolly had been looking forward to with anticipation. Our grandson Marshall followed a couple of years later. He was the last child she would have; a one boy, one girl family, just like her parents. We were happy for them.

On a Sunday in winter 1998, Dolly and I were once again lying in front of the fireplace at home on Sunset Trail, enjoying morning tea and reading the paper when she said, "Paul, check this out. British Airways is offering a complete package trip to visit London, airfare and hotel included, and the price is really a deal." We decided to bite the bullet and visit *Blighty*, also known in the past as *The Smoke*, slang terms for London, which is the sort of thing any good anglophile and owner of Jags and MGs like me would know. Thus, began our travels to England and Europe, something we enjoyed as a perk of owning our own businesses which allowed us to control our time. We had entered a period in life which let us focus on ways to enjoy life and less on earning a living. We were reasonably well positioned financially so that wasn't a problem.

Our plane landed at Heathrow and we took a train into London to find our hotel in Leicester Square. We quickly familiarized ourselves with the Tube system, which is a highly efficient underground mover of people. It took us everywhere, and then we walked and walked some more, quickly learning that being a tourist in Europe means walking…. lots of walking. British Museum, St. Martins in the Fields, Trafalgar Square, Baker Street (Sherlock Holmes wasn't home, nor was Doctor Watson), Buckingham Palace, and much more. I was in heaven. We wore our trench coats and carried our bumbershoots, feeling very British.

We visited the usual tourist spots including the magnificent St. Paul's Cathedral, which was designed by the great Christopher Wren. In metro London this church was Wren's monument, and about as grand as they get. It stood through all the bombing of London in WWII and survived. Amazing.

There's a plate in the floor of the cathedral that states in Latin, *Si monumcntum requiris, circumspice.* Translation: *If you seek his monument, look around.* This was Wren's epitaph, and I was very taken with it. When a man can leave behind a monument such as St. Paul's he doesn't need a lot of words…*just look around you* is quite enough. Our sojourn in London was a great experience, leaving us with an appetite for more travel.

In fact, the next year Dolly found another package deal from British Airways. This time, it was an offer to buy one round trip with three nights in the same London hotel as before and the second person flew free. So, we made another spring trip to England, which somehow always seemed like coming home to me. Again, we spent some days in London, then rented a car and took on the challenge of driving on the wrong side of the road and steering from the wrong side of the car. It was an adventure. We visited the Cotswold's and other scenic places in England and for art and history lovers like us, this kind of travel was a dream. Our life had become a film script, romantic, exciting, and even glamorous, just the way we liked it. We were two happy people, seeing some of the world while loving each other everywhere we went. It was all good.

Not long after our second trip to England, I was diagnosed with a heart condition called atrial fibrillation. It turned out that I was sensitive to alcohol and caffeine, both stimulants which could cause my heart to go out of rhythm, so I gave up drinking, smoking and coffee completely. Eventually, my cardiologist suggested that I have a procedure called catheter ablation which could stop or at least help control the arrhythmia. Afterwards friends said, "Now you can go back to enjoying martinis."

"Never again," I said, and when asked why, I answered truthfully,

"Because I wasn't controlling drinking very well. It had become too big a bad habit." I never touched hard alcohol again, but my doctor did allow an occasional glass of wine or two. As Dolly was, for all practical purposes, nearly a nondrinker, it was no burden. Once my mind is made up, I tend to be disciplined.

The heart procedure, which was performed in Indianapolis, had not come off problem-free, however. I spent several days in the cardiac intensive care unit. I'd been assured that less than two percent of people have ever had an issue with this procedure, but I fell into that *less than* group. They kept telling Dolly there was fluid around my heart. She finally demanded to know what the fluid was, and was told it was blood, as the pericardial sack had been accidentally pierced during procedure. Apparently, this finally fixed itself, and I was told I could go home.

Even calm, unshakable Dolly had suffered moments of real fear. She told me she was frightened she might lose me, especially when the doctors didn't want to admit what the problem was.

"I know you're okay now," Dolly said, "because I've seen you flirting with that cute nurse of yours. It's time to get you home. I think she was referring to the fact that when I was coming out of anesthetic from the procedure and looked into the pretty face of the nurse coaxing me to wake up, I said. "Am I in heaven? Are you an angel?" The lovely faced started laughing and this began many fun exchanges between us. Dolly overheard that remark (and others,) hence her wanting to take me home.

"Aw Doll," I said. "She's married and it's just for fun, and you must admit she is pretty and really funny. I can't help that I'm a normal man! And besides, a little innocent flirting is good for my recovery."

"Yep, time to get you home big boy," she said, poking me on the arm. But my problems were not over.

After being home for a time, my leg and ankle suddenly swelled up. I called my regular internist, and he said, "Get to the hospital now and I'll have someone in ER waiting for you." He'd guessed what the issue was and guessed correctly because a female tech did a venous Doppler test on me—twice. Then pointing at a chair, she said in a serious voice, "Go sit down there… gently, and *don't move*. You're going to be admitted." I had developed a blood clot. Even my always in-control girl was shaken. She realized this was a serious situation, and impairment or death from stroke was a possibility.

I don't remember how long I was in hospital, but it was not a short stay. Eventually doctors were able to clear the clot with chemistry, and once again, Dolly drove me home. This experience rattled us. If one needs a reason to remember just how much two people in love need each other, just stare the possibility of death in the face. Neither of us could imagine being without the other. We didn't even want to talk about it because the thought of ending up alone was too frightening to contemplate.

We were so much one heart for so many years that if either of us asked the other, "Do you love me?" I imagine we would have answer similarly: "Love you? I am you, and you are me. We are two become one."

Early in the new millennium, Dolly decided to stop selling printing, as she'd been offered a position at the John Blank Center for the Arts in Michigan City as the executive director's personal assistant. She had been volunteering there and now was finally going to work directly in the art world and be paid. She helped plan and hang shows, was a docent for exhibits, and learned to manage their outdoor art fair, the Lake Front Art Festival. Not long after a new building was acquired, almost immediately the executive director resigned. The board asked Dolly to take her place "temporarily" until a search could be made to find a director with fundraising and grant writing experience.

She held the position of executive director for two years during the challenging period of converting the building from office to art center use and introducing us to the community. She was, I believe, the right person for the job at that crucial period. At her request I resigned from the board so she could do her job without her husband sitting at the conference table. I remained on the building committee during the transformation. Serving as executive director of an art center was the crowning achievement of Dolly's working career, and she did a stellar job. I was extremely proud of her. I even got her a vanity license plate for her little red sport coupe: It said:

**ART BIZ** . The plate on my car read **FOTO BIZ**. After nearly two years her last day as director arrived and many were sad to see her go.

Dolly retired in 2005 when a director with professional fundraising experience was finally found. At the same time, I closed the business I'd run for thirty-seven years. It was time to ask ourselves how we were going to plan our future. First step was dinner at our favorite haunt, friend Basil Long's restaurant, *Basil's,* to toast our freedom. "Hello Social Security and Medicare…here we come." Dolly and I gathered at our usual planning spot in front of the fireplace in the house on Sunset Trail. It's interesting how many important decisions affecting our lives were made in front of that hearth. Maybe it was the true heart of our home; the fire that gives warmth while encouraging love and dreams. We both seemed in reasonably good health so fortified with cups of tea we began to consider possibilities for our future.

"The kids are grown and doing their own thing, so we are free as birds," Dolly said. "Are we going to travel more? If so, do we need this big house? You've been complaining about the maintenance, rising property taxes and heat bills. It would be so sad to sell our happy place, but maybe the time has come."

"I can't believe you're saying this," I said. "It's taken us years, nearly half our married life, to get it just the way we like it. I agree with what you're suggesting, but you love your house. Could you actually part with it?"

"If it makes practical sense, as much as I hate the idea, I suppose I'd say yes," she said. "We can get a smaller place that costs less, so we can preserve our savings and grow our investments. And this is a hot housing market, so this property should sell for a high price, and quickly. Then there's Florida to consider." Gradually, we began to create a plan and started to put it in motion. However, as happens so often in life, things didn't work out quite as intended.

Our time spent working and vacationing in Florida had caused us to consider living in that state, and the city of Sarasota specifically. We'd discovered Sarasota had an abundance of arts activities including professional performing arts. Ballet, opera, and theater, all things that interested us. In 2006 we bought a small (but pricy) house there with a screen-caged swimming pool in a recently developed community called Village Walk. Dolly's cousin Rick Butor and wife Debbie and their family, Kate and Ryan lived nearby, a plus, and part of the reason for our choice. Our new street was called Modena Place. Simultaneously, we listed (with reluctance) our beloved house on Sunset Trail. What we didn't know was this was right at the tail end of the real estate bubble. We had paid a premium price for a small house in Florida in a rapidly rising market, a quickly made decision as we feared prices were going to continue going up. This proved a wrong assumption. Offsetting that expenditure was the fact that our house in Michiana Shores had been appraised and listed at a high price, more than we expected. We thought we were on easy street, (Joking I even suggested we get a license plate that read, EZ Stret) but in fact storm clouds were gathering.

We had a friend named Gary who had become wealthy speculating during the real estate boom, so we decided to flip a condo in Las Vegas with him. It was a quick and impressive profit, so we reinvested the proceeds with our friend on an expensive unit in a newly developed condo hotel on the beach at the south end of Ocean Drive in South Beach, FL. We put this property right back on the market, adding a half million to what we'd paid for it, expecting a quick flip in a hot market. Unfortunately, that was when the real estate world turned seriously negative.

We'd no sooner listed our house up north, purchased a house in Sarasota, and invested in a property to flip in South Beach, all of them with mortgages attached, when suddenly, it became difficult to sell anything. Inflated property values were crashing. The risk we had taken is known as "leverage," (too many properties, all with mortgages.) It was a lot of debt to service. As neophyte real estate tycoons, we were bleeding money and efforts to sell Sunset Trail and Miami Beach dragged on in a soft market. Amazingly I didn't panic or suffer any anxiety. It seemed I'd conquered that malady permanently, we had adequate resources, so I just focused on our stock investments and selling two properties.

The bright side was living in Florida was being on vacation every day. We made many new friends, which was easy on our street, as everyone was very friendly. Many of our neighbors were retired but living a highly active lifestyle, and some were younger and still working. We enjoyed finding new things to see and do and spent lots of time at the beaches. We discovered the libraries and Bone Fish Grill, one of our favorite places to eat. I had towed our old MG sports car down and turned it over to Glen's MG in St. Petersburg for mechanical work. When finished, *ka-Ching* went the cash register. I found someone to do body and paint work plus the interior. More *ka-Ching*. After writing large checks, we had a very pretty MGB.

Mercifully, I'd been doing quite well in the stock market. I'd become a serious investor and holdings in Apple and many other technology companies were being very generous to us, providing substantial income that kept our boat afloat.

Dolly enjoyed a water exercise class in the village pool while I swam laps in the twenty-five-meter lap pool every day. Family and friends came to visit, and our grandchildren Veronica and Marshall flew down often. I'll never forget their first visit and the fearful expression on their young faces as they emerged from the exit tunnel of the plane. Not only were they traveling alone, but it was also their first time flying. We could see the fearful look that asked, "Will Grandma and Grandpa be there to get us?" On seeing us waiting for them, they lit up like two stars. The kids loved our home pool and spent noisy hours playing in it. We took day trips to visit places like Sanibel Island to collect shells. On a separate trip we visited Bush Gardens. Each summer, we went north for four months, renting a small love nest sized cottage from our friend, Peg L., with an additional month at Christmas, sometimes spent with my mom and sister Leona. Life was fine and would have been perfect if it weren't for those pesky mortgages.

Dolly developed an interest in orchids, so we attended flower shows dedicated to this plant. She slowly gained knowledge about these exotic flowers. Soon the deck surrounding our screen-caged swimming pool was bursting with various kinds of orchids and other plants. She'd also enlisted the advice of an elderly man who lived across from us. He too grew orchids and was knowledgeable. Books and magazines about orchids began to cover the coffee table. She was teaching me how not to kill her babies by overwatering them with the hose while I was maintaining the pool, deck, and our other potted plants. "You can water everything else but leave the orchids to me," she warned. "They require special attention." She was right. She knew more about these plants than I did. It occurred to me that perhaps she wanted orchids to be something that was hers alone. I accepted that idea.

"Yes, oh wizard of the exotic flower," I said. "I bow to your superior knowledge of the sacred orchid. I also bow down for a closer peek at what's under that wet T-shirt you're wearing, because I can see right through it. Pretty sexy for a grandma."

"Ouch! That hurt." We started to grapple with each other and ended up falling in the pool, laughing as playfully as two teenagers. How could I not love this no longer young (nor was I) but still young-at-heart woman? Perhaps that was part of our success as a couple. We had humor, love, and especially romance in our relationship, and by romance, I mean we believed in the art of love. We felt being stylish and sexy was a way of life and worked to maintain that idea. And even though we were growing old, we "thought young," and that's important. We refused to see ourselves as over the hill. After years of marriage I was still treating Dolly as if I were trying, every day, to win her love.

Certainly, that must be part of it. We somehow related like newlyweds. Dolly still dressed in style and good taste, not just for herself, but for me, continuing to wear pretty lingerie, ever the temptress. The thrill of dancing with her, the magic of a simple touch, the idea that some sexy, exciting adventure was just around the corner waiting for us. Life continued to hold the same thrill it had more than forty years ago. After all the years we still played the seduction game and our bedroom, or a hotel room would still become a playroom for grown-ups; a place to seduce and be seduced. A trip to Paris was an excuse to feel like glamourous thirty-year-old's again, because in our minds, that's who we were. A little overweight? Of course. But even in our late sixties we were still sexual beings who remained very physical with one another.

We never gave up on life; no sitting down in front of the TV to wait for death. That was not our style. I'm convinced it's important in a long marriage, to maintain the practice of romance. We tried every day, to maintain the idea that we were a sexy, stylish couple. I can only say, it worked for us.

# 17.

"There's something sad about a sign that reads,
'Cottage for Sale'"

Paul Marshall

In early 2008, more than two years after moving to Florida, we were finally offered a good price for our house on Sunset Trail. We'd recently spent what was to be our last magical Christmas season there and now had to head back to Michiana for the closing. We were staying with Gabrielle, who was living in a rented log cabin just down the lane from the house that soon would no longer be ours. On the final night before the closing, I took a blanket and pillow and walked down Sunset Trail to spend a last night alone in our now empty but much-loved house. I'd asked Dolly to join me, but she'd said, "Paul, I just can't do it. It would be too much like going to a funeral for someone I love." This was an unusually emotional response from this well-adjusted woman. Selling the house we'd lived in for forty-three years would be one of the hardest things we'd ever do. It felt like we were amputating a part of ourselves and in fact, we were.

I'd put my heart and soul into this house and walking slowly through empty rooms, in each I'd hear faint voices. Not ghosts, simply memories floating through my mind.

*"Of course, we should buy our honeymoon cottage, Paul."*

*"Guess what baby cakes, I'm think I'm pregnant."*

*"It's a girl!" and finally, "It's a boy!"*

*"Dad, would you read us a story?"*

*"Merry Christmas, my darling, brown-eyed boy."*

*"Happy anniversary, my beauty."*

*"You'll never get that giant Christmas tree into this house!"*

*"Mom, Dad, I'd like you to meet my prom date."*

The cottage on Sunset Trail was the canvas upon which our lives had been painted, our history found in every stroke of the brush. Like my father before me, I'd built large parts of the house on the hill with my own hands, creating both a home and an attachment those who simply buy a finished house will never understand. This house was a part of us. We had spent our honeymoon in these rooms; it was where we loved, struggled to become grown-ups, made babies, laughed, sometimes cried, and now we was abandoning our beloved cottage. Many times, I'd announced laughingly to friends: "In all likelihood, the day I drive the last nail into this house I'll probably drop dead." It didn't happen that way. Soon, we would hand the keys to a stranger and leave behind the greater part of our lives. Would selling our honeymoon cottage break our hearts? Oh yes. It broke mine, and Dolly's too.

But we had Florida, which was a different kind of paradise from Michiana. We tried hard to enjoy the difference and were largely successful. One of the many wonderful aspects of the state is that beautiful things grow there.

Floridians joke that you can stick an old broom handle in the ground, and it will root. I planted a gardenia tree outside our pool cage, and it grew and proved prolific, producing many flowers each year. I also became enamored of plumeria, another plant whose blossoms have a scent to rival the costliest perfumes. I'd often chose a perfect blossom from either of these exotic, perfume rich plants, to put on Dolly's pillow for her to find when coming to bed at night. This gesture won me many kisses, but in truth, I did it to see the look on her face when discovering my tokens of affection; the look saying, "I know I'm loved. After all these years, I am still loved." These small gestures were one of many things I did to keep the music playing. Dolly's gift to me was that she always looked pretty and desirable. It was important to us to be loveable for the other. Allow physical attraction to die and something wonderful is lost. We avoided the trap of losing interest in how we looked or related to each other. We still dressed both for ourselves, but also to please the other. We played at the game of love like kids.

Wanting Dolly to be happy, I tried to make our new house special. Together we purchased Florida-style furnishings and put tropical plantings in containers in our pool cage. Appropriate furniture from Michiana Shores was blended in, adding a feeling of continuity and a sense of our roots. Although Dolly was happy enough, and we were enjoying ourselves, at some point it became clear to me that Modena Place would never be Sunset Trail. No matter how hard we tried, it wouldn't happen. This would always be our second home, our vacation home. Our true home was twelve hundred miles north on a wooded lane in sand dune country and was no longer ours.

We continued to find ways to have fun in Florida. When neighbors discovered that we liked jazz, they told us about an amazing young jazz group that would be appearing in concert at a nearby venue. They called themselves Jazz Juvenocracy. Considering that the leader/trumpet player was a girl of thirteen or fourteen, they were unbelievably talented.

We met the young jazz prodigy Bit Risner and her mother, Lisa, and volunteered our talents, immediately getting involved doing promotion for the group. While seeking an idea for a poster shoot for them, I turned to Dolly with her uncanny instincts and said,

"We need an interesting location to use for the background. Any ideas?" She thought for a moment and said, "Remember that antiques and architectural salvage resale place we visited? You know, the one with a yard full of old iron gates, fences and all kinds of old architectural pieces like fancy pillars and such?" She'd hit a home run on the first pitch.

We posed the band in several settings on that property and it proved the perfect spot. It was fun to put our skills to work for these kids, and they became a happy part of our lives in Florida. We even toured with them in Europe several times when the played major jazz festivals.

On May 31, 2011, my sister Ann's oldest son Tom died of liver cancer at age forty-nine. Tom, an accomplished, athletic man, who'd earned Eagle Scout as a boy, and was now successful in business. He led a healthy lifestyle but sadly, cancer does not care who it attacks. He was a fine man, loved by all and would be missed. I was reminded that life has a beginning and an unpredictable end. Each time a tragedy like Tom's death occurred in my life, I became more convinced that life is as random as many philosophers suggest. There's no other possible explanation when bad things happen to good people. It's chance. Our lives are not planned. Logic tells me no loving supreme being would treat his creations that way. It's just bad luck when children are born with terrible diseases, and not part of some plan that's beyond explanation or logic. Reason suggested it was absurd to believe otherwise.

In October of 2012 we were called north as my ninety-seven-year-old mother was fading, something we'd been expecting and were prepared for. Although her mind was sharp, she said she was "tired" and prepared to go. Knowing her accepting attitude about death made it easier for us. She simply stopped eating and willed herself to shut down. She died at home seven hours after Dolly and I arrived from Florida. She'd been part of our lives for such a long time. She and our dad had worked hard for their family and given us so much, including that small, incidental thing called life. I remembered how, when driving past her cottage on the beach road at night I used to see the light in her bedroom glowing. It was a comforting thought to know my mother was up there reading. The pleasure of that lighted window is gone now, and I miss her sweet presence as do we all.

We lived in Sarasota for almost eight years. Imagine being on vacation in a tropical setting, where the weather is nearly always ideal, beaches go on forever, nights are redolent with the perfume of exotic flowers, and balmy air clings to skin like a moisturizer. We spent seven months of the year there and it was vacationing every day—until, that is, the evening Dolly dropped a bomb.

I was sitting on the edge of our home pool, feet dangling in the water and watching another surreal Florida sunset wash the sky in glorious Turner colors as flocks of Dolly's favorite red-winged blackbirds came to roost in the reeds of the lagoon outside our pool cage. She joined me, bringing two acrylic goblets of wine, and sat down, dangling her feet in the water next to mine. She was wearing a new bathing suit I'd never seen before, one that flattered her fuller figure which I told her was just a little more to love. The scent she wore said expensive. The piano of Bill Charlap played softly, permeating the evening air of our private little heaven with gentle jazz ballads. Peace was in this place.

And yet, something was different. Hmmm. Those subtle clues caused me to wonder if a surprise was about to occur. The bigger question was, would I like it or not? After a short silence (gathering courage?), Dolly finally spoke.

"Paul, my dear, sweet, understanding man…" (I knew it! This was going to be trouble.)

"What would you say to a move back north permanently?" she asked.

I had no hint this was coming. We'd been having a good time, so her question knocked the wind from my sails.

"I know what I'm asking is a big change," she said, "but I'd so like to be with our family more. I'd like to be there with Gabrielle, to help Veronica pick out her prom dress, to see Marshall swim in his meets, be there when Ty finishes an offshore sailboat race, all those birthday parties, and things that only happen once in life. We're having fun here, but it's all about us, just us.

We're missing time with our family that we can never get back. I also think Gabrielle needs us in her life. Tyler too." This was classic Dolly, always a loving, caring person. Once again, her values were clear. Love and family came first. She recognized what truly mattered.

She was right, of course. We were living one long vacation in Florida, while life and time raced by us up north, and we were not a part of it. I'd been so absorbed in the simple life of two lovers again, free to focus on each other and whatever pleasures we decided to pursue, that I hadn't realized I was being selfish, both to Dolly and our family.

"Gee, this is interesting," I said. "It would be a big change. Were you thinking we'd sell this house?"

"Yes," she replied. "Maybe we can buy a small cottage or condo up north. If we wanted, we could still come down in the dead of winter for a month or two and rent, so not give up Sarasota completely. If we found a property, we liked up north that didn't cost too much, we could afford to keep traveling in Europe and maybe Asia. What do you think?"

"Well my beauty, what you've said about family is true. I understand. But it would be a big change. Moving would mean a lot of work too, but if that's what you want, then let's investigate it. You do know, my love, that wherever you are, there also shall I be." Her kiss lingered until she said, "You really are a good man, Paul, and still my beautiful, brown-eyed boy." I loved when she called me that. It brought back our sweet days of youth. We finished our wine, had a light meal, and after dark, I think there may have been some skinny dippers in our pool. Well, what did you expect when the woman I loved had somehow misplaced her swimsuit? I'd have said yes to anything she wanted, of course. The love of my life could play me as on an angel's harp, and I always enjoyed the tune. She was, after all, nothing less than the music of my life.

We sold the house in Sarasota. From the moment it was listed online to a signed deal, only sixteen hours had passed. Houses like ours in the desirable village where we lived were simply not available. Up north we purchased an affordable yet interesting condo on the edge of Lake Clair in Long Beach, Indiana and were back in the old neighborhood again. Ten minutes to a Lake Michigan beach, it had two bedrooms, two and a half baths in a two-story unit with a two-car garage, wood-burning fireplace, and vaulted ceilings. We had lived with high ceilings all our life together, so this felt familiar, and was something we both enjoyed. "It has 'us' written all over it," Dolly said.

The lake side of the house was taken up almost entirely with glass sliding doors opening onto a deck, then a small patch of grass and the lake. Before we moved in, our son Tyler redecorated the interior beautifully and oversaw some remodeling of the kitchen accomplished by friend Frank Meyer. We were happy with our new digs and looked forward too many happy years on Lake Clair.


We moved in on June 1st, and in July, Dolly and I again traveled to Europe, accompanied by Gabrielle and our teen grandchildren Veronica and Marshall. We were going to tour part of the time with Jazz Juvenocracy, the young band we'd been actively involved with in Florida. They were doing their final European jazz festival tour before disbanding the group and entering college. Our grand kids got on well with the group and had a great time traveling with the band, hanging around backstage as roadies. We also spent part of the time as a family, visiting places Dolly and I wanted them to experience. Rome, Assisi, Florence, and the Cinque Terre. In Paris, we rejoined the band for a club date, then proceeded alone again, to England via high-speed train under the Channel and visited many sites including the Tower of London, which was a favorite with the kids. During our travels, we all sensed Dolly seemed a little tired and not quite herself, but she never complained (she never did), so we assumed it was nothing, but we were wrong.

# 18.

"MY HEART HAD TO BE BROKEN BEFORE
I UNDERSTOOD LOVE'S FULL VALUE."

Paul Marshall

It had been a fine trip, but not long after our return, Dolly went in for a medical checkup, and several EKGs suggested an unidentified problem. She was sent to a local cardiologist and began a series of tests to find what the issue might be. Her blood pressure had also been acting strangely, spiking up quite high and then returning to normal minutes later. On the evening of October 1, 2013, a few days before a scheduled CT scan, she went to exercise in a pool while Gabrielle and grandson Marshall swam laps. Then, being competitive, mother and son raced for fun with Dolly happily watching them try to outdo one another. Back home she told me about the fun they had swimming and then we watched a bit of TV together. Soon Dolly was falling asleep, so I suggested, "Why don't we go up my love, you're dozing off."

"Paul, would you take my blood pressure, please? I'm feeling so relaxed." As I attached the blood pressure cuff, she looked at me with complete trust, faith, and love in her eyes. I will never forget that moment. The gentle look on her lovely face was a portrait of the deep connection that existed between us; the trust she had in me to watch over her.

"Your blood pressure is nearly normal, so that's a good sign," I said. We went up the stairs holding hands, then parted, she to our bedroom, and I to my office in the spare room to write down our investment account results for the day. When I came to bed Dolly was already asleep. I had no foreboding that I would never speak to her again. The last words I can remember saying to her were, "Your blood pressure is nearly normal, so that's a good sign." But, as events would soon reveal, it wasn't a good sign, and her faith and trust in me to take care of her wasn't justified. I was blind and didn't see what was coming. She was in danger and I was about to fail her again, and this time for the last time.

The next morning, October 2, 2013, I was awakened by sun streaming through our bedroom window. I turned to kiss my beloved, and she appeared unnaturally still. Then I saw her lips were blue, and she wasn't breathing. When I touched her torso, it was slightly warm, but her legs were already cold. My reaction was denial. I'm dreaming. For the second time in my life I thought, *this just couldn't be happening. Not now. Not to us.* But I was awake, and it was all tragically real.

I shook her, begging, "Wake up. Stay with me." In desperation I began pressing on her chest with no idea what I was doing, repeatedly crying out, "Don't leave me. Please don't leave me." It was all in vain; life had left her. As the finality of death set in, a flood of anguish raced through me accompanied by a sensation of drowning. Struggling to breathe, I wanted to howl like a wounded animal in mortal pain, but nothing would come out. The sound of torment was inside my head; one long, silent scream of inconsolable despair. Heart pounding, my body felt frozen, as if I'd been injected with a numbing drug. At that moment, the only thing I fervently wished for was that my life would end now, along with Dolly's. I saw no place for me without her.

I'd never considered that my sweet girl might die before me. Statistics suggested I would go first, and I don't think I'd ever given any other outcome a moment's thought. We'd been together so long, facing many problems, and always finding solutions. But death is the ultimate problem and is without solution.

I tried calling Gabrielle and Tyler on their cell phones. Neither answered.

I called our grandchildren Veronica and Marshall, reaching them in the car on their way to high school. "Hi, Grandpa, what's up?" Veronica said.

Voice breaking, I told her. "Your grandmother died during the night and your mom and Uncle Tyler don't answer their phones. I've called 911 but need help. I don't know what to do."

"Died? Grandma's dead? Oh no. We're turning around and will be there in a few minutes. Just hang on, Pops." They quickly drove back home where Veronica, through tears, told their mother, "Grandpa called and said Grandma died and we should come to their house."

Gabrielle's response was to doubt.

"No, she didn't. Mom dead? That's not possible."

My youngest sister Leona lived nearby. I called her and sobbed out the words, "Dolly has died and I don't know what to do!" Leona's reaction was a sudden intake of breath followed by the sound of her phone hitting the floor as it fell from her hand. People like Dolly don't die; they're larger than life and we believe they will always be with us. And yet, the unbearable truth was, she was gone. Our son Tyler was located, and he too was on his way. For me, a descent into the greatest darkness I would ever know had just begun.

As directed by 911, I went down and unlocked the front door. Back in our room, I got on the bed, tears flowing, and put my arms around my darling girl's lifeless body. Kissing her cold lips over and over I began rocking her back and forth, whispering, "Why must you leave me? Please don't go. Breathe again. Come back. I'll be lost without you," as if she had a choice. This was the last time I would ever hold her. The woman whose heart and soul had been linked irreversibly to mine for fifty-five years, was dead.

When family members and emergency people arrived, I was gently encouraged to let go of her. My son Tyler, daughter Gabrielle, and sister Leona, all showing strength under stress, began managing things, staying focused on what had to be done. It was their way of dealing with terrible loss: shut off the heart, don't feel, just take care of the business at hand. Our grandchildren stood in the doorway of the bedroom with wooden faces, not wanting to enter or accept that their much-loved grandmother was lying there dead. While people moved about me doing their jobs, I stood staring at my beloved wife, a woman always laughing, always in motion, but now lying cold, and silent, all signs of life having left her now still body. Like a frightened child, I was tempted to close my eyes to make it all go away. There's no reasonable explanation for this behavior, but the mind is not reasonable when plunged into shock and grief.

Asked by someone from the coroner's office if I wanted to order an autopsy I responded, "Why? She's dead. I don't want her cut apart." To me it seemed sacrilege to allow her body to be violated in that way. A funeral home was needed. Someone gave the name of the one we'd used one year earlier for my ninety-seven-year-old mother. We were asked to leave the room as they began to put my wife's body into a black bag, which seemed to me brutal and cruel.

I stood at the bottom of the stairs as men maneuvered the cart down, the cart that held the best of me. With each step the pain in my chest grew. It all seemed surreal, as if I were suddenly trapped inside one of Salvador Dali's nightmarish paintings. The light that once was Dolly had burned out. Never again would she brighten our lives. The thought was unbearable. Officials and emergency people departed, taking her body with them. It didn't seem possible that in less than two hours, she who mattered most to me in life was being hauled away like a broken appliance. Didn't they understand? They were taking away my life and the air I breathed.

My family remained with me, but emotionally I was no longer there. I'd retreated inside myself, feeling totally alone in a world turned cold and dark. I'd reached the end, the omega, the final curtain. I wanted to die.


We were only months from our fiftieth wedding anniversary. Teens when we met, we'd been together fifty-five years. Now, while I slept unaware, death had come for her, stopping her loving heart, and taking all her dreams, and mine, away with the last breath she would ever take in this life.

She would never attend Marshall's swim meets or help Veronica pick out a prom dress. Never have fun shopping with Gabrielle or laugh happily with her dearest friend Senn. Never again would she stand on a light house finish line to wave to her beloved son Tyler as he completed another offshore sailboat race, nor would she find a gardenia on her pillow from her devoted lover. All these things and more had been stolen from her. My adored wife, lover, and dearest friend had been my morning, my day, and my warm comfort and peace at night. Along with our children, she was the most precious thing in my life. In truth, she was my life. Her tragic passing would become for me, the beginning of a long journey, sending me deep inside myself to a dark, and profoundly lonely place. I crumbled under the weight of her passing, and the terrible and inescapable finality of it.

I shamefully admit I did not manage her death well. Overcome with grief, I was not the mighty fortress a father should be for his family in a time of sorrow. I blindly staggered through Dolly's wake and funeral. Then, like a turtle, I retreated into a shell, hiding from everything and everyone, a recluse suffering unmanageable pain and a crushing feeling of guilt. Wallowing in self-pity, defeated by emptiness, I felt my life had ended. I had no desire to go on alone. Not knowing what else to do I escaped into books seeking guidance. A Grief Observed, by C.S. Lewis had been given to me by friend, Mark Sanders and I read it repeatedly. I grasped at every straw, reading Christian apologists such as Peter Kreeft. I read philosophers, always trying to find an answer to the unanswerable. My poor concerned daughter, afraid I might harm myself, would call early each morning to be sure I was still there to answer.

Wanting to avoid being on the receiving end of people's sympathy, if my doorbell rang, I wouldn't answer. Later, I'd find a casserole, or a pie left by a kind neighbor, along with a note or card. I simply couldn't face the concerned, sad eyes of well-intentioned people. I just couldn't.

I'll never know the exact cause of Dolly's death. Based on symptoms, most friends who are doctors suggest a fatal stroke. I'd said no to an autopsy; at the time I couldn't face the thought of her being cut up. I saw it as a desecration of the holy temple that was Dolly's body. The result was that she looked lovely at her wake, not caked with makeup of an unnatural color as she would have been after autopsy. My sister Leona believes she looked peaceful because her death had been instant, and she was unaware of it happening. I know people often make the *"she looks like she's only sleeping"* comment at wakes, but in Dolly's case, it was true. She looked as if she was resting peacefully. Knowing that she cared about her appearance, this small kindness might have pleased her. She looked beautiful, and yet her beauty was painful to see because soon it would be gone from my view forever.

I wanted to keep her precious face where I could see it for as long as possible. I was not ready to let her go. I would *never* be ready to let go. My heart was breaking with a pain that was relentless in its persistence. My request to stay with her through the night was denied by the funeral home. Tomorrow would be the last time I would ever see her before the lid was closed for the final time. I now know the answer to the questions, what and where is hell? Hell is the loss of one's beloved, and a far greater form of suffering than any inferno religion can conjure up. As to the question of where does hell reside? It can be found in the hearts of those who grieve. *Hell is love lost.*

Hundreds of people attended Dolly's wake. I was told the line went outside the funeral home, extending into the parking lot and even down the street for more than two hours; I never sat down in four. There wasn't enough room inside for all the people coming to acknowledge her life. It was a tribute to Dolly and demonstrated how much she was loved.

When Gabrielle, Leona and I had gone to order flowers for the wake, we chose the shop Joy of Flowers in Michigan City because I liked the name for obvious reasons. We told the owner, a man named Bernie whom we'd never met before, that we wanted his best work. We asked that all the flowers be tropical, including birds of paradise, gardenias, and of course, orchids, and we wanted creative and artistic arrangements.

"Who are these for?" Bernie asked.

"They're for Dolly Marshall," I told him. Tears instantly appeared in his eyes. "No! Not Dolly, not Dolly!" he nearly shouted. We were surprised at this show of emotion from a stranger. He then explained he knew her from Rotary Club, which she had joined as part of her job for the art center. He said that when Dolly walked into luncheon meetings you could feel the mood of the room shift. Everyone became more cheerful and many wanted to sit with her. He also told us he always made the effort to be at her table, "Because if I was, I left the meeting uplifted. She had a way of making my day better. I don't know what it was, but it's true."

"I can solve the mystery, Bernie," I said. "I've always called that gift, 'Dolly Magic.' Her joy at just being alive was addictive; her happy demeanor, irresistible; her love of people, genuine and contagious." The flowers were beautifully done for his friend Dolly. Bernie saw to it personally.

Dolly and I had agreed on cremation. Our ashes will be mingled when my time comes, so at least that part of us will be as we were in life, always together. A week or two after the funeral I came out of hiding long enough to go pick up Dolly's ashes. Walking in the afternoon sunlight toward our car I had a few tears in my eyes as I said out loud to her, "I'll bet you never thought I'd be carrying you home in a shopping bag." So began my habit of talking to her. I can nearly always imagine her answers because she always told me what she honestly felt and believed to be right, even knowing I might not like her answer. Dolly never lied.

I wrote to her cardiologist, asking if he could tell me why my wife died. He invited me to his office for a face-to-face visit and showed me ultrasound pictures of Dolly's heart and valves. He said everything looked fine and seemed to be functioning normally, so the problem did not seem to be her heart after all. Other doctors I know have suggested a fatal stroke. I asked him why she had not been hospitalized for the obviously much needed scan. Several doctors had declared there was an as-yet-undiscovered problem. Didn't that indicate a need for speed?

"Because she didn't complain of any common danger symptoms," he said. "She had no chest pain, no shortness of breath, none of the things that would indicate a serious heart issue and we were looking for a heart problem. Hospitalization did not seem called for." So, that was that. It didn't seem "called for." Personally, I would describe random spiking blood pressure readings as very abnormal and a dangerous symptom. Something had been going very wrong in her body. It's possible the problem might have been found if the scan had been completed sooner. Perhaps a stent was needed to clear a blockage or clot. It's done all the time. Yet timely intervention "didn't seem called for." After all, it was only Dolly's life at risk. Only all her dreams and remaining years hanging in the balance of their bad decisions. Doctors had dropped the ball. They were not focused enough on the danger signs. That's the truth. But then, I'd done the same thing.

If I sound bitter and angry, I am. Though everyone tells me not to do this, I blame doctors for not moving faster, and myself for not recognizing the danger signals in those blood pressure readings and rushing her off to a major research hospital in Chicago. They would have CT scanned her *at once* instead of putting her on hold for five days, possibly found the cause of the problem more quickly and saved her. I can't help but feel responsible for her death. After all, her mother and aunts had all lived into their late eighties. Dolly, as clean living as she was, expected to see one hundred. This was 2013, with medicine able to fix a plethora of issues. No excuse is acceptable to me... doctors failed her, and so did I. Her symptoms were not taken seriously enough, and the result was early death.

After she died, I lived with overwhelming guilt. I felt I had no right to be here on this earth when the best person I'd ever known had her life stolen from her.

To this day I believe her death was partly my fault. She might have been saved if only I had acted. Feeling I'd failed her, I wanted to punish myself through suffering and sadness. I deserved the pain, even welcomed it. I wanted to be miserable. I couldn't get beyond the idea that I had promised, and then failed to watch over her, whether the feeling was justified or not.

I try hard now, to accept it's just life, and perhaps someday I'll forgive myself for not having done more. For now, right, or wrong, feelings of guilt linger. I've had to learn to live with those feelings because they won't leave me in peace and probably never will. I only know she deserved better of me.

# DOLLY MARSHALL

"BEAUTY TOO RICH FOR USE,
FOR EARTH TOO DEAR."

August 21, 1942 - October 2, 2013

CHERISHED WIFE OF PAUL MARSHALL

LOVING MOTHER OF GABRIELLE AND TYLER
TREASURED GRANDMOTHER OF
VERONICA AND MARSHALL,
DEVOTED SISTER, AUNT, AND FRIEND TO MANY.

WE THOUGHT HER SONG WOULD NEVER END,
WE WERE WRONG

# 19.

"Thou detestable maw, thou womb of death…"

Wm. Shakespeare//Romeo and Juliet

Thus, did Romeo described the Capulet family tomb which he believed held the dead body of his beloved Juliet. I understand Romeo's descriptive choice in using the word "detestable" for the place that held the body of his true love. Nothing is good enough as a resting place for an angel.

Dolly's ashes went home with me, not to a "womb of death," but to a beautiful Chinese ginger jar, one she'd collected in life. I talk to her often, always fearing her responses, because if she were able, she'd be saying, "Paul, you have no need to feel guilty because I'm dead and you're not. My time had come, and you must get on with your life."

These one-sided conversations often took the form of confessing. I'd admit to her I was weak and not dealing well with her death; that I was lost without her and had become completely self-absorbed in my own pain when I should have been thankful for the long and happy marriage we'd enjoyed. I revealed to her that I felt at sea without a lifeboat, struggling in a storm of sadness, wishing but unable to believe in life after death, a life where our love would continue.

Through tears I'd ask her, "How can I confront this endless grief? Please tell me. I need to know how to live, knowing you will never again walk through our door, never lie down beside me at night?" I had a guilty sense I was only feeling pain and sorrow for *my* loss and found this somehow obscene when it was Dolly's life that was over. I feared I lacked the strength to turn away from the dark abyss that tempted me with the overwhelming desire to stop breathing. I admitted all of this to her reluctantly, knowing if she could hear me, she'd have replied in her direct and honest way:

"Get a grip, buster. You're no sissy. You can handle this; I know you can. It's true, she always believed in me. So why couldn't I believe in myself? Why did I feel this need for her guidance? Why did I not feel strong enough to stand on my own?

"I want desperately to have you point out my true course," I told her. "You were the compass of my life, my navigator, my lighthouse to guide me home. Now your light is extinguished, my compass lost overboard. I can't find my way in the darkness and feel like a boat with torn sails, sinking fast." The only response was silence from one now sleeping in a Chinese ginger jar.

After the end-of-life rituals had been observed, the next stage was well-intentioned people who wanted to help me. Predictably they'd say, "Give it time. You'll get over it." Perhaps it's true, but I didn't believe it. I wanted to shout, "You have no idea what I'm feeling, you can't know my heart, so please, just leave me alone." Again, Dolly's wise voice whispered,

"They want to help you, Paul. Let them. I know how much you love me, so I'm asking you to do it for me. It will ease your suffering." But I'd become a true master of feeling sorry for myself, and, focused as I was on my own sadness, I continued to ignore comfort from others.

Our daughter Gabrielle suffered in silence. Her deeply loved mother was dead. I'm sure she was angry and disappointed in me as I wasn't there for her, to help share her pain. Our son Ty kept his feelings private as he always does, so I didn't know what he was going through. I knew he and his mom had shared a special bond; mothers and sons do. Our granddaughter, Veronica, was silent, while our grandson Marshall wore a face of stone, both unable to speak of Dolly. Marshall asked me not to talk about her because it made him sad. Senn, her closest friend, couldn't bear to hear Dolly's name. "She's not dead, she's just not here," Senn told me one day. She was coping by denying. So many tears, so many who were suffering, and all I could feel was my own pain. I'm no poet, but wrote the following simple and modest verse in my journal kept after Dolly's death:

### The Missed Chance

I once held goodness in my arms,
an angel warm and sweet.
I wanted to say how much I loved her,
but she was fast asleep.

"Surely it can wait till morning,
my words of love will keep,
time enough to tell her then,
so, for now I'll let her sleep."

That night death came to visit us
and took my love from me.
The chance I missed will never come,
for she is gone, you see,
and all my fervent words of love?
Lost… in bleak eternity

I somehow survived the first year after Dolly's death, not very well, but I was still here. Not an hour passed when she was not in my thoughts. I found myself wishing I could tell her again how much I loved her. I wanted to tell her that every day she was mine had been a gift, a perfect day. I convinced myself that she would never abandon me and that at night she still slept invisibly beside me. I would have given anything to hear her voice call out as she came through the door, "Honey, I'm home." I would answer, "Oh Bliss," as I always did. Silly, perhaps, but we enjoyed the ritual. Small signs of affection that meant so much to us. What devoted partners we'd been in life…what true and ardent lovers.


On October 2nd, 2014, the first anniversary of Dolly's death, my family suggested we spend a day in Chicago doing "Dolly things" in her memory. We spent a large part of the day at the Art Institute of Chicago, one of Dolly's favorite places on earth. Our lunch at the institute's outdoor roof garden gourmet restaurant, *Terzo Piano* was excellent, as was the white burgundy wine with which we toasted our sweet, departed girl.

That evening found me sitting alone on a chair under the overhang of our house, shielded from the gentle rain that had just begun to fall. The burning bushes at the corner of our deck were painted with flaming red leaves, just as they had been on the day Dolly died. Raindrops disturbed the glassy surface of the lake just off our deck, making it one continuous glittering texture of little diamond splashes. Were the raindrops tears from heaven? Was it Dolly looking down on me and crying because she missed me? Such sad tears… and a rather overly fanciful musing on my part, I admit. I was beginning to feel concern that I might be going just a little bit crazy.

We had gone through so much together, but nothing ever stopped us permanently; not separation during military service, not financial stress or even our baby girl dying, nor my years of anxiety and depression. But her death was taking its toll, threatening to defeat me.

I felt a dull emptiness inside. Something vital to my life was missing. Sadly, I seldom dreamt of her at night, or if I did, I didn't remember, which was a great disappointment as I longed to have her appear to me in my dreams in the darkness of our room. What if she did materialize? Would I be able to hold her I wondered, or would she be mist and vapor? Would she be cold to my touch, or would my body heat warm her spectral presence? Magical thinking and the damnable tricks our minds play on us when we grieve. We want what we can't have; death has seen to that. The philosopher Schopenhauer wrote: *"Death teaches us about the worth of things."* He was right. Even I, Dolly's faithful husband, did not realize just how deep and intense my love for her was…not until she was gone, and her absence had shattered my heart. Only then did it become apparent to me how profound our connection was. To accept her loss was devastating.

Eventually, something shifted, and I began to think it was time to stop going down the maudlin dead-end road I'd been traveling and start to rebuild my life. I realized it's what Dolly would have wanted. I knew her so well that I'm sure she would have encouraged me to marry again, but that will never happen for two reasons: I already had the best and no new arrival could ever stand up to the comparison. And second, I have no desire for anyone new. For me it would be like cheating on Dolly as in my heart I'm still married to her. I have a family; children who love me, a brother, and sisters I love, and friends. I reminded myself that it was time to remember I was still blessed with life. I could never bring back Sunset Trail and the girl who lived there, loving me for so many years. I will always cherish that life, but if I were going to go on, I had to accept that it was over, and I can't have it back. I would never abandon Dolly; never stop loving her. She will always be one half of me, the best half. I miss her terribly, but as Gabrielle reminded me, "you have work to do."

I'd been keeping a journal of my feelings and musings and a record of the wisdom and thoughts of many poets and philosophers that, in my readings, I'd found helpful to me. Looking through that journal, I began to think I might want to try and tell our story in a book, a memoir. Was this new beginning being orchestrated by Dolly? Had she somehow taken charge? Can the beloved dead influence the thinking of the living? I shook my head to clear my brain of these mental leaps of fancy because I doubted them. I had no illusions this journey to become whole again was going to be easy and quick. I pictured a long uphill climb, and knew the trip would be arduous, but at least I had a vision of possibility that things could get better. With nervous anticipation, I felt ready to try.

After much deliberation I made a surprising decision, one I thought would have been impossible for a seriously agnostic man like me. A decision that went against all that I had come to believe. In the confused, lonely, and almost drunken state I found myself, I reluctantly yielded to the idea and the hope that perhaps there are spirits and an afterlife. Maybe I'm wrong about that question. Is Dolly waiting for me in a place where we reunite? Was it possible that religious faith might provide me some peace and direction? I decided to give religion a chance. What did I have to lose but time? Grief had thrown a fog into my thinking, making me willing to grasp at anything, even the religious faith I so fervently doubted.

Through sunshine, rain, and snow, for nearly eight months I walked several miles to attend daily mass, six times a week. My discipline was fierce. I also read Saints Augustine and Aquinas again. Sometimes I found bits of helpful wisdom and comfort. I prayed for a sign, one I could believe in, and wisdom to see clearly what the *truth* was. Was there a life after? Would I be with Dolly again? I also prayed for comfort and relief from the pain of loss. But alas, no help ever came. There was, instead, only disappointment when no saints intervened or offered comfort. And from the God so many profess to believe in, only silence and a closed door, locked and firmly bolted tight. I again accepted what I believe is the truth; there's no one on the other side of the door; there was no one behind the curtain.

Scripture says, "Knock and it shall be opened to you." I'd knocked and no door had opened. The final days of my religious journey ultimately came down to the question I'd been pondering most of my life: Is God an illusion created in the limited minds of men to fill a need and curb fear of the unknown? By applying logical thinking, and recognizing scientific fact, it seemed clear to me there was no God, at least none that has ever been proved with real evidence. Faith is a choice blindly taken by those who elect to believe in someone all powerful who is in control of their lives. They believe this deity has a plan for us, even in the face of a complete absence of proof and with all the chaos we see around us indicating the randomness of life and a lack of any logical plan. They want to believe that in times of trouble prayer will help and some power will come to the rescue. If their wish comes true, they say, "see, prayer works." If the wish does not come true, they say, "It was Gods will."

Always, there is an explanation to support the belief of the faithful. The believers also cling to the idea that life is everlasting. It's comforting to accept that a loved one lost "is in a better place," and we will all meet again in that place some lovely day.

I became convinced that *the real heaven is right here on earth*, and best experienced through love. What could be more heavenly than living life on this beautiful planet, loving each other, and enjoying all our world has to offer? How rich and valuable life is. It's exactly what people of faith believe heaven to be. We seem to have it backwards. We are together with our loved ones now and every day, so I say... Carpe Diem; Seize the day. Love one another in this life and enjoy heaven now rather than dream of a promise after death that is without any evidence or proof.

I decided to be less concerned with the concept of life after death and to try and live fully the remaining life I have on earth. To those who have faith, I want to be clear: If your faith gives you comfort, embrace it. If it fills a need for you, then use it. My conclusions and beliefs are my own. I'm on no mission to convince anyone to think as I do. I understand that for many, their religion is of great importance to them. It was to my mom and is to the older of my two wonderful sisters. If you choose and accept faith, my hope is that it gives you peace.

Emily Dickinson wrote, *"Love can do all but raise the dead."* Even love won't bring Dolly back, so I will go on missing her for as long as I breathe. To have known and loved her was a great gift. To have been loved by her an even greater one. I don't fully understand the powerful bond that existed between us. It remains a mystery to me. Oscar Wilde wryly observed: *"Women are made to be loved, not understood,"* I'll never understand what it was in Dolly that led her to love me. Perhaps the thing in us we call our soul houses a sensor mechanism and when it feels a common rhythm between two souls with a similar beat it creates an attraction. That's why I've always believed Dolly and I shared the same soul; I think we heard the same music and danced to the same rhythm She was a true part of me and I of her. It explains, at least a little, the deep connection we felt for each other. Even today, it's so strong that I know it will never end.

Sadly, I go on feeling an emptiness in the part of my life she once filled. Our love was never broken, even under stress. But when she died, I became a broken man and will remain so for as long as I can think and remember. Some days I ride over it, on others I get deeply blue. After years, it still won't let me feel anything approaching a complete peace. Still, I don't regret even one day with her and I willingly pay the painful price to have experienced what we had together.

Now I'm entering my final chapter with determination to enjoy my family and friends and remain productive as a writer. It's what Dolly would have wanted and what she would expect of me. This I'm quite certain, is true.

# 20.

"The unexamined life is not worth living."

Socrates

I have no degrees in psychology, theology, marital relationships, or grief counseling. What I write is not meant as self-help information. My observations are based entirely on personal experience, honest self-examination, research, and books read on all these topics plus of course the subject of love. In my search I've tried to understand something of love, death, and grief. As for the examination of my life and the illusive answers to the questions that arise; sometimes I find answers, but many go unanswered. I find some solutions to hard questions remain shrouded in mist. However, one thing became clear to me at the outset: never miss an opportunity to tell those you care about how much you love them. Never be embarrassed by love. Dolly and I expressed our love for each other often and in many ways. Still, I wish I'd told her even more, just how precious she was to me and how I adored her with my entire being. I wish I had held her close even more, kissed her even more, loved her even more. Opportunity not taken is a terrible burden to carry after the death of one loved in life. I know because as much as I loved and expressed my love, it wasn't enough. It could never be enough. My heart had to be broken before I fully understood that truth.

I've learned there is no perfect time to say goodbye to the one you love. I'm not sure which is more unbearable, having time to share final words of love or as I experienced it, not having the opportunity. Either way, it's heartbreaking, and I suffer to this day with wishing it were otherwise. Many have said, "If Dolly had to die, hers was the best way to go." Perhaps they're right. Still, I can't help but think she was cheated. She was a woman who lived life fully with love and had so much more joy and wisdom to share with us.

When Dolly died, I longed for death to take me. I am no longer of that mind. I've found I do have "work to do." Living alone without the woman who filled my days and nights with happiness is lonely but I'm working hard to overcome that endless empty feeling and face life without her. Living alone has some upside I suppose because you have only yourself to please. I'd trade that in an instant to have her back to challenge me when I needed challenging. When the one I loved was no longer across the table from me, nor beside me in bed, there to share our thoughts at day's end… it hurt. I spend hours and days alone. Certainly, I have family and friends nearby, but they are not with me each morning at breakfast. They are not there to plan a trip as Dolly was. Sometimes days pass when I don't speak to another person. Thankfully, my daughter now calls me nearly every afternoon around four. Our son Tyler checks in regularly and lately my granddaughter has been calling me more often. I fill my days with writing and have learned to live with loneliness, though not exactly comfortably; enduring would be a more accurate description of how I cope. Are all these feelings just self-pity? I suppose, and yet they are honestly how I feel. To say otherwise would not be the truth.

Occasionally I bump into a long absent acquaintance and not knowing our history they will ask, "And how's Dolly?" And I will have to answer with the two saddest, most painful words in my vocabulary…"Dolly died."

As I started to accept life again, I noticed that Dolly's orchids, which she'd brought up from Florida, were not looking healthy; they were in fact dying from lack of care. I'd been watering them here and there but nothing like the attention these delicate plants needed. I became obsessed with keeping them alive. They were something Dolly had touched, nurtured, and loved, and I had to save them. I knew they required special handling and discovered a place in Illinois called Hausermann's. I called and made an appointment for a visit. Upon arrival, Gabrielle and I went into reception and told the lady we had an appointment and a bunch of sick plants outside. Pointing at a cart she said, "Take that and bring the children in. I'll call the doctor." Obviously, they understood orchid lovers. We learned a lot about caring for orchids during our visit that day.

The orchids became something I could focus on that had been a part of Dolly, allowing me a feeling of closeness with her. It was a good step in dealing with grief. On occasion an orchid will open on Dolly's birthday, or our anniversary, the timing of which always excites me. I call Gabrielle and Leona with the news. I have a mass said for Dolly each Christmas morning. Why would a deeply agnostic man do something like attend a mass? It seemed important to me to continue to celebrate Dolly's life during the season our family loved. The beauty of Christmas mass, people gathering, the candles, the choir singing—it was another way to remember Dolly and celebrate her life. The mass had been a part of our lives and the culture we knew, and I have no problem with honoring the birth of the man Jesus of Nazareth. He was, by what accounts we have, a good man who preached love, something I too believe in, so I celebrate his day. I have Dolly's name read out during that part of the mass when a specific person is remembered. I continue to do this every year.

On returning home from Christmas mass one year, I discovered one of Dolly's orchids had opened. Was it a sign from her? Probably not, but it's such an uplifting thought. Even though I know it's a form of madness, I secretly try to convince myself it's her way of saying, "My darling Paul. Thank you for the mass. You are the sweetest man, and I love you for it. I miss you so much... and by the way, the orchids look lovely." I can imagine these things are real because I'm a romantic man...and why shouldn't I accept that which makes me feel better.

Another thing that helped me through grief was creating an endowment fund in Dolly's name at the Lubeznik Center for the Arts, where she had served as executive director. My family got on board and we named it *The Dolly Fund*. The mission of the endowment is to give scholarship tuition assistance to kids seven through eighteen who have artistic talent or the desire to study art in LCA classes, workshops, and camps, but whose families are financially challenged. This endowment has been successful in its mission, a fine legacy for Dolly and one more way all of us who loved her can keep her name and memory alive. It was also one more thing that helped me choose life. I realized I could honor my wife's memory in positive ways by supporting her beliefs, rather than sitting in the dark crying and feeling sorry for myself.

As a photographer I have lots of photographs of Dolly, often with family, and I keep many on display in my house. It has been suggested that I not keep her image before me as it must be painful. It's the opposite. I want to be reminded of her all the time. It makes me happy and I often speak to those images as I pass, a tiny bit of insanity? Maybe, but why not?

Years have passed since Dolly died, yet I admit the loneliness still clings like an invisible shroud. With time it has become bearable, but the longing for her never diminishes. I've simply learned to cope a bit better. I now believe all who mourn can reach some level of contentment and accept what cannot be undone. Know that it will take effort. When I speak of Dolly, even after all this time, I still choke up. Music we both liked can cause pain. Even writing this book can bring on tears. I recognize that I'm sensitized and can't stop my emotions. I'm okay with that; it's who I am. Would it have been easier for me if I had loved Dolly less? Would grief not weigh so heavily today? Or am I willing to live with her absence and my loneliness as the price of having loved an incomparable woman? For me, there is only one answer.

I would never have wanted Dolly to suffer the pain of losing her lover as I have. If it had been me that died, she would have had to experience the loss of her brown-eyed boy. I would never wish that upon her and now she'll never suffer as I have. I admit it's an unconventional way to view the problem, but Dolly will never endure the death of her spouse. From experience I know that's a blessing. I will suffer the pain for her, so she won't have to. I have found value in that.

Our life together was a beautiful voyage. Sometimes we had to endure heavy weather but what remains most in my memory are the soft nights, fair winds, and gentle seas. I wouldn't trade any of the miles traveled, not the good or even the challenging ones. They are all part of what made up who we were in our life together, the good bits and the messy ones. In our later years we became like two old trees, side by side, weathered certainly and with all the signs of a life well lived, but remaining upright by leaning a little on each other. We each had strengths that supported the other, once again proving my belief that in humans, two halves make a more complete whole. The yin and the yang. I'm grateful to her for the many things she showered on me in life, helping me when I was down, disillusioned and struggling. I needed her in those years, and she was always there to take my hand. I wanted to be her savior, but she became mine. It's my belief she was an angel…or at least a human with all the attributes of angels as we imagine them. Dolly gave us beautiful children, each pregnancy a risk to herself. Gabrielle and Tyler now continue to occupy my life, as do our grandchildren, Veronica and Marshall, who carry on our bloodline.

I'm grateful for the years we shared in an exceptionally joyful state of love. We had lots of good friends, but I have a feeling that many were really Dolly's friends. She was the most outgoing and popular girl I've ever encountered, and the most loveable. If we were invited to two parties in one night…we attended both. That was my Doll. She loved people and they loved her in return. I learned that from her. *If you want to be loved, be loveable.* Of course, she was naturally better at being loveable than I could ever be, and she did it without trying.

Music was always playing in our life, often accompanied by dancing. Cooking, laughter, her abundant joy shared, and yes, sometimes disagreements and even tears were all a part of it. All added up to a full life. So many sunset walks on the beach, so much wine sipped while dreaming on our deck as the light faded in the forest. She added incalculable pleasure to so many lives, but especially to our union and our family. Finally, I remember and thank her from my heart, for all the loving. Oh yes. . . *especially for the loving.*

Many years ago, we were with our friends, Greg, and Rebecca Kozlik. Greg, a man knowledgeable in astronomy and the cosmos, told Dolly that seventy to eighty percent of her body was in fact comprised of stardust. He was correct in his statement—I've checked the facts. Carl Sagan, the great America astronomer, cosmologist, scientist, and astrophysicist famously stated: "We are made of star-matter." Each of us is a collection of atoms made from the remnants of exploding stars; we are, in fact, star matter. Dolly instantly embraced the fact that she was STARDUST, no surprise to me because I'd always known she'd come from the stars. Angels do you know.

I'm going to take an even greater flight of fancy and suggest that the star sacrificed to provide the stardust that formed Dolly must have been a dazzlingly bright one. The atoms that combined to become this special girl were like the notes of a beautiful melody, only the best notes being used to compose the love song she was in life. She only visited this planet once, and early in that voyage she met a shy, callow boy who fell in love with her at first sight. She chose this boy to love and decided to share her life with him. Destiny had chosen me to be that lucky boy, why I'll never know. I don't consider myself special, just a kid from the southwest side of Chicago, and certainly not one deserving the love of an angel. And yet the instant we met I took one look, beheld true beauty, and sensed that here was someone unique and special standing in front of me. I sighed deeply and fell in love with a seraph with the charming name, Dolly. All this occurred before we'd spoken one word to each other. She proved all my observations true. She was the one, and I never once looked back.

She was a remarkable composition of atoms, an angel made of dust from a distant star. Sadly, as much as I wanted to, as much as I tried, I could not hold her stardust in my hands forever. She slipped through my fingers on October 2, 2013, putting a bittersweet ending to our story. Stardust was taken from me when Dolly's time here on earth ended. It was too soon. William Shakespeare helped me accept and understand why, with these beautiful, insightful words:

*"She was beauty too rich for use. For earth too dear."*

I've never found a panacea to relieve the pain of loss. There is nothing easy about it and it has no quick cure. If you have genuinely loved another and surrender them to death, to say that in one year or any other fixed time frame, grief will end would be a lie. There are no set rules for its duration. Each of us must find our own path in our own time. I have written honestly of how grief nearly defeated me. Still, I finally found my way. It wasn't prayer or magic; it was *my determination to live and do some good in Dolly's name* with what remained of my life. The going was rough for a time, but I'm still here, living a productive life, writing a book I've titled *Love & Stardust*. I hope it will entertain and perhaps even be useful and inspiring to others.

If, in this life you have known love, rejoice for it's the greatest gift of all. Yes, it hurts to part from one deeply loved; learn to accept the pain as it's the unavoidable price we pay for loving. Finally, accept, or at least tolerate what cannot be changed. As much as we want them back, the dead do not return. Keep them in your heart and love them anyway.

Family support was key to my recovery. Without it I'm not sure where I'd be today. However, in the end, more than any other thing, it was writing this book that saved me. It kept me going, giving me a reason to rise each morning, make a pot of tea, plunk my bottom in my desk chair and go to work. For me, each page was a visit with Dolly which did me a lot of good. Obviously not everyone will want to write a book to help deal with loss, so I recommend keeping a journal. Writing down one's thoughts, sad or happy, helps ease the pain and focus the mind on remembering what was good. I wrote letters to Dolly after she was gone, and many of them have inspired pages in this book. If writing down feelings sounds like magical thinking, so be it. It helped me.

I'm sure each one of us can find a pathway to acceptance of what can't be changed. For many it's religious faith and if that's your path, take it. It's no longer mine, but I know well how helpful it often is for others. To say grief was hard for me would be to understate the depth of my early despair, and yet, I've learned to endure. As debilitating as the pain proved to be and as passionate as my love is for my partner in life, and as much as I wanted my days to end when she died, I have once again found some pleasure in living. I had to go to the bottom of the well and wallow in misery for a time, but then, rung by rung, I've managed to climb the ladder out again. Adversity is not the end, nor does it have to defeat us. Considering the depths from which I began, I now believe if I can survive the test of grief, so can we all.

I am eternally grateful that I have lived, and in my life, a beautiful young girl with the face of an angel found me, and changed my life forever when she said four little words:

*"My Name Is Dolly."*

I will love her always, no matter if my days are brief or long; She filled my life, giving it meaning and now is so much a part of me that she lives in me. As I've admitted before, I have a fanciful notion that angels do sometimes become human. They are the ones who walk among us and if we try, we can recognize them because they are the genuinely good people. Sadly, we often don't realize they're special until after they're gone. I like to imagine I married an angel and while sharing with me her time on earth, she taught me a great lesson: how to love. I'm not one of the great thinkers , but I do believe in and share with you the following words as a profound truth. It's the great lesson Dolly instilled in me by example. We should heed her message well:

## "THE GREATEST THING WE WILL EVER LEARN, IS TO LOVE, AND BE LOVED IN RETURN."

# 21.

"EVEN WHEN STARS FALL FROM THE SKY,
EVEN THEN, I WILL STILL BE LOVING YOU."

*You're ever constant Brown Eyed Boy.*

One late autumn night not long ago, I stepped out into the cold darkness. Looking up into an infinite, unknowable, and endless universe filled with stars, I tried to believe that Dolly, my beloved one hundred pounds of stardust, was up there somewhere, existing in a dimension I don't yet understand but one I desperately hope to find. On the chance she might hear my simple prayer I whispered these words to her with endless longing and infinite, eternal love :

*"Keep warm my beauty, my only love, and sleep peacefully.*
*My greatest wish it that somehow, somewhere in time,*
*our souls will once again touch, even if only as*
*STARDUST to STARDUST.*
*Will I know it's you I'm touching?*
*A man can dream,*
*can't he?"*

*FINIS*

# Eulogy:

I'm including here the somewhat unusual eulogy I wrote for Dolly's funeral mass. It wrote it after her death, at three in the morning when I couldn't sleep. At the time I chose to write based on the religious beliefs we both grew up with. It seemed appropriate as Dolly's life was going to be celebrated at a Catholic mass. If God exists, and that's something I have questioned all my life, he certainly would not have spoken to us about one girl he'd made, no matter how ideal and unique she was. If I were to write the eulogy today, the facts about Dolly the person would remain, for they are all true, but it would not be based on a God as creator theme. Until there is proof, I will remain agnostic on that question. As I was emotionally incapable of reading the eulogy I wrote for my wife, it was read most beautifully at her mass by our good friend, Bryan Dunigan. I wept at my own words and was told later I wasn't alone; there was not a dry eye in the church.

*Eulogy for Dolly Marshall by Paul Marshall October 4, 2013*

One day God said, today I am going to create two children, a girl, and a boy. I will give one of them, the girl, special gifts. I will give her a nature the is loving, generous, caring, and charitable. I will make her non-judgmental, and able to give freely to others without hesitation. I will also give her a heart capable of great love. She will be one of my special girls, a golden girl, and she will spread joy in the part of my world that she inhabits. People will respond to her goodness and she will make countless friends, adding much to many lives. She will not seek nor know fame in this world, but she will be loved by all who know her during the life that I will give her. I will create this golden girl…and then in time I will send her a boy. I will have them find one another and they will feel an instant connection the moment their eyes meet. At first, the boy will be drawn to her beauty, for in his eyes she will be exceptional, but soon he will come to know this is no ordinary girl but someone unique and special. In his young boys heart, he will not yet understand that I have created him for my special girl. He will have a feeling that she is the one he is meant to love. They will be young when they meet, but that will not matter for I have made the boy to love my golden girl at first sight and he will cherish her every day of his life.

In time I will bless them with a deeply loving marriage, good and true. They will see their love as lasting forever, so when they wed, they choose to have the Latin words, AMOUR NOSTRA AETERNA (our love is eternal) engraved inside their wedding rings. The young man will find that she is his strength, his compass, his North Star, and she will guide him on his way and help him to steer a steady course. On occasion the boy will make a wrong decision and will steer their life off course, but his North Star will always guide him back to the true course. They will struggle at times, but always together, knowing pain and sorrow along the way, for no life is perfectly smooth. Suffering and mutual support will make them love each other even more.

I will bless them with two good children, a girl, and a boy. They will call them Gabrielle and Tyler and will nurture and love them. Their children will be their joy, and as they grow older, their strength, and the family will be a good one. They will also have a loving extended family and many friends that will support their life, and all will sense that this woman, this person they call Dolly, is somehow extraordinary, and they will be drawn to her. The man will know that he has been blessed. He will recognize that he has been given someone pure and true and he will love her, and she him, and they will be together nearly every day of their married life. They will experience anger and frustration at times, but they will always forgive, because for them, love truly is kind and patient, bearing all things and enduring all things.

They will be known as Dolly and Paul…always their names said together as if it were one name. People will say they have some special connection to one another, that they live in some private place and hear music no one else can hear, in a rhythm only they dance to. It is my music that they hear, and my dance they dance. I have made it so. They will have a wonderful life, not so much in riches, but rather I will give them all they need to be happy together. They will find their way through difficult trials and will always know that the greatest gift of all is that they love each another unconditionally. The girl will describe their life as one long love affair that never ends, lasting a lifetime.

There will be parties, and many will gather at the house on the hill on Sunset Trail, with singing, dancing, and music, always music. There will be special Christmas celebrations in that house, with great tall trees and much love and joyful sharing. In time, I will give them grandchildren who will be very dear to them, allowing the special girl to start more young lives on a good path. Her guidance will always be true.

As years pass, they will grow old together, always as one for that is how they choose to live. And yet, one night I will send my angels to bring the golden girl back to me. Her life will have been a good life, well lived, a loving and productive life, and I will be pleased with her. And because I too love the special girl I made I will not allow her to suffer. Breath will leave her body gently as she sleeps beside the man she loves. But when he wakes, his life will shatter into a million broken pieces. As he holds her cooling body to himself, he will feel his heart breaking and will cry out to her over and over: "Please don't leave me." Family and friends will suffer great sadness and will find that they cannot imagine life without her in it and will understand that someone special is gone and the world is less for it.

The man will be devastated. Damaged and broken, he will never be the same again. I will have thrust upon him a great weight to carry and he will feel his heart has been torn from him. Lost without his North Star, his one true love, life will seem over; he will not want to go on without her. His sadness will be profound, his grief seemingly unbearable, and he will want to die with her. The loss of his golden girl will crush his spirit, but eventually he will find the strength to carry this great weight. In time he will understand that there is a price to pay for loving, and the more valuable the gift that has been given, the greater the sorrow at its loss. He will discover the ability to endure and to help their family, for he knows that is what his beloved girl would expect of him. She will never leave his thoughts and will haunt his heart every day for as long as he lives. His memories of her will all be beautiful, as she was beautiful, but they will also be tainted with the sadness of loss. It is the price he must pay for having known the perfection of the priceless gift I gave to him in life…

I gave him my golden girl to love.

# AUTHOR COMMENT

Some critics, if they approve of a memoir about love and loss, often seem to prefer it having been written with little emotion on display. They seem to favor a memoir factually told, like a reporter might report in a newspaper. They'll use words like *honestly presented*, or *brave and truthful*, while thinking privately, *and thank the gods of writing, without too much sentimentality.*

And yet when someone whose heart is broken because they've lost their true love writes unashamedly, with honest emotion, baring his or her soul while telling exactly how they feel, those emotions are called self-indulgent, overdone, and full of self-pity. I don't understand that. What has happened to our culture when it's frowned upon to express and share true sincere feelings? When did personal suffering become the dreaded *self-pity,* and something to be ashamed of?

Sharing feelings without reservation, telling what loss really feels like, is far more honest than unemotional reporting. Why is sadness and relentless pain a thing to be embarrassed by? A man in love, a man like me, is going to feel sorrow when he's lost the one who mattered most to him in life. I know this from personal experience. For me it's normal behavior to share my feelings honestly. They are not something I'm ashamed of nor do I sweep them under the doormat. I don't belong to the school of stiff upper lip that says, never show your feelings in polite society.

Love is a powerful human emotion and yet much of masculine society has made it something to be embarrassed by. When did movies about love become the negative "chick flick?" Are only women allowed to feel and show love? Many men are so busy defending their precious masculinity they have forgotten how to have and show a tender side; they're embarrassed by it. How sad because in fact real men can and do cry. I'm one of them. When a great love is lost to death, the pain can be nearly unbearable. Grief is devastating, a thing that crushes the soul. I know this from experience.

In my life I loved only once, and the loss of my wife was the hardest thing I've ever had to endure. Perhaps I'm not like everyone else, because in this book I've exposed my emotions truthfully, and if that's indulgent self-pity, so be it. I'm not ashamed to speak of love and loss and don't mind if some don't feel comfortable with my writing. I know I have told you the truth of my experience, honestly and from my heart.

PM